Venture Capital Handbook

ISBN 0-13-065493-0

90000

9 780130 654939

FINANCIAL TIMES

Prentice Hall

In an increasingly competitive world, it is quality of thinking that gives an edge. An idea that opens new doors, a technique that solves a problem, or an insight that simply helps makes sense of it all.

We must work with leading authors in the fields of management and finance to bring cutting-edge thinking and best learning practice to a global market.

Under a range of leading imprints, including *Financial Times Prentice Hall*, we create world-class print publications and electronic products giving readers knowledge and understanding which can then be applied, whether studying or at work.

To find out more about our business and professional products, you can visit us at www.phptr.com.

VENTURE CAPITAL HANDBOOK

AN ENTREPRENEUR'S GUIDE TO RAISING VENTURE CAPITAL

UPDATED AND REVISED EDITION

DAVID GLADSTONE

LAURA GLADSTONE

FINANCIAL TIMES
Prentice Hall

AN IMPRINT OF PEARSON EDUCATION

LONDON • NEW YORK • SAN FRANCISCO • TORONTO • SYDNEY
TOKYO • SINGAPORE • HONG KONG • CAPE TOWN • MADRID
PARIS • MILAN • MUNICH • AMSTERDAM

Library of Congress Cataloging-in-Publication Data Available

Acquisitions editor: Tim Moore
Production editor: Rose Kernan
Cover design: Nina Scuderi
Cover design director: Jerry Votta
Manufacturing buyer: Maura Zaldivar
Manufacturing manager: Alexis Heydt-Long
Marketing manager: Dan DePasquale

2002 Prentice Hall PTR
Prentice Hall, Inc.
Upper Saddle River, New Jersey 07458

The publisher offers discounts on this book when ordered in bulk quantities. For more information, contact: Corporate Sales Department, Prentice Hall PTR, One Lake Street, Upper Saddle River, NJ 07458. Phone: 800-382-3419; Fax: 201-236-7141; E-mail: corpsales@prenhall.com

Printed in the United States of America

10 9 8 7 6 5 4 3 2 1

ISBN 0-13-065493-0

Pearson Education Ltd., *London*
Pearson Education Australia Pty. Ltd, *Sydney*
Pearson Education Singapore, Pte. Ltd
Pearson Education North Asia Ltd., *Hong Kong*
Pearson Education Canada, Inc. *Toronto*
Pearson Educacíon de Mexico, S.A. de C.V.
Pearson Education—Japan, *Tokyo*
Pearson Education Malaysia, Pte. Ltd

CONTENTS

v

CHAPTER 4   A THOUSAND QUESTIONS 101

Chapter 5 Meetings and Negotiations 141

CHAPTER 6   THE COMMITMENT LETTER 177

CHAPTER 7   DUE DILIGENCE 211

CHAPTER 8   THE CLOSING 243

CHAPTER 9   WORKING TOGETHER 271

CHAPTER 10 THE EXIT 309

INTRODUCTION

This book has been great fun to write, and, with this revision, it is ready for another 15-year run. One of the teachers currently using the book in her class calls it a classic. When the book was written almost 20 years ago, there was no indication that *Venture Capital Handbook* would become a classic. But with the tremendous increase in venture capital and the many new and young businesses looking for VC, the book has proved its worth by filling a need for guidance in this field.

The chief strength of the book is that it is a "nuts and bolts" approach on how to raise venture capital. It talks about the process in straight talk without a lot of theory or war stories. It shows the reader how to win the game of raising venture capital.

It has been gratifying to see *Venture Capital Handbook* be so useful to so many entrepreneurs and small business owners. Some entrepreneurs, in letters to the author have claimed to have raised great sums of money using this book. It is wonderful that there are so many business schools that use the book today, and it is gratifying to know that so many people are studying how to raise venture capital. It would be fun to know how many billions of dollars have been raised by venture capital firms by using this book. It would be quite a rush to know exactly how many businesses came into existence because of this book.

We know the book is having an impact because our venture capital friends make snide comments to us about "giving away the secrets of the business." It seems that we have made it more difficult for them to gain the advantage over the entrepreneur. But we are sure that this book has also made it easier for them to work with some of the entrepreneurs who have read it because the book gives the reader some insight into the world of the venture capitalist.

In this second edition, we have a father–daughter team doing the revision and updating the book for the current times. It has been easy to update the book because so much of the business of raising venture capital has not changed. We both work at a new fund we created called Gladstone Capital Corporation. Our Web page is www.gladstonecapital.com. Come visit our Web page and learn about our fund and more about venture capital.

Acknowledgments

Many people made this book possible. Most of them are our friends in the venture capital industry, many more are the friendly entrepreneurs with whom we have worked over the years. We wish there were enough pages to list them all here, but if we tried to do that we would most likely miss some. So, we are just going to say thanks to all of you for your help in making this book a success.

Best wishes and good luck with all your investments.

1

ANYONE CAN RAISE VENTURE CAPITAL

YOU CAN GET THE VENTURE CAPITAL NEEDED FOR YOUR BUSINESS.

A SUMMARY OF WHAT IT IS ALL ABOUT.

There is more venture capital money available today than at any other point in history. Each year large financial institutions, such as pension funds and insurance companies, are committing to invest billions of dollars to the area called venture capital. This category of investing has been growing at such a feverish pace that it is now one of the primary categories that institutions must invest in. This book has been written so that you can explain your business idea to the venture capital community in a way that they will understand and thereby facilitate your fundraising efforts. However, if you do not have a compelling story about how you will make money for the venture capital investors, than this book will not help.

Every business has venture capital. Venture capital is the money at risk. It is the long-term capital in a business that permits a business to grow and prosper. Most entrepreneurs are not savvy about how to raise venture capital and do not understand the process necessary to raise it. The first step that an entrepreneur usually takes is to approach a bank for a loan. Most entrepreneurs soon discover that banks make loans where the risk of loss is negligible. The banks must act in this manner because they are regulated by governmental agencies. So most banks are not in the business of providing venture capital.

After being turned down by a bank, the entrepreneur usually asks friends and family to provide the initial investment in the business. Sometimes friends will provide enough money to get the business going, but most often they do not provide enough money to make the business a success. Undercapitalization is the leading reason that small businesses fail.

At this point the entrepreneur must begin the arduous task of raising the necessary capital from the venture capital community. And a similar story can be told for those entrepreneurs who want to buy a business or finance the growth of a business that they own. Banks will lend only so much money to an existing business, so in most cases a business will need venture capital in order to achieve its growth objectives.

This book tells you how to raise money from the point of view of professionally run venture capital funds and how to make the relationship work for you. There is nothing easy about raising venture capital or working with venture capitalists after you have their money. This book will help you endure the process of finding venture capital and living with venture capitalists (VCs) once you have their money. Since you will have to live with this relationship for a few years, it is important that you understand the relationship and how to pick a compatible venture capital investor. Remember that the venture capital investment in your company is not just an investment; it is a partnership between you and the venture capitalist.

Venture capital investing is a difficult business, with the decision to finance a business a complex process. Certain critical elements must be present in a business proposal before it will receive venture capital backing. This book explains those elements and in so doing answers the question, "How can you raise venture capital to start a business, to buy a business, or to grow an existing business?"

I'LL BACK YOU

"I'll back you if you have a good idea that will make money for both of us."

That simple sentence contains all the ingredients necessary to obtain funds from a venture capital company. Analysis of the parts of the sentence will give you an understanding of venture capital.

In the middle of the sentence is the clause, "that will make money." It is pretty obvious what that means. Venture capitalists are not interested in investments based on motives of faith, hope, or charity. A venture capital company is run exclusively for profit. Even though some investments made by venture capital companies perform so poorly that they may look like charitable contributions, you should rest assured that the original intent was profit. If you are offering anything except profit, you should not approach the venture capital investor. Many times an entrepreneur thinks that if the entrepreneur offers the venture capitalist some additional benefit, it will induce the venture capitalist to make the investment.

For example, the venture capitalist who is considering financing a Broadway play may be offered an opportunity to meet some famous actors and actresses. One venture capitalist was told that if he invested in a particular company and it succeeded, he would be remembered forever in history as having financed one of the greatest inventions in this century. While the venture capitalist is not above a little glamour, greed and avarice, are the primary motivations in making an investment in your company.

Let's turn to the part of the sentence that says, "for both of us." Surprisingly enough, venture capitalists are not interested in a project that will make money solely for them or for you. They look at every situation as if it were a partnership. Your interests and those of the venture capitalist must be congruent, or the venture capitalist will not make an investment. As a result, any investment opportunity in which only the venture capitalist will make money or only the entrepreneur will profit is not considered a good investment from a venture capital standpoint. Both parties should be able to make money.

Now turn to the hard part: "a good idea." Good ideas are easy to find. Thousands of good ideas are floating around. The problem with all good ideas is that very few can be turned into profitable businesses. Finding an idea that will make money is not easy. Finding a good idea that has a large profit opportunity is extremely unusual. Explaining how profitable a good idea can be for an investor is also a difficult assignment. It will be easier for you to communicate your ideas to a venture capital company if you follow the procedure outlined in this book. If you follow the directions, any venture capitalist will understand what your company is about and how your idea will make money. A good idea always has what venture capitalists call a "compelling story" behind it. You must have a compelling story for the venture capitalist, or you will not get the backing.

Finally, look at the beginning of the sentence, "I'll back you." It is the most important part of the sentence. The venture capitalist must be convinced that you and your management team can make the idea happen and make money doing it. This will be your most difficult task—explaining why you and your team are the ones who can make it all happen. And it is the team that the venture capitalist is interested in most. Venture capitalists invest in teams, not businesses. It is the most important part of your compelling story. You must convince the venture capitalist that your team can take the good idea and turn it into a profitable business.

WHAT IS VENTURE CAPITAL?

It is easier to begin the description of venture capital by explaining what venture capital is not. The loan that a bank makes to a business is not venture capital. The stocks and bonds an investment company buys on the New York Stock Exchange do not involve venture capital. A real estate investment company buying apartment buildings, shopping centers, and so on, is not investing venture capital.

However, a subsidiary of a large corporation that makes investments in a small business could be using venture capital. Some investment companies that buy new issues of publicly traded companies might also be considered investors of venture capital. If you and a group of friends get together and put some money into a small business to get it off the ground, your investment may be a type of venture capital. If you loan some money to your brother who is opening a new type of store, that money may be considered venture capital. If you buy stock in a private company that is starting to manufacture a new type of machine, the money you invest is traditionally known as high technology venture capital. The equity money put up to buy a business is considered venture capital. The money invested in a new company that shows a potential for fast growth is venture capital.

As you are now beginning to understand, a venture capital investment is characterized by high risk. It doesn't matter how the investment is structured, whether it is an equity investment that generates long-term capital gains or a high risk loan that gives the venture capitalist a 25 percent return on the investment. If high-risk loans qualify, then you might ask yourself, "What is the difference between a finance company and a venture capital company? After all, a finance company makes loans at a high rate of interest." The difference between the two is management assistance. You will find the venture capitalist more involved in your business than a finance company. Venture capitalists frequently review your operations and constantly make suggestions. They are, in essence, your business partners. When you acquire venture capital you are acquiring additional brainpower to help your corporation achieve the goals that you have established. It is important that you acquire a good VC to help you, not just to provide the money you need.

Now let's return and get an overview of how venture capital fits into the investment community. In that community, venture capital is a segment of a category called private equity. It is known as private equity because it deals with investing money in private companies not public ones (such as those listed on the New York Stock Exchange or the NASDAQ). And within the category of private equity are three categories that we will talk about in this book: venture capital, mezzanine capital, and buyout capital. Think of these three segments of private equity as being very different, as different as bond managers and stock pickers. And remember, if you are seeking money to start a business, don't show up on the doorstep of the LBO funds. They will not give you the time of day. You need to understand the structure of the private equity world so you don't end up approaching the wrong source and wasting your time.

Venture capital is defined as money that is invested in new companies. This investment category is reserved for money that is invested in new ideas and very new businesses. When you hear discussions about venture capital you here people talk about start-ups and about first, second, or third round financing. This is the world of high-tech (high technology) investing. Venture capital comes from the early investors in the personal computers, in disk drives, in software systems, in the Internet, in new telecommunications companies, and in new biotech companies. It is a very exciting world with spectacular returns for investors and some tremendous losses. The people in this category are part gambler and part futurist.

On the other hand, the providers of buyout capital are known simply as leveraged buyouts or LBO. These investors are very different from the professionals that provide venture capital. The buyout folks are the ones who buy big and small businesses with the existing management of that business (a "management buyout" or MBO) or with a new management team. In the recent past these LBO funds have raised enormous sums of money for their companies. And it is only recently that the venture capital managers have begun to raise similar large amounts of money for investing in new businesses.

Now the third type of private equity is mezzanine capital. "Mezz" capital, or subordinated debt as it is sometimes called, can be a form of venture capital or LBO funding. It derives its name because it is in between the senior debt and the common stock investors in a business, just as the mezzanine floor in a department store is in between the ground floor and the first floor. This "in between" money is usually more risk averse than the money received from venture capital or LBO funds. Mezzanine capital is most commonly found in the capital structure of companies that receive later stages of venture capital and it is found in a buyout when the bank that is making the senior loan will not lend as much as the LBO fund is seeking. So the mezzanine fund will make a subordinated loan to your company that is below the bank in the capital structure but superior to the equity from the LBO fund. Mezzanine funds are also providers of substantial amounts of growth capital. When a growing business cannot get all the money it needs from a bank, it usually seeks out a mezzanine lender to borrow from. As you would suspect, the mezzanine lender charges a lot more than a bank, but much less than the venture capital firms or LBO funds.

For the rest of this book, we will be talking about venture capital and will use the term as most people commonly refer to it today. In a general sense, it means all forms of high-risk capital that finances a new business, a buyout business, or an existing business experiencing strong growth—or venture capital, buyout financing, and mezzanine capital. So don't get confused when the term venture capital is used in its popular sense. When people say venture capital they really just mean high-risk capital and a source of private equity. Usually, when it is used by a professional investor, venture capital means the capital that goes to start-up companies and other very early stage investments. However, in this book we will stay with the familiar use.

WHEN DID VENTURE CAPITAL BEGIN?

Investing in new companies and new ideas has been happening since the dawn of human civilization. The industrial revolution was funded by venture capital. But when did venture capital begin to be practiced as a stand-alone business in its current format? This apparently began sometime after World War II. After the war, there were few institutions that made venture capital investments. Most venture capital came from wealthy individuals (otherwise known as "angels") and from a few pools of capital that were managed by the larger Wall Street brokerage firms in New York City. But during that time, there were a few firms that sprang up that invested only in early-stage technology situations. This was the beginning of the venture capital industry. Those early practitioners were the forerunners of the industry as we know it today. With the passage of the Small Business Investment Act of 1958, the U.S. government began to assist the budding venture capitalist. Venture companies that qualify with the U.S. Small Business Administration (SBA) were and, are today, able to borrow money from the SBA at lower rates as long as they invested their funds in small businesses. More than a thousand of these small business investment companies (SBICs) were formed. But as time passed, many of the managers of SBICs left their firms and founded venture capital funds not associated with the government. Today the SBIC program run by the government is only a small part of the venture capital industry. But it, too, was a founding partner in the growth of the VC industry.

Those individuals who first left the SBIC industry in the 1970s formed partnerships that raised money from individuals, banks, and pension funds. Those early investors were daring souls. They put their money in with no control and waited for years to see if the investments that were made would make money. They did. With that early success, pension funds and insurance companies gradually committed more money to this category, and the VC industry grew to giant proportions. As the new century began, the industry was in full bloom and showing signs of maturity. It is one of the great strengths of the U.S. capitalist system.

TYPES OF VENTURE CAPITAL

Today the venture capital industry has four types of firms: private limited partnerships, a few publicly traded funds, corporate arms of public companies (and some of these are banks), and wealthy individuals. Here we are looking at the industry by its corporate structure. Let's look at each.

PRIVATE LIMITED PARTNERSHIPS

By far the largest identifiable pool of venture capital is in the form of private limited partnerships. These pools of capital can be as small as $50 million or as large as $8 billion. These partnerships are the investment vehicles that source their funds from pension funds, university endowments, large foundations, insurance companies, corporations, and some wealthy individuals. The managers of these partnerships are general partners (GPs) and the investors are limited partners (LPs). The limited partners make a commitment to invest their money over a two-or three-year period, and the partnership is set to be liquidated after eight to ten years. These limited partners are passive investors.

The general partners run the partnership and find the investments. They make investments on behalf of the partnership. The limited partners are passive investors with little or no control over where the funds are invested. So when you seek funding from these pools of capital, you will be dealing with the general partners and will probably never meet a limited partner. The general partners are the ones taking the risk and making the big bucks. They are the ones that the press writes about. Most of them have egos the size of a mountain. There are more than two thousand private limited partnership style venture capital funds in the United States and many more in Europe and Asia. There are hundreds of billions of dollars in this category.

One key thing to remember here is that funds are limited partnerships with a limited life. When you get money from these funds, it is not permanent capital. They will want it back in a few years. You need to plan to pay them back even though they invest by buying common or preferred stock. They need to have the capital back because their limited partnership will need to be liquidated in ten years or less. So in a sense, this is "hot money." You get to use it to grow your business fast and then you need to give it back and give back a big profit with it.

Publicly Traded Funds

Public venture capital funds are scarce. You can count the number of publicly traded companies dedicated to venture capital by using both hands. This area has never developed, and, given the current outlook, it is not likely to develop. You can think of the reason why they don't develop this way: if a general partner of a private venture capital limited partnership can raise the money privately from pension funds, why would that general partner ever want to deal with all the hassle of being public? So this category has very little capital and only a handful of funds.

Sometimes these public funds are called incubator funds because they take the small business under their wing and provide a lot of management direction. While they are a good source of funding if you can find them, don't waste a lot of time looking for money in the public sector. There are only a few billion dollars in this category, and most of this money is in mezzanine funds. If you are looking for mezzanine capital or subordinated debt, for a later stage business, then the public companies may be a good place to look.

Corporate Venture Capital

Corporate venture capital can be similar to the partnerships just described, or it can be a program set up inside the company. It is usually set up as a separate arm of the corporation to invest in businesses that are related to the business of the corporation. It is sometimes a "window" on new technology for the corporation. Many of the large technology companies have a VC arm. They may have different names, but they are looking for deals. The amount of money available to be invested in venture capital by the corporate world is difficult to identify, because a corporation can dip into its cash reserves and finance any investment it wants to. So there is no identifiable pool set aside that can be counted.

These corporate venture capital operations are usually staffed by professionals who report to the CEO. There are tons of money in this category. Unfortunately, many of the investors from the corporate side are interested in owning your company rather than being a venture capital investor. You must be careful, or you will find yourself an employee of the large company. There are hundreds of corporate venture capital funds.

An interesting subset of this category is the venture capital arm of some of the large banks. Most of the venture capital arms in the banks are part of the very large bank holding companies. They may be funded with money from the holding company, or they may be the major investor in a pool of money managed by the bank's employees. In recent years these pools of capital have grown dramatically. Major banks have seen that they need to be in this category to be looked upon as a major bank. So as with all the other categories that banks have moved into (such as investment banking and advising on mergers and acquisitions), the bank's parent companies have become venture capitalists.

It's not surprising that with all the assets controlled by the major banks, they play a large role in supplying capital to buyouts, start-ups, and growing businesses. So the statement at the beginning of this chapter that banks do not provide venture capital is not quite true. The banks don't do it through their loan department, but some employees of some major banks at the holding company do provide venture capital. Ah well, there seems to be an exception for every rule.

ANGEL INVESTORS

Wealthy individuals also supply a large amount of venture capital. Known as angel investors, this category has increased dramatically during the past ten years. There are a number of organizations that foster these investors, but mostly these angel investors are just out there financing businesses. There is more money for early-stage investments in the angel category than in all the other categories combined. But since it is so hard to find, one is left with only crude estimates of how much money is actually out there. It is a lot by any measure. In order to tap into this area you need to find a couple of good books that discuss the market. You need to talk to some local business people. Someone in your community will know some of the angels and how to contact them.

So let's see where we are. In the past 20 years there has evolved a group of professional managers of pools of venture capital funds that might be found managing any mutual fund. These venture capital funds have evolved into some of the best analysts of early-stage investing and leverage buyout investing in the world. Not only can they pick winners, but also they can add great value to the process by helping the small business attain goals that would have been unattainable without them. In your quest for backing, you will meet some of the best and the brightest minds in the world.

A word from the wise: It wasn't until the late 1980s and early 1990s that the venture capital community became a large industry. There are now more than 2,000 institutional venture capital funds. This is your primary target for raising money. Professional managers run these corporations or partnerships just as any other corporation would be run. From an entrepreneur's standpoint you should deal with the institutions or professionally run venture firms rather than the nonprofessional individual groups. Sometimes a nonprofessional individual investor can become quite possessive and limit the potential of a small growing business. Often the corporate investor wants to own and control the business. If you are raising money, go to the professional venture capital fund for money.

WHERE CAN YOU FIND VENTURE CAPITAL?

Two published lists are available to help you to find the right venture capital company for your situation. The first list is from the trade association of venture capitalists. A current list can be obtained from that trade association by writing to them or going to their Web site at www.nvca.org. Their address is:

The National Venture Capital Association
1655 North Fort Myer Dr., Suite 700
Arlington, VA 22209
(703) 528–4370

The second list contains the names of firms licensed by the SBA, which are known as Small Business Investment Companies (SBICs). If you want to obtain a listing, write to their trade association or visit their Web site at www.nasbic.org. Their address is:

National Association of Small Business
Investment Companies (NASBIC)
1156 15th St Suite 1101
Washington, D.C. 20005
(202) 833–8230

There are several publications that list all the venture capital companies. Each of these charge a fee for the list or their service.

Pratt's Guide to Venture Capital Sources is the old-line publication that has been around forever. It is published by Venture Economics, a division of Securities Data Publishing in Boston, MA. It is a good listing of venture capital funds. You can see an array of products on the subject by going to their site: www.sdonline.com.

Galante's Venture Capital and Private Equity Directory is published by Asset Alternatives, Inc. in Wellesley, MA. Their Web site is www.assetnews.com, and they can be reached by phone at (781) 304–1400. This is a very good listing, and they have a lot more on their site.

You are going to need a list to work from, and a trip to the library may give you one of the listings above. If you cannot find a copy at the library, then shell out the money to buy one. Buying the CD from either Pratt or Galante is the way to go. The CD lays it all out for you.

How Do Venture Capital Companies Invest in Businesses?

As you look through the list of VC funds, you will see them fall into two distinct categories based on the form of investment they are willing to make in your business: those that are lenders and those that are equity investors. In general, the lenders are themselves leveraged, meaning they have borrowed a great deal of money from either the government or private sources. The equity funds, as their name implies, have not borrowed any of their funds. The equity is from their limited partners or from their stockholders, and their money is used to buy equity securities in small businesses. On the other hand, lending venture capital companies borrow most of their funds. As a result, their investments in small businesses have to be loans or convertible debentures. They must have interest income from the small business in order to pay the interest on their own borrowings.

You should review each of your potential venture capital investors and determine whether they are lenders or equity investors. If you are seeking equity, you probably should not approach a leveraged venture capital fund.

Small businesspeople often ask why the lending-oriented venture capital funds do not invest equity in their small businesses. It is easy to illustrate why they do not. No individual should go to the bank and borrow money at high interest rates to buy equity in a small company. The individual will have to make the interest payments on the debt at the bank. Also, it may be a long time before the money invested in a small business matures so that the individual can repay the bank debt. When you approach a lending-oriented venture capital fund, think of it as an ice cream store. It has only one flavor of ice cream, chocolate (debt). If you are looking for vanilla (equity), you are out of luck.

The equity partnerships invest primarily in the form of preferred stock and sometimes common stock. They have very patient investors that do not need current income like the leveraged VC funds. So they can buy equity in your company and wait for the growth to make them a lot of money. But be aware that the equity partnerships are buying growth with their investment. They want you to grow your business very fast and they expect to make a lot of money when they sell out. They are interested in your company only if it can grow fast and if they can see a time in the future when they can sell their equity and trigger a gain.

WHAT TYPES OF BUSINESS DO VCS BACK?

Somewhere along the way, the venture capitalist will try to define your business situation according to a set of categories used by the venture capital community to stereotype each business situation. These categories are discussed next.

START-UP STAGE OR FIRST-ROUND FINANCINGS

As the name implies, these are businesses that are just being formed. These are the most difficult situations to finance because few people are willing to believe in an idea. The fact is that not many new ideas have the potential to make money. It is especially hard to communicate a new, money-making idea to a venture capitalist because every venture capitalist is constantly bombarded with ideas—some of them good, some ludicrous. Rather than obtaining funds from a venture capitalist, you may have to beg, borrow, and steal from friends and relatives in order to obtain the initial seed money to get your idea off the ground. Remember, a start-up is only an idea with no prototype product, just some words on a piece of paper. It usually takes two to three years before the company attains a cash flow break-even point. Anyone investing in a start-up is taking a huge risk and will be looking for a tremendous reward.

In recent years more venture capital companies have been making more investments in start-ups. A much larger percentage of venture investments are now start-up investments, whereas only a few years ago the number of start-up financings was small. But alas, most of the early stage money is for high-technology companies, not regular businesses. Because so much money is now looking for start-up situations, there is a good chance that a venture capital company will finance your start-up. The money is there for a compelling story.

DEVELOPMENT STAGE OR SECOND-ROUND FINANCINGS

Once you have proved that the idea can work by means of a prototype, an economic study, a marketing analysis, or some other means, you are in a position to have a good shot at obtaining financing from the venture capital community. However, your selling ability still needs to be extremely sharp in order to convince people that the idea that works in a proto-type can be brought to the marketplace at a profit. By this time, your company is usually one to two years away from cash flow break-even. As a result, the venture capital company will want a considerable return on its investment for taking a high risk. After all, some companies never reach cash flow break-even after this stage of their development.

EXPANSION STAGE OR THIRD-ROUND FINANCINGS

At this stage of development the company has created a product or service and is marketing it with some degree of success. The company needs additional funds to finance expansion of the business. In most of these cases venture capital is abundant. The entrepreneur will be in a good negotiating position to obtain the best price for the needed capital from the venture capital community. A company in the expansion stage is usually near the break-even point or perhaps no more than one year away from breaking even. You will not have to give up as much of the equity in your company if your venture has reached this stage in its life cycle.

The only thing that will make it difficult for you to get money here is a cold or dead IPO (Initial Public Offering) market. If there is an active IPO market for your company, the venture capitalist will throw money at you. At one point in the late 1990s many Internet and telecommunications companies went public at this stage of their financing and the venture capitalist reaped huge rewards. However, the crash in the IPO market in 2000 put a stop to it. Timing is everything.

GROWTH STAGE OR FOURTH-ROUND FINANCINGS

The company that is running well and is generating a profit but needs additional capital in order to continue its strong growth will have the venture capital community drooling to invest; that is as long as you do not structure the deal so that they cannot make any money. A company at this stage of development is near break-even and may be making money. It needs money to grow quickly. Strong profits are just around the corner. In this situation you may have to give up only a small amount of equity unless you are raising a large sum of money. You may consider "going public" at this stage.

LEVERAGED BUY-OUT FINANCINGS

In some cases an existing company may be purchased by an entrepreneurial team. The entrepreneurs come to a venture capital company in order to obtain additional equity to purchase the business. Sometimes the entrepreneurial group that is managing a division of a large conglomerate can buy the division away from the conglomerate by using the venture capitalist's funds. In independently owned small businesses a leveraged buy-out occurs when a nonowner management team buys the company from the original owners. Any of these situations is called a leveraged buy-out or LBO because most of the money is invested into the company as debt. Many venture capital companies are seeking these types of investments in either the debt or the equity.

TURNAROUND SITUATIONS

Some venture capitalists finance turnarounds—that is, companies in trouble or even in bankruptcy. These turnarounds need money and management assistance. Turnarounds are hard to finance, and only a few venture companies specialize in this activity. Most people in the venturing industry agree that there are a hundred ways to fail in a turnaround. The difficulty is that you can think of and plan for only 20 of them. The other 80 are waiting to pop up at the most unexpected moment. You have to have lots of luck to handle turnarounds. The business presentation to the venture capitalist for a turnaround situation must emphasize the new management team—how they can make the company profitable and what they will do to make the company become profitable quickly.

PUBLIC OFFERINGS

Some venture capital companies and venturesome mutual funds will buy equity in a new issue or second-round public offering for a business on a path of high growth. This happens only from time to time. What interests the venture capitalist in a public offering is strong growth and a hot stock market. Some people call this the fifth round of financing.

WHICH INDUSTRIES DO VENTURE CAPITALISTS PREFER?

Most venture capitalists will tell you that they want to invest most of their funds in high-technology products or services. In the late 1990s the Internet and telecommunications were hot.

And in that same period biotech was very hot and attracted a phenomenal amount of venture capital. In the late 1980s and the early 1990s the LBO professionals invested in a flood of deals. Many of them crashed in the recession of 1991–92. But the biotech business came back strong in the 1990s and has been overshadowed only by the technology area. The Internet has had a tremendous impact on venture capital investing. As a new way to reach consumers and suppliers, it has produced some spectacular successes and some incredible failures. It is very similar to the boom and bust that happened in the early 1980s with the introduction of the personal computer.

The mezzanine lenders were consistent investors over this period and sometimes got squeezed out of an investment opportunity by aggressive bank lenders. Mezzanine lenders seem to be a permanent fixture in the marketplace now and invest in companies in need of third-and fourth-round financings. Since mezzanine lending or subordinated debt is analogous to riskier bank lending (i.e., they need cash flow to pay back the subordinated debt), most mezzanine providers cannot lend to companies in the early or first-round stage of financing. Therefore, mezzanine lenders are attracted to more mundane businesses, like manufacturing, distribution, and proven service businesses, with cash flow.

Most venture capitalists do not finance retail operations such as dress shops or muffler stores. Generally, if you have a new concept for a retail store, you will find your innovation falling on deaf ears at the venture capital community. A number of venture capitalists in the Small Business Investment Company (SBIC) community will finance retail operations. Over the years there have been several new venture capital funds that specialize in retailing, and there have been some new ones in medical products.

In the wholesale distribution area there are no venture capital firms except for a few SBICs that specialize in this area. You will again find it difficult to finance an innovation in distribution. A few venture firms specialize in financing projects concerned with natural resources such as coal mining or oil well drilling. Again, this is a difficult area to finance within the venture capital community. Entertainment projects are also difficult to finance. A group of specially licensed Small Business Investment Companies financed entertainment ventures for a while, but these seem not to have prospered.

Service companies used to be difficult to finance, but with the rise of the service economy in the United States, things are bright for the service companies. The easiest companies to finance are those with high-technology products or services.

Finally, only a very few number of venture capital firms have financed real estate. Most are precluded by their charter from investing in real estate development projects.

As you look through the full category of business ventures, you will not find any funds that will look at all types of businesses. This means that you will have to find the right type of venture fund to finance your venture. This may take a lot of trial-and-error work, but hopefully this book will limit your time and efforts in this area. Don't take your start-up business plan to an LBO group. Don't take your second-round financing to a mezzanine group. If you need equity, don't bother with the lending venture capitalist. If you have a telecom deal, don't go to the Internet-oriented funds. If you have a new restaurant concept, don't bother the high-tech VCs. Like all industries, the venture capital industry has a lot of specialists and few generalists. You will have to find the one that fits your deal, but, more important, don't waste your time going to venture capitalists that don't invest in your kind of business or your stage of development.

WHAT TYPES OF PRODUCTS OR SERVICES DO VENTURE CAPITALISTS PREFER?

Venture capitalists prefer technology because there is an opportunity for strong, quick growth. Since it seems obvious from the foregoing that venture capitalists like technology products and services, what type of growth products and services do they prefer? There are four such categories: revolutionary, innovative, evolutionary, and substitute products. Revolutionary products are extremely difficult to finance anywhere. The light bulb, the television, the telephone, the camera, the phonograph, and the early automobile are examples of revolutionary products that changed life dramatically. The personal computer industry developed from the financing of a revolutionary product: the mainframe computer. Another industry that could be considered revolutionary is the one derived from genetic engineering. And the Internet is another revolutionary product. Such revolutionary products absorb enormous amounts of capital. They have a very long development time before one can realize a substantial profit. Most venture capitalists would prefer to finance the services and products that use the revolutionary change that is occurring.

Venture capitalists prefer innovative products. By innovative one means that a product is the next generation in a series or an application of a revolutionary product to a specific situation. For example, the instant camera, the personal computer, the color television, and the fluorescent light are all next-generation stages after their predecessors.

The application of the Internet to business and to consumer needs is a good example. And the application of new communications products to business and personal needs is another good example. The change was large enough to generate demand but small enough not to create a need for extensive education. Many venture capital firms prefer evolutionary products such as a cheaper instant camera. These firms want to be one year ahead of the competition rather than five or ten years ahead of the competition. With an evolutionary product and an aggressive management team, venture capitalists believe they can stay one or two years ahead of the competition and make significant profits.

Still another group of venture capitalists do not finance any of the foregoing categories, but instead prefer substitutions. These are the people who finance a fast-food restaurant that substitutes chicken for burgers. They are the leveraged buy-out specialists that back an aggressive new group to buy a stodgy old firm and substitute a repackaged product for the current one.

All venture capitalists are looking for sizable markets. If your product is competing in a marketplace that is very large, you will have a better chance of receiving financing. However, if your product is in a marketplace that is growing 10 to 15 percent a year and total gross sales are only $100 million to $300 million, the venture capitalist will not see the beauty in being the market leader in such a small market. Your best bet is to try the mezzanine lenders to see if you can induce them to invest.

How Much Venture Capital Is Available?

Over the past 20 years, dramatic things happened to increase the amount of venture capital. First, venture capital came from individuals. When the tax laws were changed so that the capital gains tax was reduced substantially, more people were willing to invest money in venture capital firms. The investors were seeking outstanding long-term capital gains because the tax on these capital gains is much lower. This brought a great deal of money into the venture capital industry.

The great change that has helped create more venture capital occurred in the pension fund area. The U.S. government decided that pension funds may invest a small percentage of their total assets in high-risk ventures such as venture capital companies. In practice this means that up to 10 percent of a pension fund's assets may be invested in the venture capital community. And up to 2 percent can be very speculative. Two percent may sound small, but it is large; when multiplied by the trillions of dollars in U.S. pension funds, it is huge. Because of these two changes, the venture capital industry is receiving substantial attention from professional investors. Venture capital firms are able to raise money quite easily. For the entrepreneur there is a great deal of money available to back a great opportunity.

Opportunities Available for Entrepreneurs

At this point in time a great opportunity is open to entrepreneurs. Staggering changes in the U.S. economy have created numerous opportunities for small businesses to spring up.

The United States is changing from an industrial nation to an electronic-information nation. Fewer and fewer people are being employed in industrialized businesses such as steel, the automotive industry, and the like. On the other hand, the electronic and information processing industry, the telecommunications industry, and the biotech industry have all shown sharp growth rates. Where there is growth, there is opportunity and the money will follow.

The restructuring of many large corporations and the megatakeovers have brought opportunities. Big corporations are spinning off some of their small subsidiaries in order to generate cash to pay off the mountains of debt they have created and LBO funds have been willing to pay high prices for businesses. Entrepreneurs with an itch to own a business are willing to pay high prices for businesses. Because of these high purchase prices, more small business owners have decided to retire early and sell their businesses. For every seller today there are five trying to buy. It is an excellent opportunity for entrepreneurs who want to buy and own their own businesses, but they must be careful not to pay too much.

CAN YOU RAISE VENTURE CAPITAL?

With so much money available, you would think that money would be easy to obtain. However, there continues to be intense competition for money among entrepreneurs and small businesses. The reason: many people are seeking financing for their new ventures or their growing small businesses. The baby boom that worked its way through our colleges in the 1960s and early 1970s is now at work in business. These middle-aged men and women are reaching the end to their careers. They have reached an age in the workplace that leads them to sell their businesses. There are many young workers who see the difficulty of rising inside of a large organization. They see that there are only so many vice-presidential slots and presidential slots in the 1,000 largest U.S. companies. There are only so many opportunities to make a great deal of money inside large businesses. Many young people are realizing that they have to start their own businesses now if they are ever going to do it at all. Others know that they need to leave their jobs and buy an existing business if they are going to make a fortune. This book has been written for those of you who are ready to start a business or buy a business. This book will give you an edge over others seeking funds from the venture capital community because you will understand the process better.

There is one large impediment to your progress in obtaining venture capital financing. There is a lack of senior venture capital officers to review your proposal. Because of the extreme growth in the venture capital community, there are fewer seasoned executives to manage the billions of dollars that have been invested into the venture capital business. As a result, you will probably work with a junior officer until a critical decision can be made as to whether the venture capital firm will invest or not. You may hear yes, yes, yes, from the junior executive, only to receive a resounding no from the senior management after your deal is discussed at their management meetings. There is no way to avoid this problem. The best thing to do is to work as quickly as possible toward obtaining a decision from the senior management. And always have your business proposal working in more than one venture capital fund.

How Much Money Should You Seek?

How much money you should seek to finance your business is always difficult to determine, particularly in the early stages of development. A useful equation to remember is that the more money you raise, the more equity ownership you must give up to the investor. Of the four stages of development (start-up, development, expansion, and growth), the start-up stage is the most difficult to raise funds for. It is difficult to raise enough money in the initial start-up phase to carry the company through to the growth stage. So at each stage of the development you will have to go back to the venture capitalist or other investors in order to raise additional money, and each time you do you have to give up an additional piece of equity ownership.

In seeking money you must seek enough to do the immediate job at hand. That is, you must seek enough money to make significant progress so that the next round of financing will cost you (in terms of ownership) much less than the initial financing. If you sold 30 percent of your company in the first round of financing, you would have to make enough progress so that in the second round you would give up only 10 to 15 percent of the ownership.

There are horror stories about entrepreneurs who have approached venture capitalists and asked for the money they needed to take them through the start-up phase. The venture capitalist, acting in an unethical manner, states that he wants the entrepreneur to cut back on the amount of cash needed by trimming the business's budget. The entrepreneur trims the budget to the bone. With less money from the venture capitalist, the entrepreneur still tries to make a go of it. When the entrepreneur runs out of money before reaching a significant milestone, the entrepreneur returns to the venture capitalist and asks for additional funding. Since the milestone has not been reached, the only way the entrepreneur can raise the necessary cash in order to make the milestone happen is to give up an even larger amount of equity. Often the entrepreneur gives up control of the company for the original amount of money the entrepreneur initially asked for—leading to a loss of control of the company to the VC. This book will help you avoid that pitfall.

Besides selecting an ethical venture capital firm, you should make sure that you raise enough money in your first financing to make it through to the next stages of development. If you have achieved your stated goals, you will find it easier to switch to a different venture firm or outside investors in order to raise additional capital. You will be in the driver's seat, not the provider of capital.

WHAT TYPE OF FUNDS ARE YOU SEEKING?

There are only four basic ways to obtain venture capital financing. Each has its advantages and disadvantages. Usually an advantage for you is a disadvantage for the venture capitalist. Each of the four alternatives is discussed in turn.

COMMON STOCK

Most people would like to sell common stock in their company. The price is always the question. The venture capital firm cannot gain control through common stock unless it owns 51 percent. Therefore, there are fewer opportunities to sell common stock in a company without making additional concessions. You may be able to sell stock, but the venture capital firm may require that all stock be placed in a voting trust that the firm will control if your projections are not met. Also, the venture capital firm will want representation on your board of directors. You will have to keep this in mind when trying to sell stock. The venture firm may seek other means to control the company if you get in trouble. This problem is discussed later in Chapters 5 and 6.

PREFERRED STOCK

Venture capitalists may agree to purchase preferred stock in your company under certain conditions. First, they may want dividends paid on the preferred stock, probably in the range of 6 to 8 percent. Most often this dividend is deferred until the preferred stock is redeemed. This is often explained by the venture capitalist as a "preferred return." This means that the venture capitalist gets a return before the common stock investors like you. Second, the venture capitalist may want your company to repurchase the preferred stock after a specified period of time. This arrangement will assure the return of their money in case your company does not grow quickly. Finally, they will always want the preferred stock to be convertible into common stock so that they can share in the equity ownership if your company performs well.

CONVERTIBLE DEBENTURE

Most of the lending venture capitalists will be willing to buy a convertible debenture from your company. The debenture is a loan to your company that is convertible into common stock. The conversion price, the interest rate, and the covenants of the loan agreement are all the items you will have to negotiate with the venture capitalist. Most of the buyers of this security are mezzanine venture capital funds. These terms are discussed in Chapters 5 and 6.

LOAN WITH WARRANTS

Many of the lending-oriented venture capital funds (mezzanine funds) will make loans to your company if you agree to let them have detachable stock options, known as warrants, to buy stock in your company. In this way, if their loan is paid off, they will still have the option to buy stock in your company. Warrants are discussed in later chapters. Most of the lending venture capital funds are somewhat like junk bond buyers. This was a popular type of investment in the late 1980s, and it caused some serious problems for some buyers of the junk bonds. Since the late 1980s the market for privately placed junk bonds with warrants has grown strong and is now a discrete market niche of the bond marketplace. For the smaller transactions these junk bonds are sold to the mezzanine funds in the venture capital marketplace.

HOW WILL THE VENTURE CAPITALIST BE INVOLVED?

When it comes to the venture capitalist's involvement in your business, there are two types of venture capitalists: passive advisers and active partners. Most lending venture capital companies are passive advisers. They get monthly financial statements and talk to you on a regular basis, but they never get involved in your business. The equity-oriented venture capitalists are much more active. They will sit on your board of directors, and they will come to regular management meetings. They are not just investors but rather they are your partners and expect to have a say in the direction of the company.

Some venture capitalists limit their advice to areas in which they have strong expertise, such as the financing of your company, the growth of the company, and matters involving projections and employees. Usually the passive adviser does not become involved in your business unless you have operating trouble. If you do have trouble, he will become very active in trying to manage your company in order to save his investment.

On the other hand, the active venture capital director will want to help you run the business. Usually the venture capitalist does not help on a day-to-day basis, but may be at the business once or twice a week. Some venture capital firms even supply part of the management team to companies they have invested in. Some venture capital companies have consultants on their staff who will help you with the marketing plan. They will charge a fee for this consulting arrangement. Most venture capitalists will be actively involved in hiring any of the top management team. Some venture capital funds have management recruiters (headhunters) that work for them, finding good people to join your team. Most venture capital managers spend at least 25 percent of their time recruiting good people for the companies in which they have an investment.

Some venture capital companies play a more active part than just direction. They actually seek to control the company, either directly by having their company manage the small company or by controlling the board of directors or the voting stock. This may not be entirely bad for you. If you have an idea that is tough to finance and that needs a great deal of ingenuity to bring it to the marketplace, try to find a venture capital company that provides this type of complete assistance. If the venture capitalist truly has people that can help achieve your goals, then it may be in your interest to accept assistance as part of the financing for your idea.

There has developed another kind of help for early stage companies. Called incubators, these venture capital funds have rented extra space and offer offices to the companies they have financed. In addition, once in the incubator, the venture capital fund provides accounting people to keep the books and prepare the financial statements. They provide lawyers to set up the corporate records and negotiate contracts for the small business in the incubator. Once the small business begins to take off, then the small business "graduates" from the incubator and finds new space and hires its own lawyers and accountants. Usually the entrepreneur will give up a lot of equity ownership to start his or her business in an incubator.

HOW TO SELECT A VENTURE CAPITAL COMPANY

Before you approach any venture capital company, you should determine the type of venture capital fund that best fits your situation. First, using the list of the venture capital companies in Appendix 1, determine which firms are closest to your location. Venture capital companies prefer to invest in companies located nearby. You will save yourself a large amount of time if you choose a venture capital company that is located close to your business. Many venture capitalists on the East Coast of the United States are surprised when they receive a proposal from a small business on the West Coast. They ask, "Why didn't this small business receive financing from a West Coast venture capital firm?" It seems unlikely that a small business would come that far in order to find venture capital.

If you are unable to raise the capital from your local venture group, then you need to explain why you are seeking capital outside your area. One reason may be that the local venture capitalists do not wish to invest in your industry. Another reason may be that the distant venture capital firm is a specialist in a certain type of business. You should explain that you have traveled 3,000 miles to find a specialist and a partner, rather than just to find capital.

Once you have selected a few venture capital firms that are close to your business, you can begin the second phase of selection. You should ask around town about their business ethics. You may want to ask local lawyers or accountants about the firm. Do these firms live up to their commitments? Are they involved in a great deal of litigation? Are they profitable companies? Do they have money to invest? These are all questions you should be asking others about the venture capital companies you are considering. You might run a credit report on the funds just to find out what is in their credit file. You may check the courthouse records to see if they have suits against them. After all, once you have obtained money from a venture fund, you will have to live with the venture capitalist for a very long time. Find out as much as possible about the one you finally choose before you obtain the funds. Every company has a Web page, and you should read it all to learn about the venture capitalist.

In talking with the venture capitalist you should ask the managers of the fund to tell you about some of the fund's investments. You should call the entrepreneurs of those companies mentioned to ask how they are being treated by the venture capitalist. When you talk with a venture capital company, you may ask for a bank reference or other references. Again, it is important for you to select a venture capital company as a partner, not just as an investor. Be careful in selecting the venture capital company that you will take money from. The company doesn't go away after it invests its money. Investigating the venture firm is discussed in detail in Chapter 7.

SHOULD YOU PHONE THE VENTURE FIRM?

Now that you understand what you are trying to finance and what type of venture capital firm you may wish to seek out, the question arises, Should you phone the venture capital company to determine if they are in the business of financing your type of venture? You should telephone if you follow the guidelines set out below.

When calling a venture capital company, remember that it probably receives 50 to 100 phone calls per day plus many unsolicited business plans and letters. Your phone call should be to the point. Explain the type of deal you are trying to finance, ask if the venture capital company has funds available, and finally, ask if it will be able to review your business proposal during the next week. If the answer to all three of these questions is yes, then do not take up additional time; send in a summary and business proposal as set out in Chapters 2 and 3 of this book. Of course, if the venture capitalist wants to discuss your situation, begin selling your concept.

The point here is that venture capitalists are not important people who are unapproachable, but they are very busy people. They receive hundreds of telephone calls from entrepreneurs as well as crackpots with crazy ideas. Be sensitive to the time pressures of the venture capitalist and the venture capitalist will appreciate your tact. The following telephone call is considered by venture capitalists to be a helpful opening telephone conversation:

> Receptionist: Mr. Capitalist, J.P. Entrepreneur is on the phone and wants to talk about you investing in a new company.

> Venture Capitalist: Hello, this is A.V. Capitalist.

> Entrepreneur: Mr. Capitalist, this is J.P. Entrepreneur. Just call me J.P. I am calling to find out if you have an interest in a business that needs financing.

> Venture Capitalist: Can you tell me about the business?

> Entrepreneur: Well, Mr. Capitalist, my best friend and I started a small software company about six months ago. We now have the beta test site completed, and we have received preliminary indications of interest from a number of major corporations that believe this will solve a number of computer security problems. We have applied for a patent on this process, and we believe it will be granted. What we are looking for is $3,000,000 in order to complete the software and hire a sales staff to begin selling the software. Do you have money available for this kind of investment?

> Venture Capitalist: Yes, we do have funds available, but what kind of funds are you looking for? By this I mean are you seeking common stock or loans?

Entrepreneur: Well, we are completely flexible on this issue. We would, of course, like to sell common stock. However, we realize that some venture companies don't buy common stock and we would be open to discussion as to whether it is a common stock or preferred stock.

Venture Capitalist: Fine. Do you have a proposal put together outlining what you are trying to accomplish? Does it have projections, résumés, and those kinds of things?

Entrepreneur: Yes, we have a business proposal with a summary, and I would like to send it out to you. I would like to know how long you think it would take for you to have an opportunity to review it so that we could come by and discuss how we might work together on this project.

Venture Capitalist: Well, I am tied up this week but beginning next week on Monday or Tuesday I should get to your proposal and should be back to you by the middle or end of next week. If you really want me to rush, I may be able to squeeze it into this week's work.

Entrepreneur: Oh no, I think that timetable fits with what we are trying to do. We hope to have something, at least a preliminary commitment from a venture capital source, within 30 days, and we would like to work with your group because we have heard so much about you.

Venture Capitalist: Fine. Send it to my attention. I assume you have our address.

Entrepreneur: I have the address as listed in your Web site. Is that correct?

Venture Capitalist: Yes, that is correct, but send it to me via e-mail. My e-mail address is ven@capitalist.com

Entrepreneur: Thank you very much for your time. I will get this in the e-mail today, and I look forward to speaking with you next week.

Venture Capitalist: Thank you and goodbye.

This conversation is ideal from the venture capitalist's point of view, because the entrepreneur gave the venture capitalist an inkling of the business that sparked his interest. The entrepreneur was flexible as to the type of investment capital he was seeking and did not ask for an overnight determination of the venture capitalist's interest. The conversation was short and to the point. The venture capitalist could have asked more questions about the project if he had wished to, but he decided to wait for the proposal. Some entrepreneurs want to explain their business on the telephone and ask if the venture capitalist is interested in financing the business. No venture capitalist can give a positive response on the telephone. A venture capitalist must have a well-documented proposal before the team at the venture capital fund can give the entrepreneur encouragement.

Some venture capitalists are not approachable without an introduction, meaning that they are looking for someone they know and trust to introduce them to the entrepreneur. This will make your job more difficult because when you call the firm where "Mr. Big" is the general partner, you are likely to get a very junior associate who does not appreciate your great business idea. In order to get to the general partner, you will have to find someone who knows the general partner and can reach the general partner on the phone and ask the general partner to take your call. Even then, the general partner may pass your proposal off to a junior associate. Unfortunately, the venture capital industry has grown so dramatically that it is difficult for the small businessperson to reach the top of the heap inside some of these large venture capital funds.

Certain venture capital firms make it a policy not to talk to the entrepreneur. Instead, the assistant to the general partner will ask the entrepreneur to mail in the written proposal and will explain that the venture capital manager will not talk to anyone until he has reviewed the proposal. When these venture capital firms receive the proposal, they log it in with a number and begin their processing. This is not an unusual procedure, and you should not be taken aback by such treatment. However, if you are treated poorly and not given an opportunity to discuss your proposal with anyone, even after you have sent it in, then it is best to move to another venture capital company.

OTHER QUESTIONS FOR THE VENTURE CAPITALIST

The conversation just mentioned covered some but not all the facts that you may want to know about the venture capitalist before you proceed. The first and most important question is, "Are you investing money in companies?" If the answer is not a resounding "yes," then you do not want to spend any more time talking to this venture capitalist.

The second most important question is, "Do you have time to review my proposal?" Most venture capitalists are pressed for time. They may have several companies in trouble and may be trying to work themselves out of a loss situation. They may have made commitments to another company and may be involved in due diligence in that situation. If the venture capitalist is too busy to review your proposal within a week to ten days, you may want to consider discussing your proposal with other venture capitalists. In the preceding conversation the venture capitalist indicated he would review the entrepreneur's proposal at the beginning of next week. Such a date should not be interpreted in absolute terms. If you don't hear by the date indicated, then give the venture capitalist a few more days before you call.

A third area you must question the venture capitalist about is your industry. Does the venture capitalist have an interest in your company's industry? If you are in a rather mundane industry, the venture capitalist may not be interested. On the other hand, it may be just the industry he has been seeking as an investment. A related question is, "Have you ever invested in this industry?" If the venture capitalist has already invested in the industry or looked at potential investments in the industry, the venture capitalist understands the economics involved.

If you can find a venture capitalist who has such experience and understands your industry, you are weeks ahead of the schedule for receiving your money. A venture capitalist with experience in your industry will not have to go through the learning period necessary before investing in an industry.

A fourth subject to discuss with the venture capitalist is that of contacting other venture capitalists. Most venture capitalists would rather review your proposal without having others review it at the same time. It is better for you, however, if you select several venture firms and send them your proposal. To do this tactfully, do not ask if he minds if you contact other venture capitalists, but perhaps phrase your question as follows: "Do you have any friends in the venture capital business who might also be interested in reviewing my proposal?" Or, if the venture capitalist says the fund is interested in your industry, you might ask whether the fund would like to work with any other venture companies that also know the industry.

You should let the venture capitalist know that you are sending your business proposal to several other venture capital firms. The venture capitalist should not expect to be an exclusive. On the other hand, do not push the idea that the venture capitalist has to move quickly or the fund will miss this golden opportunity to invest in your firm. Remember, venture capitalists have dozens of places to put their money, and if you become pushy, your company will definitely not be one of them.

Other items you need to determine about your venture capital partner is the matter of due diligence. Chapter 7 covers how you can determine whether a venture capital firm is the one that you want to deal with. Most venture capital firms are run by honest professionals. However, some are not. Don't neglect your due diligence in investigating your potential venture capital partner.

How Long Does It Take to Get the Money?

A final key question concerns the time it will take to obtain funds. The amount of time from your initial contact until the time of a legal closing—when you receive the money—can be as short as a few weeks or as long as six months. The time involved depends on many factors. In general, the procedure takes six to ten weeks. You must remember that there is more to the business of venture capital investing than listening to a sales pitch from an entrepreneur.

First the venture capitalist must review a written business proposal if the venture capitalist is to understand your business, your industry, and your management team. The length is not a critical factor, but every venture capitalist wants a written proposal. It is vital to understand that the venture capitalist wants to know something about your business before there is a meeting with you. Therefore, the venture capitalist needs a written business proposal.

After reviewing the business proposal, the venture capitalist will decide whether to have a meeting with you. The next step is to hold an initial meeting and discussion of the business proposal, which cannot always take place immediately. As mentioned before, venture capitalists work under extreme time pressures. They have hundreds of business propositions sent to them on a monthly basis. Taking half a day to discuss your business idea is a large time commitment on the part of the venture capitalist. Once the initial meeting has taken place, the venture capitalist will want to check out all the things you have claimed in your proposal.

If your proposal is successful, the final step is to obtain a commitment on the part of the venture capitalist, which normally involves a meeting of her/his partners to make a decision on your opportunity. Also, the legal documents have to be drawn, and signatures have to be obtained on these documents before the formal legal closing on the commitment takes place. This book discusses these stages in detail so that you will understand what a venture capitalist must go through before she/he can invest in your venture. You need to know about these processes so that you can facilitate each of them to get your money.

By far the largest amount of time in this process will be devoted to the investigation of your industry by the venture capitalist. You can minimize that time by picking a venture capitalist who has already invested in your industry or a similar industry. The process can also be simplified if the venture capitalist has reviewed, but not necessarily invested in, several deals in your industry. Such contact will reduce the time needed to understand the industry and your situation. You can shorten the time further by writing a complete business proposal as set out in this book.

MYTHS ABOUT VENTURE CAPITAL

A number of myths should be dispelled at the outset. They are as follows.

MYTH 1

Venture capital firms want to own or have control of your company and tell you how to run the business. Nothing could be further from the truth. No venture capital firm intentionally sets out to own control of a small business. The venture capitalist seeks more than 50 percent of a company only when the venture fund needs to have that much of the company in order to justify the amount of money the venture fund is investing in your business. This is a question of return on investment.

Venture capitalists have no desire to run your business. They do not want to tell you how to make day-to-day decisions and have you report to them on a daily basis. As you will see later in this book, venture capitalists are busy keeping up with their investments and seeking new investments. They want you and your management team to run your company profitably. They do want to be consulted on any major decisions, but they want no day-to-day say in your business operations.

MYTH 2

You must have an introduction to the venture capitalist from one of his or her friends in order to obtain financing. For some venture capitalists this is true. However, in most cases you do not need an introduction to the venture capital management from anyone. A business proposal that is well prepared is the best introduction you can have. Gone are the days when you needed an intermediary to introduce you to a rich investor before he or she would invest money into your venture. Most venture capital firms are run by middle-class, non-elite individuals. To be sure they have big egos. But most of all they are interested in good investments. They are not interested in your social contacts or introductions. Later on in your relationship, if you have mutual friends or know people of similar background, such contacts will enhance your credibility; but there is no need to have an intermediary to get your idea across to the venture capitalist or to gain financing.

Myth 3

Venture capital firms are interested only in new technological discoveries. Actually, in the majority of cases venture capital companies are not interested in revolutionary ideas that change the way people live. These kinds of ideas take 10 to 20 years to develop. I doubt that any professional venture capitalist would have backed the electric light bulb. It took a far-sighted person to see that someday everyone would replace his or her oil lamps with light bulbs.

Revolutionary ideas are very difficult to finance because the return on investment takes so long to realize. The venture capitalist is more interested in an add-on technology. Venture funds want to invest in a new type of computer, a new silicone chip, a new marketing technique using the Internet, or something that will involve moderate change. It is true that venture capitalists tend to be oriented toward high technology, but a better way of viewing their orientation is to say that they are interested in companies that promise high growth. If you have a company that has a potential for high growth, then you can attract venture capital money.

Myth 4

Venture capitalists are satisfied with a reasonable return on investment. No venture capitalist expects a reasonable return on the venture funds investment. The truth is, these people expect very high, exorbitant, unreasonable returns. They can obtain reasonable returns from hundreds of publicly traded companies. They can obtain a reasonable return from many types of investments not having the degree of risk involved in financing a small business. Because every venture capital investment involves a high degree of risk, there must be a corresponding high return on investment. Expect the venture capitalist to require a very high rate of return.

You may believe that your business is a special situation, and that the strong potential and high demand for the product assures the investor of a very low risk of failure. You may believe that if you could only accomplish certain events in your business plan, everyone would be rich. Your optimism and inability to see a potential failure are expected of you as an entrepreneur, but ask yourself, "If this is such a low-risk investment, why can't I get a loan from a bank in order to finance the company?" If you come seeking funds from a venture capital firm, the venture fund expects to take a risk and to receive a very high rate of return on its investment.

MYTH 5

Venture capitalists are quick to invest. On the contrary, it takes a long time to raise venture capital. On the average, it will take six to ten weeks from the initial contact to raise your venture capital. If you have a well-prepared business proposal such as that discussed later in this book, you will be able to raise money in that time frame. A venture capital fund will see 100 to 500 proposals a month. Out of that number, ten will be of some interest. The venture capitalist will read those ten business proposals. Out of those ten, two or three will receive a fair amount of analysis, negotiation, and investigation. Of the two or three, one may be funded. This funneling process of selecting one out of a hundred takes a great deal of time. Once the venture capitalist has found that "one," the venture capital team will spend a significant amount of time investigating possible outcomes before they will fund it. Your proposal will be weighed against the many alternate investment opportunities available. Make sure it stands out and is well prepared so you can receive your funds quickly.

MYTH 6

Venture capitalists think that management is a secondary consideration. Not true. Venture capitalists back only good management teams. In fact, the most important reason a venture capitalist will invest in a business is belief in its management team. A strong and experienced management is essential to obtaining funding from a VC. If you have a bright idea but have a poor managerial background and no experience in the industry, try to find someone in the industry to bring into your team. The venture capitalist will have a hard time believing that if you have no experience in that industry and no managerial ability in your background, you can follow through on your business proposal.

However, you do not necessarily need a complete management team the day you write your proposal. Many venture capitalists have staff members who can help you with certain areas of your business. However, most of them would prefer that you have your management team pulled together before you get the venture off the ground. A good idea is important, but a good management team is even more important.

MYTH 7

Venture capitalists need only basic summary information before they make an investment. In actuality, a detailed and well-organized business proposal is the only way to gain a venture capital investor's attention and obtain funding. If you think that you can hastily write a two-page summary and have a venture capitalist fund your investment, you are sadly mistaken. There are stories of people having only a slide show of 15 slides that have raised venture capital. Those are the exception. Venture capitalists want a good summary as a start, but the summary is not a substitute for a sound, well-thought-out business plan.

Every venture capitalist team, before they become an investor in a entrepreneurial team, wants the entrepreneur to have thought out the entire business plan and to have written it down in detail. It may never come true and the company may change directions, but on day one the venture capitalist wants to know how you will succeed.

A well-prepared business proposal serves two functions. First, it informs the venture capitalist about your idea. Second, it shows that you have thought out your intended business. It shows you know the industry and have thought through all the potential problems.

And don't forget that the venture capital community is not homogeneous. There are VCs that specialize in certain industries and others that have certain sectors. There are VCs that look for early-stage investments and those that look for companies in a later stage of development. There are all types of VCs with a variety of motives. You need to perform research on each one to make sure you make a good selection. Your motive is to raise capital and to find a good partner.

OBJECTIVE

The objective of this chapter has been to give you the skills to identify the proper venture capital firm and decide if it has an interest in reviewing your business proposal. This is usually a simple task, since venture capital firms will review any proposal. You must identify the best venture firm to review your business proposal. You must also be sure that this venture firm has money and the time to review your proposal.

Now that we have presented the basics of the venture capital community and you understand how to determine which firm may be best for your business situation, you are ready to prepare the two documents that you will be sending to the venture capital company: the summary and the business proposal.

2 SUMMARY PRESENTATION

CAN YOU SUMMARIZE WHAT YOU INTEND TO DO?

A GOOD SUMMARY HAS LESS THAN A THOUSAND WORDS.

Any venture capital fund with money to invest is under constant assault by entrepreneurs seeking money to back their ideas or their businesses. Virtually hundreds of people and ideas are vying for the opportunity to be reviewed by a venture capital fund. Therefore, it is absolutely imperative that the presentation being made to the venture capital fund be excellent.

The presentation must be of a high quality in order to have a competitive edge over all the other proposals arriving on the venture capitalist's desk. The only response a poorly presented business proposal will receive is a toss into the trashcan. The most crucial part of the presentation is the summary because this is what sparks the interest of the venture capitalist. It must not be more than three pages long. You may attach to the summary a complete business proposal, but venture capitalists prefer not to plow through the details of a business proposal until they understand the business from a summary proposal. Three out of four venture capitalists will read only the summary and will not take the time to review a full proposal. A venture capitalist may read as many as twenty proposals in a day. Out of about a hundred proposals per week, maybe ten proposals are read. The others are usually so poorly prepared that they are only cursorily glanced at. Your goal is to be in that top 10 percent and have your proposal read. The summary will make the difference.

WHAT DOES A SUMMARY LOOK LIKE?

I will now show you an effective summary format. The format is a composite of many I have seen. I have used this format for seeking additional financing for many of the companies we have invested in. What follows is a disguised financing request, based on an actual company in which funds were invested and in which the investment made a tremendous amount of money for everyone. The numbers, name, and people have been changed completely:

Company: E Press, Inc.
8888 Avenue of the Americas
New York, New York 10005
Telephone: (212) 555–1212
www.Epress.com

Contact: Joseph Entrepreneur, President (J.Entrepreneur@epress.com)

Type of Business: Internet preparation of material and printing of materials requiring quick turnaround.

Company Summary: A new company has been formed to purchase the assets of a small printing company. The existing company uses the method of setting type common to the industry today. The company has invented a new way to set type using the Internet. The company needs some additional funds to complete the process and set up the system to drive a special machine that will produce digital copy for printing at remote locations. The customer sends the document to the remote printer via the Internet, and it is set up to print. Then it is set up on the Web site for the customer to review and approve. Once it is approved, it is printed and delivered back to the customer in several hours.

This method will make the current process obsolete. All existing customers will be serviced with the current method of printing until the new system is ready. By keeping the customer base and converting them to the new process the company will have the ability to jump-start the process of getting customers for the new process. If the invention fails then there is always the ability to pay back some or all of the investors' funds from the existing business.

Management: Joe Entrepreneur, President, has been in printing for 12 years. He has worked in all phases of the business. He has been working with the Internet programs to set type for the past year. He has a B.A. from a New York university in accounting. He is 32 years old.

Jim Black, Vice-President, has been in the computer field for eight years. He has been a programmer, systems analyst, and management consultant on computer applications. He has been working on a computer program to prepare type via the Internet for one year. He has an engineering degree from a large Boston college.

Product/Service and Competition: E Press will begin by continuing to offer conventional printing services. Once the Internet can be used to print the document, the company will offer the customer the quicker turnaround for its printing. Customers can use the actual digital, camera-ready copy for corrections and can make corrections quickly.

Funds Requested: $2.8 million in common stock for a 40 percent ownership.

Use Proceeds: $600,000 as down payment of the business; $200,000 accounts payable; and $2 million to carry the company's research and development budget to develop the computer program. The purchase price is $1.8 million—$600,000 in cash, and $1.2 million in a five-year 8 percent note.

Projections:

PROJECTIONS	CURRENT YR.	YEAR 1	YEAR 2	YEAR 3
Revenue	$2,900,000	$6,000,000	$29,000,000	$83,000,000
Net Income	$389,000	$600,000	$3,900,000	$26,000,000

Exit: The company will go public in three years. If the company does not go public in five years, then the investors can exchange their ownership for three times their investment and be paid out over three years.

WHY IS THE VENTURE CAPITALIST INTERESTED?

The venture capitalist has interest in this situation from a number of perspectives. First, and most importantly, the VC sees a management team that has experience in both printing and in personal computers, and he sees the benefits of combining the two talents in order to initiate a new approach to an old industry. Second, he sees profit opportunities, as this company has the potential to grow beyond the projected $6 million to as high as $80 million or $100 million. The third aspect that the venture capitalist sees is uniqueness. It is not unique that computers can print from a digital file, but it is unique to use the Internet for delivery and corrections to avoid delay. Finally, the venture capitalist is interested because the VC sees a viable exit strategy in becoming a public company. Should the company be able to hit the projections it has set out to achieve, it should be able to have a public stock offering and give the venture capitalist an opportunity to liquidate the fund's position at a considerable profit.

How to Complete a Summary

Now let us look at each category used in the above summary to see what is needed, because you should understand how each section is to be prepared and what the venture capitalist is looking for.

Company

You would be surprised to learn how many people fail to include a name, address, e-mail address, or telephone number on their proposals. It sounds stupid, but it happens. In one instance, we received an extremely interesting proposal but could not find a return address. Unfortunately, I did not read it until the day after it came into the office and by then the envelope had been thrown away. Too bad, whoever you are!

Most of the time the name and address are in the package but not in a conspicuous location. One must wade through page after page looking for this basic information. Do not let this happen to you. Put the company's name, address, e-mail address, Web site, and telephone number up front on the first page of the proposal and also make it the first item on the summary sheet.

Contact

Many proposals list a number of people in this section but do not indicate the person to contact. The venture capitalist is not sure if the VC is supposed to talk to the president, the vice-president of finance, or someone else. You should indicate on the front of the proposal the person within your company who is responsible for raising the money along with the special telephone number, e-mail, etc. at which that person can be reached. Usually it is the president of the company, but sometimes another person is the ongoing contact. And if you have an investment banker, there needs to be a second line that will let the VC know about the broker.

Leave a number where you can be reached. A number that is attended only part of the time is useless. Have an answering service answer for you if you do not have a permanent number. Using your cell phone number is fine, too. And if you have a beeper, it is also helpful. Always include the e-mail address so the VC can get you via e-mail. A venture capitalist will try to reach you only so many times before giving up.

TYPE OF BUSINESS

Here you need no more than ten words, just enough to let the venture capitalist zero in on the industry. Because there are a number of industries in which many venture capitalists will not invest, identifying your type of business saves a lot of time and agony.

You may also wish to identify the stage of your business, such as start-up, development, and so on, as discussed in Chapter 1. This information will permit the venture capitalist to respond more quickly. If the venture firm has a policy of not investing in turnaround situations, for example, it's better to receive a quick no rather than a delayed no.

BUSINESS SUMMARY

Here you are trying to give a thumbnail sketch of the company's history to date. Give a little background on the company and emphasize some of its strong points. The objective is to get the venture capitalist interested in your company. If you have more than half a page in this section, it is not a summary. Be brief!

MANAGEMENT

Although this is the most important section of the entire presentation, the information does not need to be covered in detail in the summary. The more you can emphasize the entrepreneur's experience in the industry, the better the presentation will be. List the top two or three people and give a two-sentence background statement for each. The venture capitalist will want to investigate management in detail, but the summary is not the place to itemize all the accomplishments of management.

PRODUCT/SERVICE AND COMPETITION

In this section, first give a short description of the product or service. Second, show why that product or service is unique. If it is not unique, then explain why this product or service will succeed over all the other products and services that are offered in the marketplace. You need to discuss the competition briefly in order to show the niche that it occupies in the industry. Do not write more than a half page here.

FUNDS REQUESTED

Briefly state how much money you want to raise. And, for goodness sake, *do not* give a range! For example, do not say $2 million to $4 million. Pick a number and show why you need that amount. Also, state the type of funds you are raising. Is it equity? Is it debt? Remember, not only is it easier to raise debt financing, but you will give up less equity in your company with debt financing. It is important to state what type of funds you are seeking, because some investment companies do not make equity investments. They make only convertible subordinated debentures or loans with options to buy stock. If you are flexible, then don't worry about structuring the deal; just state your preference and add that you are flexible. If the venture capitalist likes your proposal, the VC will come back and suggest a restructured deal.

COLLATERAL

If you are seeking debt, you should state whether any collateral security is available for the loan request. Loans with collateral are easier to obtain than those without collateral. If there is none, state "none." The more collateral you have, the less equity you will have to give up.

USE OF PROCEEDS

One need not be extremely specific on the use of proceeds in the summary. That will come later in the full business proposal. Here you should indicate how the funds would be used. Avoid broad terms like "working capital" or "to pay expenses"; it is better to be more specific and to indicate whether the funds will be used to pay salaries (and put in a dollar amount), build inventory (and put in a dollar amount), pay accounts payable, and so on. This gives the venture capitalist an idea of how the funds will be used.

FINANCIAL HISTORY

This section seems to be fairly self-explanatory, but remember that it is important to put down the actual figures in columnar form alongside the list of items to be included. If the company is a new one, obviously the historical section will be dropped.

FINANCIAL PROJECTIONS

Most venture capitalists would like to see five years of projections even though they realize the fifth year is based on wild speculation. It gives them a clearer idea of how much money they could make if everything goes right. Again, use a columnar format.

EXIT

As has been mentioned before, the venture capital company does not want to be a minority stockholder in your company forever. It would prefer to realize a capital gain soon after investing its money. In practical terms, its horizon is three to seven years. That is, somewhere after the third year, the company would like to begin receiving a capital gain on its investment. This means a public offering of stock in which you and the venture capitalist can sell some shares. This means selling part of the equity position owned by the venture capitalist, or all of its equity position, to a third party or perhaps back to the company. You need to keep this problem in mind, because the venture capital company will not invest if there does not appear to be a way out somewhere down the road. Chapter 10 discusses this in detail.

STRUCTURE

This section needs to be included after the foregoing items if it is a complex investment structure. For example, you may be investing in common stock and you may have an investor friend who is investing in preferred stock. You are now trying to raise debt financing from a venture capital company. There will also be a loan from a bank. In that case, the structure might look like this:

INSTITUTION	AMOUNT
Bank	$2,000,000
Venture Capital	$2,000,000
Preferred Stock	$200,000
Common Stock	$100,000
Total	$4,300,000

Many venture capital companies have indicated that they eventually put each of their investments into a summary format similar to the one above. They do this for their own record keeping, for presentation to their investment committee, or for discussion purposes. To give your deal a head start, prepare an effective summary.

WHAT KIND OF COVER LETTER IS NEEDED?

Many investment companies want only a summary and do not want a full business proposal. Along with the summary, entrepreneurs need to submit a cover letter that sets out some basic introductory information. And if you are submitting it via e-mail, then you don't need any more than the following information in the e-mail with the plan attached:

Mr. A. V. Capitalist, President
Venture Capital Corporation
123 Main Street
Washington, DC 20006
Re: XYZ Corp. Financing

Dear Mr. Capitalist:

Attached is a summary of the financing I am seeking for my company. If you have an interest in providing this or similar financing, l would be pleased to send you a full business proposal. Please call or e-mail me if you have any immediate questions.

Sincerely,

Joseph "Joe" Entrepreneur
123 Main Street
McLean, VA 22102
(703) 555–1212

Some venture capital companies are taken aback when such a query letter is attached to the summary. They perceive it as part of a mass mailing. That is, it may suggest that the person seeking the money is sending the summary to hundreds of venture capital companies to determine if any of them are interested in the business. If your query letter has that look, you may be doing yourself a disservice by discouraging the venture capital company from taking the time to review the summary. Other venture firms routinely respond to a query letter by saying, "We are interested. Please send me your business proposal." This response may merely mean the venture capitalist has a cursory interest. The VC may turn down the funding requested after looking at your full proposal for only two minutes.

In order to avoid the look of a mass mailing and to ensure a speedy response, you should select several venture capital companies located close to you, of the type you believe to be interested in your company, and mail them a query letter, a summary, and a business proposal as set out in Chapter 3. By giving them the full treatment, you will dispel any suspicions about your being in a mail-order operation.

Personally, I like to see the complete package—that is, the summary with the business proposal attached to it. With that material in hand, I can continue to review the company after examining the summary. In other words, providing the potential investor with the business proposal as well as the summary speeds up the process tremendously because the venture capitalist does not have to write or call you to ask for the business proposal. If time is a critical factor in obtaining support money, you should send the business proposal along with the summary. If the venture capital company turns you down, you can always ask the venture capitalist to mail the business proposal back to you.

STRATEGIC USE OF SUMMARY

It is obvious that the purpose of the summary is to entice the venture capitalist to read the entire business proposal and "fall in love" with your company. The summary then becomes an advertisement for your company, much like the advertisements placed in a singles magazine. You hope to entice someone into making a considerable effort to contact you.

You should treat the summary as an advertising document. It is a sales pitch for your company, your idea, and you. Never send out a summary or a business proposal that is a rough draft or anything less than a complete, professional piece of work. To do so is to make a halfhearted attempt at selling your idea and company. Instead of a rough draft, you should have a polished copy with dynamic words and an effective selling orientation. After all, you are the one who has to sell this idea. Thousands of ideas out there are competing for the same funds that you are seeking from the venture capital fund. Without a strong selling document you will never meet the venture capitalist and have a chance to discuss your idea.

When you have finished writing your summary presentation, sit back for a few minutes and think about it. Try to determine if it really stands out, if it makes an exciting statement, and if it suggests that your situation is an opportunity the venture capitalist cannot miss. If your summary accomplishes these things, then you have satisfied the basic requirement of the summary. Remember, the basic idea is to sell your idea to the venture capitalist.

Rather than talk about how wonderful your management is, you should mention the actual achievements that management has accomplished to date. By eliminating superlatives you will avoid giving the impression that you are a salesperson first and an achiever second.

ANOTHER KIND OF VENTURE CAPITAL

The summary for subordinated debt is quite different from the summary for equity from a venture capital fund just covered in the preceding section. Subordinated debt lenders or mezzanine funds lend money and have an option to buy stock in your company, whereas venture capitalists make equity investments by means of common or preferred stock. The previous summary would be used to request an equity investment. In contrast, the summary that follows is oriented toward a mezzanine fund. We made the investment along with others, but it had a poor return. The summary is a disguised version of one that was presented to us some years ago. The numbers and people as well as the stage of development have been changed completely:

Company: TT Corporation
123 Main Street
McLean, Virginia 22101
Telephone: (703) 555–1212
www.ttcorp.com

Contact: Jane Entrepreneur, President
(j.entrepreneur@ttcorp.com)

Type of Business: Manufacturer of switching gear for telephone equipment.

Company Summary: TT Corporation was founded two years ago by Jane Entrepreneur, an individual with seven years' experience in the communications and switching-gear industry. The company's first product was a multipurpose laser switching unit attached to telephone systems permitting the buyer of the unit to use several low-cost telephone services. The company has reached profitability after its second year of business, and estimates show that it will be very profitable in three years.

Management: Jane Entrepreneur, with seven years' experience in manufacturing telephone switching equipment, founded the company in 2000 and has served as President since that time. She previously worked for a large communications network conglomerate and several other communications corporations. She is a graduate of a San Francisco technology university with a degree in electrical engineering.

John Smith, Executive Vice-president, has been with the company for one year. Previously he had seventeen years' experience in the field of telephone switching gear and related equipment. He has written two books on the subject and has been granted six patents for work in telecommunications. Currently he guides the company in all of its marketing operations. He has an M.B.A. degree from a large university in California.

Product/Service and Competition: TT Corporation manufactures a unique laser-driven switching box that can be adapted to all forms of telephone communications equipment. At present no companies other than TT Corporation are in the business of manufacturing these add-on communication boxes. It is doubtful that anyone will enter the business in the next two years. If competitors do enter, TT's patents should give it a monopoly on certain types of installations.

Funds Requested: $5 million convertible subordinated debentures at 13 percent interest and convertible into 10 percent ownership of the company.

Collateral: Second secured interest in the assets of the business subordinated to a local bank debt of $19.75 million.

Use of Proceeds: The company has currently outstripped its line of working capital at the bank, and its low equity base prevents the bank from increasing the line of credit beyond the current status. The company will use the $5 million initially to pay down the bank loan and negotiate a larger line of credit ($25 million) with the bank so that more working capital will be available to the company.

Projections:

PROJECTIONS	CURRENT YEAR	YEAR 1	YEAR 2	YEAR 3
Revenue	$35,000,000	$65,000,000	$130,000,000	$240,000,000
Net Income	1,000,000	10,000,000	25,000,000	63,000,000

Exit: The company will attempt a public offering in two years. If there is no public market and no prospect for a public market in the near future, then the company will offer to buy back the stock owned by the venture capitalist in five years. A predetermined price could be set ahead of time, if desired by the venture capitalist.

WHAT MAKES IT EXCITING?

There are three reasons why the foregoing summary is exciting to a venture capitalist. The first bit of information that is music to the venture capitalist's ears is the fact that both individuals have had previous experience in this area and have been working in this company for almost three years. Second, the product is unique. As discussed under "Product/Service and Competition," the product is manufactured only by this company, and there appears to be no potential competition on the horizon. This background usually makes the venture capitalist more comfortable about the operation and about the prospects for the future. The third is the crowning touch to this exciting summary is the financial projections. Not only has the company turned the corner from its actual financial statements, but it is now projected to have strong earnings. Obviously the venture capitalist will be led to believe that in the years ahead the company will go public or be sold to a large company. The projections would probably not excite a true-blue venture capitalist, but they suggest a good return on investment to a mezzanine fund that lends money.

PERSPECTIVE FOR YOUR SUMMARY

Both of the summaries discussed in this chapter have followed a specific format. The format that we will discuss next has worked well for people seeking money in the venture capital field. You should use the format that you believe will present your company in its best light. The format we present here may not be the one to accomplish this. However, be aware that the venture capitalist is seeking the four basic items we have described. You may cover some of the items in greater detail than others, but you should mention all four.

Uniqueness: You should mention the uniqueness of your product or why this situation is special.

Management: You should indicate that you have a competent and experienced management team.

Profits: You should indicate that there are substantial profits available for your company.

Exit: You need to take into account the venture capitalist's desire to have an exit.

These are the four basic items that venture capitalists look for immediately. You need to cover all four in your summary. You should cover them in sufficient detail. If you fail to cover these four items, the venture capitalist may merely put your proposal on the "back burner" while the VC reads some other proposal.

The summary document will be the most important piece of paper that you will create. The summary must interest the venture capitalist. It must act as a hook and pull the VC toward reading the entire business proposal.

Write your summary proposal before you write your full business proposal. In doing so, you should place in the summary only the essence of your entire business proposal. Then when you write your business proposal, make sure you substantiate and expand on everything in the summary proposal. Once you have finished your business proposal, return to the summary and rewrite it to make sure the summary is consistent with your business proposal.

Once you have finished the summary and the business proposal, you will want to have a friend read the entire product. Your friend should be asked to keep in mind certain questions during this reading. First, did it grab the reader's attention? Did it say, "This is a tremendous investment opportunity?" Second, was it easily understood? If your summary is not easy to understand, you can be sure that the business proposal will not be easy to understand either. The third question should be, "How can the summary proposal be improved?" Remember, constructive criticism can be of great assistance.

WHAT DO VENTURE CAPITALISTS THINK ABOUT SUMMARIES?

Venture capitalists believe that summaries should be exciting, that they should turn the reader on. Writing a summary is not like writing a novel. It doesn't take a talent for creative writing. And it doesn't take a talent for clever writing, as composing a jingle or a catchy phrase does. Still, the summary should be exciting. What excites you about the situation should come through in the proposal summary, not in the form of superlatives but in the form of a strong sales pitch backed up by facts.

You may have seen the prospectuses printed to sell stock in small businesses. These prospectuses must conform to the requirements of securities laws as enforced by the Securities and Exchange Commission (SEC). Usually, the writing is "dry." The prospectus merely outlines how the investor can lose money. There is rarely a sense of excitement. In making a presentation to a venture capital investor, you are not bound by the SEC requirements to make your proposal drab. You can make it exciting. It can be a sales document as long as you reveal the facts, and all of the facts.

CONFIDENTIALITY OF YOUR GREAT IDEA

From time to time, an entrepreneur will call a venture capitalist and discuss an idea in vague terms. After the venture capitalist has asked several questions, the entrepreneur will ask how to assure that the venture capitalist will not steal this great idea. In an effort to prevent piracy, many entrepreneurs ask the venture capitalist to sign a nondisclosure or confidentiality agreement. The agreement provides that the venture capitalist will maintain confidentiality with regard to the business situation presented by the entrepreneur.

Most venture capitalists will refuse to sign such nondisclosure agreements. They will give you every assurance that they will maintain the confidentiality of your special situation and, in most cases, this is true. Any venture capitalist that steals ideas faces the risk of a lawsuit and a bad reputation. A venture capital firm that deliberately divulges confidential information in a proposal could be considered liable if the act proved to be detrimental to the entrepreneur. However, the greatest repercussion for disclosure of confidential information would be the damage caused to the venture capital firm's reputation, since many people would find out about it and entrepreneurs would not send the firm business opportunities. In most cases, you can rely on professional integrity of the venture capital firm not to use or distribute the information you have given him. Sometimes VC firms have their own confidentiality agreement, which would be in your best interest to sign.

Many times a broker will ask a venture capital firm to sign an agreement to pay his fee if the firm is financed. Virtually all venture capital firms will refuse to sign these agreements, simply because they do not want to obligate themselves to pay any brokerage fees. Most venture capital firms will honor any directive given by the small business being financed. That is, if the small business tells the venture capital firm to pay the broker out of the proceeds of the investment proceeds, then it will be paid by the venture capital firm out of the proceeds.

As in any business, if you are dealing with a professional venture capital group, then you do not have to worry about confidentiality, and brokers do not have to worry about losing the opportunity to make a fee. Venture capitalists are in the business of making money for themselves, but they do not mind other people making money.

OBJECTIVE

In your own summary, you need to develop strong ideas that will make the venture capitalist wish to be an investor in your company. The summary should make the VC want to read and study the business proposal. As we discuss the items in the business proposal in Chapter 3, you will understand more clearly the desires of the venture capitalist company as well as the things you need to do to keep his or her interest going once the VC has been sold by the summary.

3

THE PROPOSAL

CAN YOU PUT TOGETHER AN
INTERESTING PROPOSAL?

A COMPLETE PROPOSAL IS ONE THAT
SELLS YOUR COMPANY.

Many people telephone an investment officer of a venture capital fund and try to set up an appointment so they can explain their financial needs and the potential of their company. Most venture capitalists will resist such visits until after they have received the business proposal. Without the proposal, or at least a summary proposal, the venture capitalist has no idea of the details of the business. If you do meet, the venture capitalist will not be prepared to ask intelligent questions. So what is the point of the meeting?

Some people show up at the office of the venture capitalist with an inadequate business proposal in hand and want to talk about their business. Sitting in a meeting with them, the venture capitalist fumbles with the papers and stumbles through the business proposal before understanding the situation. Such visits make it difficult to have a productive meeting.

On the other hand, after reading a sound business proposal, the venture capitalist usually knows if the partners at the fund will want to invest in the business you are presenting. If the venture capitalist (VC) does not wish to invest, the VC can save the entrepreneur a trip to the venture capital company. If the venture capitalist wants to invest, then the VC is prepared to discuss the company in detail when the meeting occurs.

Some entrepreneurs believe that if they can only meet with the venture capitalist, they can "sell" their idea. This attitude is especially common in cases where the venture capitalist has read the business proposal and notifies the entrepreneur that the VC does not have an interest in investing. I have never seen a "sale" happen in such circumstances.

Entrepreneurs often believe they can meet the venture capitalist, present their idea orally, and receive financing. A meeting with the venture capitalist cannot substitute for a well-prepared business proposal that has a compelling story. After reading a strong business proposal, the VC knows precisely the type of investment they will want to make, as well as what questions still remain unanswered. For most venture capitalists, then, the business proposal is the turning point in the decision to go forward, to invest time and energy in trying to analyze the situation, and to work out a deal with the entrepreneur.

If the entrepreneur is invited to the office of the venture capitalist to discuss the business proposal, the venture capitalist is probably seeking a way to make the investment. The entrepreneur is 50 percent on the way to obtaining funds if the entrepreneur is invited to meet with the venture capitalist. Because of the emphasis placed on the business proposal by the venture capital community, every entrepreneur must understand the vital importance of having an excellent business proposal with a compelling story.

The business proposal is similar to the business plan, except that it is shorter and contains fewer details. A full-blown business plan could be several hundred pages long. It would have sections on the financial plan, the marketing plan, the production plan, and personnel needed to carry out the plans. It would discuss the strengths and weaknesses of the company in all business segments. It would discuss strategies, long-range objectives, and short-run objectives.

A business proposal is much like any other proposal in that it proposes something to someone. In the case of a venture capital proposal, it suggests how the venture capitalist and you can both make money. A business proposal is an abbreviated business plan with an emphasis on showing an outsider how the company will succeed. In many ways the business proposal is a promotional document meant to sell your company to an investor—in this case the venture capitalist. When you write your business proposal, remember that it's a promotional document. It is the sales literature for your company, and it must be compelling.

SHOULD YOU USE A BROKER OR CONSULTANT?

Many "consultants" and "financial brokers" prepare business proposals. The business proposals prepared by these people are known by their generic name, "packages." Brokers usually charge a great deal to assemble packages. Unfortunately, this fee is normally required in advance, and when the consultant is finished with the package it is usually a poor imitation of a business proposal. Many financial brokers merely send out sketchy information supplied to them by the entrepreneur. This usually ensures that the venture capital management will turn down the proposal.

The reason a financial broker cannot prepare an effective business proposal is simple. Brokers rarely know your business as well as you do. The business consultant cannot write a proposal without the help of the entrepreneur. By using Chapters 2–4 of this book you can create a business proposal that will present your business in its best light. The proposal will be submitted to a venture capital company, not a bank. Bank proposals are different, and there are many good books on preparing them. By using this book you will be able to deal directly with the venture capital source.

Of course, it is wise to have your banker, your accountant, and friends review the proposal. They may be able to suggest another point of view for you to consider. If you must use a business broker or consultant, please read Chapter 11 before you pay out a single cent to them.

MOST IMPORTANT QUALITY OF A BUSINESS PROPOSAL

The most important quality of your business proposal is succinctness built around a central compelling story. A business proposal that is longer than 30 pages, excluding the financial exhibits, is probably too long. One that runs over 50 pages is definitely too long. The idea behind a business proposal is to impart the main ideas important to the venture capitalist. Chapter 4 covers the additional information you will need to prepare, and this Chapter covers the key sections of the proposal.

The business proposal format set forth on the following pages has been organized for a traditional, straightforward company. A business proposal can be organized in any manner. Most of the components listed in the following pages should be included in every business proposal; however, some items should be deleted if they are not applicable to your situation. You should not cover those that are not significant. For example, a service company would delete many sections dealing with production. The organization and presentation of the components can be rearranged to place important items first. Some items can be combined under a single heading.

What follows is the description of a complete business proposal. When you read it you might ask why you should do all this work for the venture capitalist. The fact is that if you do not, the venture capitalist will have to do it before the VC invests in your company. By doing the work for the VC, you speed up the process and you make sure it is correctly presented. Also, remember there are many business proposals arriving on the desk of the venture capitalist. If yours is to win out, the proposal should eliminate as much work as possible for the venture capitalist. Make it easy for the venture capitalist to invest in your company and you will be ahead of the pack.

Many venture capitalists will not invest in a company that does not have a strong business proposal. They believe that if the entrepreneur cannot prepare an effective business proposal, the entrepreneur cannot possibly be a competent entrepreneur. Other venture capitalists will not lean that far, but every venture capitalist agrees that a well-prepared business proposal is a sign of an intelligent person that cares about growing their company.

You must look at your business proposal as a legal instrument too. Legally, you want to prepare a complete business proposal. If you leave out material information, then the venture capital investor may have a strong reason to sue you personally if the venture fails. Everyone understands that the venture capitalist is an adult. A venture capitalist has the ability to review proposals and make a professional judgment. The VC is, by every standard, a sophisticated investor. But you should remember that security laws dictate how a private placement of securities must be carried out.

Of course, you cannot include fraudulent or misleading information in your proposal; moreover, you are supposed to fully disclose any material item about your business. The disclosure must be in writing to the purchaser of the securities. If you fail to disclose a material item, the venture capitalist may be able to demand all of his money back; even worse, if the business fails, he could have a legal basis to sue you personally. Therefore, as you prepare your business proposal, begin by including too much information. Later, when you begin to pare it down to size, remember not to delete those items that will be material to a reasonable investor.

In general, the major sections you should cover in your business proposal are

1. Summary
2. Description of the business and its future
3. Management team
4. Description of the financing you seek
5. Risk factors of investing

6. Return on investment and exit

7. Analysis of operations and projections

8. Attachment: historical and current financial statements

9. Attachment: projections

10. Attachment: illustrative information

Let's discuss each item in turn.

PART 1: SUMMARY

The summary should be the first item a venture capitalist sees. The summary was discussed in Chapter 2. It gives the venture capitalist an initial impression of you and your proposal so it should be typed perfectly and presented clearly. Economy of words and crispness are key here. If the venture capitalist is not captivated by the summary, your business proposal may go in the trash. Hit the compelling story hard.

PART 2: BUSINESS AND ITS FUTURE

This section covers a number of key topics that will help the venture capitalist understand your business. Each item is important in its own right, but throughout this section there must also be a general, if not specific, attempt to show how your business is unique. Show the reader what makes your business special in the world of business. While reading this section, the venture capitalist will try to determine the "keys to success" for this industry. In other words, the VC will try to identify these two or three things that must be executed very well in order to be successful in your business situation. Note the numbering system has headings with a single number and subheadings have decimals such as 2.01.

2.01 General. Begin with a paragraph that starts with the sentence, "The company's principal offices are located...," and put in the address, the telephone number, and the individual who should be contacted, as well as the standard industrial classification (SIC code) for your industry, if you know it. The SIC codes are established by the National Bureau of Standards, and its codebook is available in most libraries.

2.02 Nature of the Business. In this part give a general synopsis of the business that you are in. For example, you might say, "The company designs, manufactures, markets, and services minicomputer-base software-controlled medical diagnostic equipment used in outpatient monitoring." A pithy sentence describing what your company does is probably the best beginning. Next, you should describe the product or service in general terms. You want to make sure the venture capitalist understands your product or service in as few words as possible.

2.03 Business History. In this section you should tell when the company was incorporated, specify when it introduced its first product or service, and list the most important milestones (with dates) through which the company has passed. The business history section of the report must be brief and to the point. If it is more than a page, or at the most, two pages, you have included too many historical asides. There may be a special reason for including a long historical section if the company has had a colorful past, but by all means be brief. The venture capitalist will talk to you about the business history section in order to understand your business. At that time, you can go into many details.

2.04 Business of the Future. Spell out in chronological sequence the plan for the company and indicate critical milestones. In essence, the venture capitalist wants to know how you move from where you are today to where you intend to be in five years. The form of this section of the proposal is open to a great deal of freedom even though it must be brief. You may simply state that you intend to continue producing your two basic products for the next five years and that in year three you will introduce another similar product. In that case, your business of the future would be brief and to the point. On the other hand, if you expect to go through innumerable changes before you reach your final point of stability, you should indicate what changes will take place. The venture capitalist wants to know precisely what the company will have to do to be a success.

2.05 Uniqueness. Every business proposition to a venture capitalist should have some unique property. Is the management team unique? Is the product or service unique? Is the production process unique? Is it based on unique financing? All these items could be included. The important point is that something should make this company stand out from all the other investment opportunities available to the venture capitalist. Venture capitalists do not like to invest in "me too" companies. They want a company that has a unique business position.

In a separate section such as this, or in various sections throughout the business plan, you should stress the uniqueness of your company. If your business involves a new product, a patent on a process, or some other particularly unusual feature, then it should be covered in a separate section such as this. Besides including this section, the entrepreneur should interlace the business proposal with the strengths of the company.

2.06 Product or Service. In this section you must describe the product or service precisely, in terms that will leave no doubt in the mind of the reader as to what you produce or plan to produce. If you have several products or services, describe each in a separate paragraph. You should describe the price of the product, how the price was determined, and the amount of gross profit.

Entrepreneurs tend to treat pricing of their product too hastily. Spend enough time to think through all the factors affecting your pricing of the product and make sure that you can explain, in straightforward, logical terms, the rationale behind the pricing. Is it priced because competition has forced prices in that direction? Is it priced high because you can get away with it? You must be prepared to answer these questions.

2.07 Customers or Purchasers of the Product. Describe in detail the customers of the product: who uses it, what they use it for, and why they buy your product or service. Do they buy your product because of price alone, or are there other considerations? What need does the product or service satisfy for the customer? In this section you also need to list the top three purchasers of your product, along with the dollar volume and unit volume of their purchases. You can do this in columnar form, the first column containing the company, the second the dollar volume, and the third column the number of units purchased. You will be furnishing the venture capitalist with a complete purchaser's list if he or she becomes very interested in your company. This section of your proposal will give the venture capitalist an idea of the business at an early stage in your dealings with him.

2.08 Industry or Market. Here you should describe the general marketplace for your product: the total dollar volume, the rate it has grown, and the overall demand for this product or service. A projection for the future size of the marketplace is necessary as well as an explanatoin of how you determine those projections. You may use a tabular format such as:

YEAR	INDUSTRY SALES	% INCREASE
Last Year	$1,000,000,000	N/A
This Year	$1,200,000,000	20%
Next Year	$1,440,000,000	20%
2nd Year	$1,800,000,000	25%
3rd Year	$2,250,000,000	25%

In stating industry sales, make sure you don't fall into the trap of stating industry sales for the entire marketplace when, in effect, your product will be sold to only a very small part of that industry. The classic example is the company that is going to manufacture computer disk drives. In its business proposal it lists the entire computer disk drive market as its marketplace. Actually, the computer disk that it is going to manufacture is compatible with only one manufacturer. That manufacturer has only a 10 percent share of the market. Venture capitalists are eager to know the details of industry sales and the penetration of the industry with your product. You will need to be an expert in this area.

2.09 Competition. Here you must describe all the competing products and the various companies that produce them. Pay particular attention to the dollar volume that they are selling, the percentage of the market that they have, and the financial strength of the company that is your competitor. You should also describe precisely how your product is different from their products. A typical description of a competitor might be:

AJAX MFG. Ajax Mfg. is a $300 million company with one division selling widgets to this industry. The division had sales of approximately $14 million last year, which indicates it has 12 percent of the market. Ajax's other business has suffered, and currently Ajax seems to be draining this division of capital because Ajax has not introduced a new product in four years. Its product is obsolete and lacks many of the features of our machine. Our machine has a three-dimensional matrix, whereas theirs is two-dimensional. Our machine is microcomputer driven; theirs is manual. Ours is only 10 percent more expensive.

If you have no competition, then describe why you do not have competition. A reason for no competition might be your patent position. If you think there might be competition in the future, then you should indicate each probable competitor and when he might enter the market. Most entrepreneurs do not know enough about their competition. A venture capitalist will be leery of your analysis if you do not understand your competition. Be aware, too, that most venture capitalists believe every product has some type of competition.

2.10 Marketing. This section must contain information about your marketing process and the channels of distribution. That is, how does the product leave your plant and arrive in the hands of the ultimate user? Will you have a direct sales force or use distributors? What brokers or intermediaries are involved in selling your product? What is the relationship of your company to these intermediaries? You must describe any special arrangements you have entered into in order to market your product.

Most venture capitalists are poor market analyzers. They fancy themselves as marketing men, but they are not. In explaining the marketing of your product, you will have to take one step at a time so they can understand the marketing process.

If you are marketing to state, local, or federal government almost exclusively, most venture capitalists will be nervous because your company will be subject to the whim of governmental appropriations. You will need a convincing explanation to overcome the objections to the marketing of most of your products to the government. Further, if you have a sole customer, it may be difficult for the venture capitalist to accept your marketing dependence on one customer. The risks are too high.

2.11 Production. Here you need to describe all stages of the production process and whatever affects production. A key point here is production costs. How did you arrive at the cost of goods sold?

2.12 Production Characteristics. This section should focus on the production characteristics. Is it a difficult or a sophisticated production process? Are there many components or just a few? How much value does the company actually add to the product? How much is purchased in subassembly format? What components are crucial to the production process? The venture capitalist wants to determine the difficulty of the production process. Is it a standard production process, or does it have many difficult tasks? If it is a complicated process, will people with special skills be needed to carry it out?

2.13 Labor Force and Employees. In this section you need to describe the number of employees you have, your relationship with the work force, and whether it is union or nonunion. Also, categorize members of the work force in terms of white collar, blue collar, and so on. If the work force is unionized, you should describe the union contract, the relationship with the union, and when the contract will expire. The venture capitalist will want to determine how difficult it will be to acquire and maintain your employees. If your employees are hard to find, you will have to explain how you intend to attract and keep good employees.

2.14 Suppliers. In this section describe the companies that supply your company with raw materials or other necessary items. At this point in the proposal, you need to list the three or four top suppliers and the items they supply. You will want to do this in columnar form, the first column listing the suppliers, the second column listing the dollar volume of the supplies, and the third column showing the product supplied to your company. Later, you will be required to provide the venture capitalist with a complete list of suppliers of major components. The venture capitalist will use the list to call suppliers and verify your list.

2.15 Subcontractors. If subcontractors or other people complete part of the work in bringing the product to the marketplace, describe them and the relationship with them. In this section you should list several of the subcontractors and the dollar volume of work you are contracting with them. Later you will need to supply the venture capitalist with a complete list of subcontractors, names, addresses, telephone numbers, and volumes so the venture capitalist can contact these subcontractors.

2.16 Equipment. Describe in some detail the equipment that you have or intend to buy. Give a general idea of the fixed assets and their value of resale. Describe the total dollar volume and number of units that you can produce using the existing equipment. Identify any long lead time in acquiring machinery.

In this section, the venture capitalist wants to know if your equipment is difficult to obtain. If it is and you reach capacity, the company will have to wait for a long period of time before it can acquire additional equipment in order to increase capacity. The venture capitalist will want to know if the equipment is complicated and requires a special skill to operate. If so, you will need a special work force in order to operate the machines. The question is, "How difficult is it to find such a special employee to operate the machine?" Finally, if the machinery is used for a special purpose, it will be difficult to sell. Therefore, its collateral value is worth much less. All these points are important to the venture capitalist.

2.17 Property and Facilities. Describe the real estate that the company owns, or the lease that it has for its offices and plant. Describe the size of the plant in square feet and the price per square foot. You must describe the equipment that you have or intend to buy; describe the fixed assets in detail.

Here the venture capitalist wants to know that the plant is sufficient to take care of the growth of the company. If you will have to move out of the plant in a year, the company will have difficulty continuing to expand at a rapid rate. Some venture capitalists don't like to invest in companies that have to move within a short period of time. They believe such moves are disruptive and can destroy the company's growth.

2.18 Patents and Trademarks. You must describe in detail any patents or trademarks held by the company or those it intends to apply for. You may wish to describe why a patent has been granted in order to emphasize the product's uniqueness. At some point in the process you may want to give the venture capitalist a copy of your patent so he can read it and determine for himself why you have a unique patent or trademark. You should not put a copy of the trademark in the business plan unless it is key to describing the uniqueness.

2.19 Research and Development. Here you should indicate the amount of money for research and development, specifically the amount that has been spent in the past, and the amount that you intend to spend in the future. You should describe precisely what you intend to accomplish with the funds spent on research and development.

It is every venture capitalist's nightmare that he will somehow misjudge the entrepreneur and invest in a consummate researcher, rather than an entrepreneur who wants to develop a product. The research entrepreneur will spend millions researching and developing new product variations of the existing product. The venture capitalist wants an entrepreneur who can make the transition into a marketing and production company that is trying to make money.

2.20 Litigation. Describe any litigation the company may be involved in now, including suits against the company and those the company has filed against others. Be sure to mention any potential litigation that may be contemplated. Venture capitalists are litigation shy. If they find that a company has been involved in a great deal of litigation, they are apt to turn down the request for funds. After all, if everybody is suing you, there must be something wrong with the way you operate your company. On the other hand, if you are the type who sues others at the drop of a hat, there must also be something wrong.

The venture capitalist will have every reason to wonder if you won't end up suing him very soon after he has made his investment. A company with a history of litigation will have to explain the details to the venture capitalist in order to help the venture capitalist overcome his natural reservations about companies with such a background.

2.21 Government Regulations. Describe the governmental agency that regulates the company and describe the relationship with the government. In this section describe how you plan to comply with regulations set down by the Occupational Safety and Health Administration. Most venture capitalists can tell stories about excruciating experiences with a federal or state agency that had one of their portfolio companies tied in red tape for months or even years and that in some cases destroyed the company. If your business comes under a great deal of governmental regulation—for example, by the Food and Drug Administration—you will have to use extra persuasion to convince the venture capitalist that you know how to operate in a regulated environment.

2.22 Conflicts of Interest. Describe any potential conflicts of interest, such as a director who is also the owner of one of your suppliers. Describe any transactions with management in which management has sold something to the company for a price that may or may not be reasonable. If you do not reveal conflicts of interest and the venture capitalist uncovers them, you lose credibility instantly. It is better to meet this problem head on and reveal it to the venture capitalist at the outset. Show how the company is better off by being involved in a potentially conflicting situation than it would be otherwise.

2.23 Backlog. In this section you should indicate the amount of backlog outstanding for the company's products. List the items requested and the size of the order. You can also give the venture capitalist a good idea of the backlog by listing the top three or four customers and their backlog of orders. Do this in columnar form. The first column should contain the name of the company that has placed the order, the second column the dollar volume of the orders, and the third column the number of units ordered. Later in your meeting with the venture capitalist, you should show him a complete list of the backlog so he can see where the orders are coming from and who purchases the product.

2.24 Insurance. List the insurance carried by the company or intended to be carried by the company, including fire, casualty, product liability, flood insurance, fidelity bond, life insurance on key employees, and so on. However, list only the insurance that is important to the operation of the company, not health insurance, dental plan, or the like.

2.25 Taxes. Mention any special taxes that are levied against the company. If you are already in business, mention any outstanding taxes, such as payroll taxes or income taxes.

2.26 Corporate Structure. In this section you should mention whether it is a stock company, a partnership, or a Subchapter S, and whether it is 1244 stock. Tell where the company is incorporated, where it is licensed to do business, and what trade names it uses. You should mention if it is a parent company with a subsidiary. If it is a complex situation in which a parent owns part of or all subsidiaries, you should use block diagrams and show the separate legal entities and draw lines between them with percentages on them as shown below.

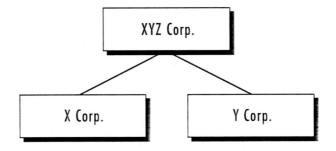

2.27 Publications and Associations. As a point of information, the venture capitalist may be interested in trade associations for your industry. He may also want to know which trade magazines and trade newspapers are good ones, so that he may use back issues to learn more about your business.

PART 3: THE MANAGEMENT

In this section you should describe the management, the directors, and all others who are key to the operation of this business. Usually, there are no more than three key people in a very small firm and fewer than six in a larger one. Remember, the venture capitalist is looking for key people. You should refrain from using superlatives to describe the key people, but do not be shy about mentioning achievements.

3.01 Directors and Officers. List all the officers, directors, and key employees. You should include the full name of each individual, his or her position, and age. An example is as follows:

DIRECTORS		
Joseph Entrepreneur	President	42
Donna Dont	Chief Financial Officer	34

3.02 Key Employees. In this section you should identify the three or four individuals who are key employees and give a summary, in resume style, of their background and where they have worked. It is important to demonstrate that these key people are achievers.

There is a considerable body of psychological literature on achievers, but not much on entrepreneurs. Some people argue that achievers are born the way they are, whereas others believe the attributes of achievers can be learned. The point is simple in your case. You must present yourself as an achiever to the venture capitalist, or you probably will not be financed. Further, the more you have achieved in your industry, the more the venture capitalist will be motivated to finance your company.

3.03 Management Fidelity. It is difficult to demonstrate your honesty on paper. But a positive statement like the one that follows will be a big plus.

No member of the management team, no director, or any major investor in the company, has ever been arrested, convicted, or charged in a material crime; and further, not one has been bankrupt personally or has been associated with a bankrupt business of any kind. Personal credit reports will verify that all individuals have excellent credit ratings and have no overdue debt outstanding.

Obviously, what you are trying to communicate to the venture capitalist is that you and your team are as clean as a whistle.

3.04 Remuneration. In this section you are to list all key employees, directors, or officers who will receive any payment whatsoever. You should list in tabular form the names of the individuals, the capacity in which they will be serving, and the salary or remuneration that they have received or propose to receive. Under the heading of remuneration, you should include all fees, director's fees, consulting fees, commissions, bonuses, salary, and so on—in other words, total remuneration by your company. An example is:

Name	Position	Amount
Joseph Entrepreneur	President	$200,000
Donna Dont	CFO	$150,000
Sam Smith	Head of Marketing	$100,000

3.05 Stock Options. You should tabulate all stock options that are now outstanding. Beside each person's name you should indicate the number of shares that have been granted, the average exercise price, the number of shares that have been exercised since the options were granted, and the number of options still outstanding. Where options are outstanding to a corporation, you may wish to note why they are outstanding at this point. An example is as follows:

NAME	AMOUNT	PRICE	EXERCISED	OUTSTANDING
Joe Entrepreneur	200,000	$1.00	None	200,000
Donna Dont	100,000	$1.00	None	200,000

3.06 Stock Option Plan. In this section describe the general stock option plan that exists at the company and how many options the plan has in it or will have in it at some date in the future.

3.07 Principal Shareholders. In this section list in tabular form the name of the individual, the amount of shares owned beneficially or directly, all shares under option, the percentage this ownership represents with regard to all the shares outstanding, and the percentage of ownership that will exist after the shares have been exercised. Also indicate the price paid for the ownership.

NAME	SHARES	% OWNERSHIP BEFORE FINANCING	% OWNERSHIP AFTER THIS FINANCING	PRICE PAID FOR OWNERSHIP
J. Entrepreneur	400,000	50%	40%	$200,000
S. Smith	400,000	50%	40%	$200,000
V. Capitalist	200,000	0	20%	$2,000,000

3.08 Employment Agreements. List in detail any employment agreements that the company has with any of the employees, and state specifically what the arrangement is with each employee. Employment agreements are not appreciated by venture capitalists. Most often they are used to ensure that top management will not be fired and will continue to obtain a high salary. If you have a legitimate reason for employment contracts, state it in this section.

3.09 Conflict of Interest. This item is listed once again to make sure that any conflict of interest transactions that have transpired are revealed fully. In this section you should reveal transactions that management has had with the company. For example, a director may have contributed services to the company, and in return the director may have received stock or stock options in the company.

3.10 Consultants, Accountants, Lawyers, Bankers, and Others. In this section you should mention the names of your consultants, if any, and your accountants, lawyers, and bankers, along with their telephone numbers. If a special fee is being paid to any of them or if any of them are on a monthly retainer fee by the company, mention it in this section. The VC will be impressed if you have some good names here.

PART 4: DESCRIPTION OF THE FINANCING

In this section you will describe the type of financing you are trying to obtain, along with some related items.

4.01 Proposed Financing. It is difficult for an entrepreneur to set the price for a new investment; many have made a mistake of setting the price too high. A high price will turn off the venture capitalist. Many writers of business proposals will leave out this section assuming that they would like to get in the door of the VC firm first and negotiate price later. This is an acceptable practice. However, before you meet with the VC you need to think about the items discussed in this section. The subject will be a main topic at some point of your meeting.

If you want to include your discussion of pricing, then you need first to describe the loan, the options, the preferred stock, the common stock—whatever it is you are trying to sell to the venture capitalist. Be sure to provide enough details so that there will be no question about what you are selling.

If you are proposing a loan, explain the term of the loan. Is it five years or ten years? Will there be an interest-only period? What interest rate are you seeking? Will the interest rate be variable or fixed? Will the loan be convertible into common stock or preferred stock? All these items need to be covered. If you are open to suggestions on the structure, then state this important point in this section.

If you are selling preferred stock, what dividend will you pay? Will the dividend be cumulative (meaning that in case you do not pay it one year or one quarter, then you must make it up in some other year or quarter)? What redemption will there be of the preferred stock? For example, after five years will you have to begin redeeming the stock over a number of years to give the investor his money back? Is the preferred stock convertible into common stock? If so, what is the conversion price? What restrictions are there on these shares, and does the preferred stock have voting rights? Does it control the board of directors? What preferential treatment will it have?

If you are selling common stock, will there be a dividend on the common stock? Will the dividend be cumulative in case you miss it? Will a redemption of the common stock be required after a period of time in order to give the investor his or her money back? What price will the investor pay for the common stock? Will there be restrictions on the shares? What voting rights will holders of common stock have? What registration rights will holders of common stock have? That is, can the venture capitalist make you register the stock and in so doing make you become a public company?

If you are offering stock options under any of these conditions, you need to consider the price that the venture capitalist will pay for the option when he purchases the option from your company. You must also consider what price the venture capitalist will pay to exercise the option into common or preferred stock. How many shares will the options exercise into? What is the expiration period of the option? Five years? Ten years? You should spell out all these things about the stock options. If you are flexible as to the type of financing or the terms of the financing, state your willingness to negotiate in this section.

4.02 Capital Structure. Here you should describe the common stock, preferred stock, and long-term debt that is currently outstanding so that the venture capitalist will know the general capital structure of the company. For example:

TYPE OF SECURITY	BEFORE FINANCING	AFTER FINANCING
Bank Debt	$4,000,000	$2,000,000
Long Term Debt	$2,000,000	$2,000,000
Preferred Stock VC	0	$2,000,000
Common Stock	$ 600,000	$ 600,000

In the case above, $2 million of the funds raised from the venture capitalist is being used to pay off the bank debt. You need this section only if the financing is complex.

4.03 Collateral for the Financing. If you are seeking a stock sale, omit this section. If you have gone to a VC that buys subordinated debt, list the debts that will be senior to this subordinated debt. If you are seeking debt that will have some security, explain what will be used to collateralize this debt. For example, the debt could be secured by a patent.

4.04 Guarantees. Here indicate the personal or corporate guarantees that will be given to the venture capitalist for his investment. If there is to be a personal guarantee, you will be required to supply a personal financial statement on the guarantors. If a separate company is to guarantee the loan, you will need to provide a separate financial statement on the company guaranteeing the investment.

4.05 Conditions. Describe any conditions of the financing. For example, must the company provide a seat on the board of directors for the venture capital company's representative? Will the company have to live by any ratios? What milestones must the company achieve?

4.06 Reporting. Describe what reporting you intend to make to the investor with regard to this financing. For example, will you provide a monthly profit-and-loss statement, a balance sheet, and an annual audit?

4.07 Use of Proceeds. Specify where you intend to apply the funds. Do not use the amorphous name "working capital," but specify how the funds will be spent—for example, purchasing of inventory: $2 million; increase in accounts receivable: $1 million; and meeting payroll: $2 million. Be as specific as possible.

4.08 Ownership. In this section, indicate the number of shares outstanding and the number that would be owned by the venture firm if this financing occurs. Indicate the price paid for the ownership and the percentage of ownership the venture company will have of the company. Use a tabular format. An example is as follows:

SHAREHOLDER	BEFORE	AFTER	%	PRICE
Existing	800,000	800,000	80%	$1,000,000
Venture Capital	0	200,000	20%	$2,000,000

4.09 Dilution. Here you want to describe the degree to which the new investor is diluted in terms of book value. Compare the cost per share that the venture capitalist will be paying with the price paid by others.

4.10 Fees Paid. In this section indicate whether you will pay any brokerage fees and whether you will pay the legal fees of closing the investment. Specify what other fees you will pay or are obligated to pay. Be forewarned that most venture firms expect you to pay all fees.

4.11 Investor Involvement. The venture capitalist will want to have the right to attend board meetings and in many cases will want to become a member of the board of directors. The VC may want one or two or even three board positions. You may wish to have the venture capitalist more actively involved. This is the section in which you describe the amount of investor involvement that you are seeking or would like to have from the venture capitalist.

There may be other opportunities for the venture capital firm to offer services to your small company. You may wish to set these out in this section. For example, you may want the venture capital firm to provide you with assistance in the area of finance and may offer to pay a fee for this assistance. You may require a particular type of financing, such as an industrial revenue bond. You may offer the venture capitalist a fee for placing the bond—for example, 2 percent of the amount being placed. Generally speaking, this section deals with the type of involvement you expect the venture capitalist to serve in the future.

PART 5: RISK FACTORS

In this section you want to describe the major risk that an investor will incur by investing in your company. This section spells out all the drawbacks. Do not offer positive comments, except at the end of each paragraph. Some areas you may wish to cover are as follows:

5.01 Limited Operating History. If the company is new or has recently been organized, then the lack of operating history will be a significant item to discuss.

5.02 Limited Resources. The company may or may not have enough resources to continue operations for a prolonged period of time if everything does not work out as planned. Mention this as a potential risk.

5.03 Limited Management Experience. If management is young or new to this industry, you may need to discuss the experience level of management.

5.04 Market Uncertainties. You may wish to describe the market uncertainties that exist with regard to sales.

5.05 Production Uncertainties. Here you should describe any production uncertainties that may exist. Perhaps a prototype has never been built on a production assembly line, and therefore there are some uncertainties as to whether it can be built.

5.06 Liquidation. Here you should present a liquidation analysis of your company. That is, if the company were to get in trouble and had to be liquidated, what might it be worth on the auction block?

5.07 Dependence on Key Management. You need to explain either on paper or directly to the venture capitalist later what changes you expect when any of the key managers die. Who will step into his place? Who could be designated to run the company if the top person died? If you do not cover the subject here, you can expect the venture capitalist to ask you the favorite question, "What happens if you are run over by a truck tomorrow?" Some entrepreneurs write a corporate "will." In it they describe what is to be done with the company when they die.

5.08 What Could Go Wrong? Here the venture capitalist wants you to put on his hat and try to look at the business as an investment. He expects you to address the question, "What could go wrong?" The related question to answer here is, "How could the venture capitalist lose his money?" In other words, the venture capitalist wants you to use your objective, analytical skills to analyze your own business situation. He wants you to point out the major problems that can arise. As soon as you have pointed them out, you must indicate how you are going to solve them.

5.09 Other Items. You should mention such items as your estimated financial reserves, the lack of a public market for the shares, economic controls or other government regulations, control of the company by noninvestor stockholders, and the lack of dividends. You should mention these points if they are material, rather than wait for the venture capitalist to bring up these questions.

PART 6: RETURN ON INVESTMENT AND EXIT

In this section you need to discuss how the venture capital investor will eventually receive cash for the investment the VC makes in your company. Remember, the venture capitalist's objective is to liquidate the investment some day and end up with all cash and no investment in your company. There are three generally accepted methods of giving the venture capitalist liquidity. You should cover all three, but should also indicate which one is the most likely exit for your investor.

6.01 Public Offering. The first possibility is a public offering—that is, the company could go public by offering its shares in the public marketplace. Part of the shares or all of the shares owned by the venture capitalist would be sold in the public offering. You may wish to discuss this with a brokerage firm before you discuss it with the venture capitalist.

6.02 Sale to Another Company. Second, the company could be sold to a large company, usually a conglomerate. In the case of this option, you should actually mention some conglomerates or large companies that you believe would have an interest in acquiring your company.

Most businesses are sold either to strategic buyers or to financial buyers. It will be difficult for you to name any financial buyers that would be interested in your company, but you should be able to list a number of strategic buyers. A strategic buyer is a company that is in your business and would like to grow by acquisitions, or a strategic buyer could be a larger company that is in a similar business to yours but is likely to want to branch into your area. In your study of the market for your product and the competition, some of your competitors could be strategic buyers.

6.03 Buyback. Finally, you may offer the venture capitalist a "put" according to which your company will be required to buy the equity owned by the venture capitalist on the basis of a predetermined formula. Buyback formulas are covered in Chapter 6. In this case you will have to demonstrate that at some point in the future your company will have the ability to buy back the stock owned by the venture capitalist.

6.04 Return on Investment. Return on investment (ROI) will be important to the venture capitalist. You need to show what return the venture capital fund can expect if it invests the amount you are requesting. For example, you might say, "If an investor buys 30 percent of the company for $3 million and after four years the company is a public company with pretax earnings of $10 million, then $10 million times a price earnings multiple of 12 for our particular industry is $120 million as a value for the company; take 30 percent of that and you have $36 million for the investment of $3 million or about 10 times.

Assume that the 30 percent ownership is sold after four years; then the IRR for investing $3 million and in four years getting back $36 million is 86 percent. If only all the VC's investments gave this high IRR. IRR stands for internal rate of return and most calculators and spreadsheet programs (e.g., Lotus and Excel) will calculate IRR when you input the numbers set out in this paragraph.

PART 7: ANALYSIS OF OPERATIONS AND PROJECTIONS

Here you will present your own analysis of the company's prior operating history as well as projections for the future.

7.01 General. In this section you need to start out with some general profit-and-loss information, which will be based on financial data from your company. For example, for the last three years and for the next three years in the future, take net revenues, cost of sales, operating expense, interest expense, and income. Project them forward and give historical information for them so that one can see at a glance where the company has been and where it is going. Most people attach a spreadsheet or include a disk that has a spreadsheet, but you can also give a summary here. For example, the chart below shows the projections:

ACCOUNT	PRIOR YR ($)	THIS YR ($)	NEXT YR ($)	YEAR 2 ($)	YEAR 3 ($)
Revenue	1,000,000	4,000,000	10,000,000	40,000,000	100,000,000
% Change		300%	150%	300%	150%
Gross Margin	100,000	400,000	1,000,000	5,000,000	15,000,000
Operation Expense	300,000	400,000	600,000	1,000,000	3,000,000
Net Income	(200,000)	0	200,000	4,000,000	12,000,000
Current Assets	100,000	400,000	2,000,000	3,000,000	7,000,000
Municiple and Equities	300,000	500,000	1,000,000	2,000,000	3,000,000
Land and Building	0	0	0	0	0
Current Liabilities	400,000	600,000	1,000,000	2,000,000	5,000,000
Long-term Debt	100,000	400,000	1,000,000	1,000,000	5,000,000
Equity	20,000	600,000	2,600,000	8,000,000	35,000,000

7.02 Ratio Analysis. In this section you should take the net revenue, cost of sale, operating expenses, interest expense, and net income and compute them as percentages. That is, use 100 percent for net sales, then calculate cost of sales as a percentage of sales, and so on. Place these percentages in columnar form so that one can see the percentage ratio. You will want to have this in your spreadsheet.

7.03 Results of Operation. In this section you should discuss the results of operation and projections. Why have the results increased or declined? Tell why they will go up in the future. Discuss why the percentages might change, and mention any momentous events such as the year a new product was introduced or the year in the future when you will have large research and development expenditures, for example. In other words, you need to explain the numbers that you set out in the preceding section and should mention the attached financials and projections, which you are about to discuss in the next part of the proposal.

7.04 Financial Conditions. In this section you should discuss in detail the current balance sheet. Describe the liquidity of the company. Tell why there are significant increases in certain items such as accounts receivable, accounts payable, and so on.

7.05 Contingent Liabilities. Describe the company's contingent liabilities such as an unfunded pension plan, or a lawsuit from a company contending that one of its former employees working for you has brought corporate secrets with him.

PART 8: ATTACHMENT: FINANCIAL STATEMENTS

This is not a section so much as it is a collection of supporting documents. It should consist of complete financial statements. If your financials are not certified by an independent public accountant, they should be reviewed by an independent public accountant. You should have consolidated balance sheets, a consolidated statement of income, a consolidated statement of shareholders' equity, and a consolidated statement of changes in financial position. You should add appropriate notes of explanation to the financial statements. This exhibit should include the last several years of financial statements, as well as current financial statements that may or may not be audited by an accounting firm. These should all be attached as Exhibit 1—Financial Statements, and your business proposal should mention these exhibits.

Whatever you do, don't submit a business proposal that does not include current financial statements. Too many business proposals arrive with old (six months or more) financial statements. If you are to demonstrate that you are operating a stable business, you should present its current financial statements. Some business proposals present financial statements that are a year old. How can anyone make a decision to invest in a company on the basis of financial statements that are history? Some entrepreneurs do not seem to be aware of the fact that financial statements are of prime importance in operating a business. Needless to say, this type of entrepreneur does not receive the backing of venture capital companies.

PART 9: ATTACHMENT: FINANCIAL PROJECTIONS

This section, too, contains a spreadsheet exhibit. It should consist of the annual financial projections for the next five years, as well as a detailed monthly cash flow statement for the next twelve months. Anyone looking at the situation should be able to determine precisely the cash flow situation. The cash flow statement should show the inflow of this financing as cash inflow. These statements should be attached to the business proposal and should be marked Exhibit 2—Financial Projections and Exhibit 3—Cash Flows. Appendix 3 shows a typical format you may use for both projections and cash flows.

Please make sure you put a lot of time and energy into this section. You and the venture capitalist will spend a lot of time discussing these projections. In essence the entire business proposal that you described above is translated into numbers in this section. If you have a poor set of projections and cannot explain them you will reduce your chances of raising money from the VC. Clearly, the more detailed your projections, the more it looks as if you know your business. But remember the venture capitalist will do his own projections, so don't be offended if a VC's number differs from yours.

PART 10: PRODUCT LITERATURE, BROCHURES, ARTICLES, AND PICTURES

You should include pictures of the product and literature about the company that will show off your product or service. Written descriptions in the business proposal are essential, but pictures will also help sell your proposal. A general article about the industry or about competitive products compared to your product is a useful addition. Newspaper articles or magazine pieces on the company are probably unnecessary and do not say much to a venture capitalist. It is advisable to leave them out. Sending along tapes, records, or other promotional audiovisual items is a waste of money and time; do not do it.

DO YOU REALLY NEED ALL OF THIS?

The business proposal discussed above represents a thorough approach. You do not need to include everything that has been listed. What you must put into your business proposal are the material and key elements about your business. If there are only two key employees, you do not need to list the top ten people. If you operate a service business, you don't need to discuss production problems. Your proposal does not have to describe all the minute details of the business. It does need to include those aspects of the business that any investor, including you, would want to know before investing in the business.

When you begin writing your business proposal, you should cover all of the foregoing aspects in detail. That means you will have a very large draft proposal. Once you have finished that draft, you should weed out the parts that do not add materially to the proposal. The main goal of the business proposal is to present the major aspects of the business and to avoid or merely touch on the nonmaterial aspects of the business.

WHAT IS THE VENTURE CAPITALIST REALLY LOOKING FOR?

When all is said and done, what is a venture capitalist looking for when he reviews a business proposal? Many venture capitalists will tell you that they look for good management—that is, they immediately examine the management teams in depth. I think that most venture capitalists first look for what is special about this situation. In other words, they want to know why this company will make a lot of money. What is the compelling story behind this investment?

Basically, they are interested in the uniqueness of the idea or product or service and in management's ability to make it all happen. That means the venture capitalist will first look at the uniqueness of the product and what the team plans to do to capitalize on this uniqueness. Therefore, it would be wise for anyone preparing a complete business proposal to address the question of uniqueness in several places in the proposal.

UNIQUENESS

Since uniqueness is the first thing the venture capitalist will look for in the business proposal, let's see where it can be mentioned. Uniqueness can first be covered in Part 2 of the business proposal, "Business and Its Future." The question can be taken up directly under "Product or Service." You can even have a section entitled "Uniqueness" as covered above. There may also be unique aspects of marketing and production. You should certainly comment on the unique qualifications or skills of the management team; it is not enough to say that they are good people.

MANAGEMENT

Most venture capitalists consider management to be the key to every successful venture capital investment. This is the second thing the venture capitalist will be looking for, but the VC will place more emphasis on this area. The old saw of the venturing business is as follows: You can have a good idea and poor management and lose every time; conversely, you can have a poor idea and a good management team and win every time. Let us look at what is meant by "good" in this context.

The first thing a management team must have is experience. Unfortunately for young people, venture capitalists believe entrepreneurs should be between the ages of 30 and 45. There seems to be a 15-year open window of a person's lifetime, which the venture capitalist believes, is the best entrepreneurial age. Younger than age 30 usually means that the entrepreneur lacks management experience or the knowledge needed to conduct a strong growth-oriented company. Older than 45 usually means that the entrepreneur has the experience but lacks the drive and ambition. Certainly, there are exceptions to this pattern, but these are the general expectations of the venture capitalist.

Anyone preparing a business proposal should pay particular attention to the backgrounds of the management team. Explain in detail who they are, what makes them tick, and why these entrepreneurs among all the people in the world can take this unique product or service and make a great deal of money with it.

PROJECTIONS

Money is the third key subject covered by a good business proposal. It is incumbent upon the entrepreneur to set out strong growth projections for the company. These financial projections must not only be reasonable in terms of the percentage of growth that occurs each year, but they must also be realistic when compared with the many projections presented to the venture capitalist by other companies. Every entrepreneur should spend a great deal of time making, evaluating, and understanding his financial projections. Some entrepreneurs have an accounting firm prepare the projections on the basis of assumptions made by the entrepreneur. This is probably a poor approach because the venture capitalist will undoubtedly interrogate the entrepreneur to see if the entrepreneur understands the projections and the underlying assumptions. If someone else makes the projections, the entrepreneur will not be able to explain them adequately or convincingly. The venture capitalist will continue to question whether it is possible to expect the amount of growth indicated.

Many venture capitalists routinely cut the sales and earnings of a projection in half, and assume that these reduced figures are more realistic to expect. It will be incumbent upon the entrepreneur to persuade the venture capitalist that the projections are achievable.

EXIT

How the venture capitalist will exit from this situation will be a critical factor influencing his decision to invest. He wants to know how he will get out before he gets in. The venture capitalist does not want to be a long-term owner in the company. He wants to invest his money, ride with the deal for a while, and then exit. There are three basic exits:

1. Public offering, whereby the venture capitalist sells his ownership to the public.
2. Sale of the company, including the venture capitalist's ownership to someone else (usually a large company).
3. Sale of the venture capitalist's position back to the company, to you personally, or to a third party. You must cover this point in detail in your business proposal.

Remember, you need to cover (1) uniqueness; (2) management; (3) projections; and (4) exit. To miss any of these points is to set yourself up for rejection by the venture capitalist.

HOW TO PACKAGE YOUR PROPOSAL

In the retail food business, the package is as important as what is inside the package. Retailers must emphasize whatever will attract the buyer because it is a buyer's market. Thousands of retail products are vying for the consumer's money. The same is true in the case of venture capital. Thousands of proposals are vying for the venture capitalist's money. The packaging can draw the venture capitalist to your proposal.

You might write a great business proposal, but if its physical appearance is sloppy, it might not be picked up by the venture capitalist for weeks, and when it is picked up, what a sight! The venture capitalist's first impression of the proposal would be so colored by the poor packaging that he might turn down the business proposal without reviewing it in detail.

It cannot be emphasized enough that a venture capitalist receives hundreds of telephone calls and dozens of business proposals every week. If your business proposal is to compete with all the others sitting on the VC's desk, you must have a distinctive proposal. So you need to know the basics of how to package a winning business proposal.

Copies

You should not send an original to the venture capitalist. You should have crisp, clean copies, preferably on white paper with margins wide enough for the venture capitalist to make notes. A margin of one inch on all sides is the standard. The copy paper you use should be of high quality; it should not be the old variety that has an oily touch and a foul smell. It should provide a crisp, clean imprint on every page. Colored paper is optional. It does not impress most venture capitalists, but it might appeal to a few. You can copy on the back and the front or just on the front of each page.

Style of Type

You should not use an unusual style of type such as script. A type that is easy to read is essential if people are to process your business proposal quickly. The type should be dark and sharp in the original and in the copies. Submitting handwritten items is forbidden unless it is absolutely necessary.

Graphs and Pictures

Generally speaking, graphs are fine if they are of high quality, but they are usually not essential in a business proposal. Bar graphs of sales are not as effective as numbers. Pictures of the product or literature on the product should be attached to the business proposal in order to give the venture capitalist a better idea of the subject, but such material should be of good quality.

COPYING ARTICLES

You should copy articles carefully in order to make sure the copies are of good quality. A poor-quality copy of a newspaper article will not invite the venture capitalist to read it. Generally, articles are not recommended as part of your proposal.

COVER

If possible, the cover on your proposal should be an attractive color. Also, the cover sheet should be of heavy paper so that your proposal will stand out from all the others sitting on the venture capitalist's desk. Perhaps a bright yellow page with your logo in the middle and name at the bottom would invite the venture capitalist to pick it up and read it immediately. Once he opens it up, of course, the summary sheet should grab attention and draw the VC into the proposal. You might wish to use a picture of the product on the first page in order to attract attention. Again, you are selling, so make sure your product's package catches the eye of the venture capitalist.

BINDING

There are many ways of binding business proposals today. A staple probably will not hold your business proposal together. If an ordinary staple will hold it together, it is probably not long enough. Certain heavy-gauge staples are acceptable, of course. If such a staple is not available, you have three options: you can use a three-ring binder, have the proposal professionally bound, or put a large clip on it so that the venture capitalist can take the clip off and turn the pages. Of the three options, most venture capitalists prefer a professionally bound proposal. Otherwise, most would prefer to have a large clip. Most venture capitalists dislike three-ring binders only because they are almost impossible to store. While most venture capitalists prefer professional binding, they are perfectly willing to take any of the three options if they receive a professionally prepared proposal.

HOW MANY VENTURE CAPITALISTS SHOULD BE CONTACTED?

Entrepreneurs normally make one of two mistakes in contacting venture capitalists. Either they contact too few venture capitalists, or they contact too many. The typical entrepreneur in the first situation contacts one venture capitalist, asks the VC to review the proposal, and then waits patiently for a response. This can consume a huge amount of time, especially if the venture capitalist happens to be occupied with something else. The venture capitalist may have a portfolio company or, heaven forbid, many portfolio companies in trouble. The VC may like your proposal but may not have the time to spend on it.

At the other end of the spectrum, some entrepreneurs prepare a summary sheet and mail it out to 500 venture capitalists, assuming that this is the best approach. Although this is one way to contact many venture capitalists at once, it seldom moves them, because the mail-out is not taken seriously. The best procedure to follow is to select the half dozen venture capital firms nearest your company or those most likely to invest in your industry. Send them the summary and the full business proposal with a concise but pleasant cover letter. After the proposal has been out for one week, call each of the venture capital companies and ask them if they have received the proposal and if they are interested. This telephone reminder will move them along a little faster.

Every venture capitalist who claims to be "interested" and would like to meet with you should be approached with skepticism. You should spend some time on the phone with the VC to make sure there is a strong interest. If the VC seems to be genuinely interested then by all means set up an appointment to meet with him or her. The quicker you can get to a face-to-face meeting, the sooner you will know how interested the VC really is.

Some venture capitalists, having quickly read the proposal once, will tell the entrepreneur that they are interested in the deal. The entrepreneur, hearing the words, "Yes, I am interested," usually overreacts and assumes that the venture capitalist is ready to write a check. The entrepreneur is ready to board an airplane to visit the venture capitalist. You can avoid wasting time on such trips by asking the venture capitalist to clarify his intentions on the telephone. For example, if the venture capitalist says, "Yes, I am interested, but we can't make any commitments for six months," you might not see the need to visit him via airplane.

On the other hand, the venture capital firms might say they are interested in your proposal but after a few minutes of discussion, they might learn that the technology is more involved than they had perceived, and thus might decline. In short, a follow-up telephone conversation can help to clarify the venture capitalist's interest.

Discuss by telephone what the VC has in mind. If there seems to be some common ground on which you can put together a deal, then you should visit the venture capitalist. Running off to visit each venture capitalist will consume a great deal of your own time, so be sure it's worth the trip.

To be sure, most of the time you will not get a return call and will have to begin the arduous task of calling the venture capitalist to see if they are interested. Getting the attention of the VC is a terrible job. You will call and all too often will not be able to speak with anyone. Persistence pays off here. Just keep calling and trying to get to see the VC.

Most venture capital funds have Web sites with the names and e-mail addresses of the managers of the fund. Also on the Web site are discussions of what the VCs are looking for when they invest. Many sites have descriptions of the companies that they have invested in. You should read the site and customize your proposal to fit what they are looking for. Of course it is not possible to change a computer software company into a biotech company, but it is assumed that you are not sending your computer software business proposal to a biotech venture fund. The point is that if the VC has invested in a company that is similar in some ways to your company, it would be good to compare your company with that past VC investment.

You can submit your business proposal to the VC via e-mail. Most are receptive to this form of submission, and some of the high-tech VC funds prefer this form of submittal. Unfortunately, there are quite a few venture capitalists that do not read the e-mail that arrives at the e-mail address listed on their Web site. So be sure that you are getting your business proposal to the VC if you submit it via e-mail. A call to the venture capital fund will put you in touch with a receptionist. Usually the receptionist can tell you if the venture capitalist will accept a business proposal by e-mail. In addition, the receptionist can name some other people inside the firm who may be available to read your proposal.

SYNDICATIONS

Often, venture capitalists will tell you that their fund is interested in investing in your company, but that the fund can invest only part of the money that you need and the rest will have to be syndicated with other VC funds. This means that the VC will look for other venture capital firms to join the investment in your company. The first question you should ask in this situation is, "Will you be the lead investor?" This means that the venture capital firm will act as the leading investor and will help persuade other venture firms to invest in your firm.

Syndications are extremely common in the venture business, and many venture firms routinely syndicate all their investments with other venture firms. It is important for you to determine who will have to persuade the other companies to join the syndication. In some cases, the venture firm, as the leading investor, will go with you to other venture firms or will meet with a group of them and will help sell your idea to them.

In other cases, the venture firm will merely act as the first investor to commit funds, and all the others will have to do so on their own, in a separate action. This means you will have to be the syndicator and you will have to find the other venture firms to join the group. Of course, any firm that commits funds to you will have a list of other venture firms that they are interested in having in the investment with them.

Quite often, the leading investor is paid something for assisting in the syndication. Investment bankers, of course, are paid 5 to 10 percent for putting together a syndication of venture capital firms to invest in a small business. On the other hand, if the venture firm acts as a principal and syndicator, the fee is usually less. The typical fee to the venture firm will be 2 to 3 percent of the money it is raising through other venture firms. Sometimes, the VC will share part of those fees with the other venture firms that are investing.

As mentioned, syndications are common in the venture capital business. However, in many instances they are difficult to organize because each venture firm will have its own way of analyzing your deal, its own way of making a commitment to you, and its own lawyer to close the loan. You will have to juggle all of these people in pulling together the investment into your firm. Although a syndication can be put together (and this is done frequently), it is a complex and time-consuming endeavor.

Objective

Once you have created the proposal, it should sell you and your concept. If it does not accomplish this, you will not be given an opportunity to meet with the venture capitalist. Your objective is to create a business proposal that will lead to a meeting between you and the venture capitalist. That meeting is the subject of Chapter 5. Don't squander the opportunity to meet with the venture capitalist by giving him a number where you cannot be reached, especially one that rings and is not answered. A venture capitalist will try several times and then will stop trying.

Remember, you are selling to the VC, so be available or have an answering service take your calls. Carry a cell phone or a beeper. No one likes to arrange meetings leaving voice mail. Of course if you can begin chatting via e-mail, then arranging a meeting time will be easy. Before you meet with the venture capitalist, you should prepare yourself for the many questions he will have. Chapter 4 deals with the questions most often asked by a venture capitalist and shows you how to answer some of them.

4 A THOUSAND QUESTIONS

CAN YOU ANSWER A THOUSAND
QUESTIONS?
BE PREPARED BY ANSWERING ALL
THE QUESTIONS IN THIS CHAPTER.

It would be wonderful if the venture capitalist (VC) would read your business proposal and, without another thought, write out a check for the amount you requested and call you in to give it to you. Unfortunately, this will never happen. You will have to earn the money by proving your company is a good investment. The venture capitalist will have a thousand questions for you to answer before considering investing in your company.

Before you submit your business proposal to a venture capitalist, you should have some friends read it—your accountant, if possible, and perhaps your banker. From these readings should come questions that will help you clarify your business proposal so that it can be easily comprehended by the venture capitalist. The questions these friends ask will also prepare you for the venture capitalist's questions.

Questions are the subject of this chapter. Every venture capitalist will ask a thousand questions about your business, about you and your background, and about your plans for the future. You can answer some of these if you prepare a good business proposal. Other questions will be asked when the venture capitalist meets with you (more about this meeting in a later chapter).

In order to prepare you for the many questions of the venture capitalist, this chapter presents a number of questions under the same headings used in Chapter 3 on the business proposal. Before moving on to these various headings and the corresponding questions, you should understand the four basic areas in which the venture capitalist will concentrate the questions. These critical questions will give you an overview of what the venture capitalist is seeking. Later, the specific areas of your business proposal will be discussed and the questions that might arise will be suggested.

WHAT ARE THE MAJOR QUESTIONS?

The venture capitalists will focus their questions on four basic areas: uniqueness, management team and compelling story, financial projections, and exit. Let's look at them individually.

UNIQUENESS

Every venture capitalist receives thousands of business proposals every year. If you saw the desk of the VC, you would see lots of business proposals sitting there to be read. Many of the proposals received are sound but lack strong growth because they lack uniqueness. Sure, the company may grow at 10 percent a year, it may be a good small business, but let's face it, most small businesses are very poor investments for the investor. They are poor because they never pay dividends and there is no place to sell the stock. One could own 49 percent of every small business in the United States and starve to death, because the stock pays no dividends and there is no one to sell the stock to. So what will make your company grow?

The VC is looking for growth, and growth is usually related to some unique situation. The venture capitalist will repeatedly ask such questions as "What makes this situation special?" and "Why will it succeed?"

The VC is looking for a compelling story. Why will more people buy your product or service? Why is your product or service better? What are the drivers that will make your product or service sell? Among all the businesses of the world, why does this business have high growth potential?" Always be prepared for this type of interrogation and, conversely, never miss an opportunity, when asked a question that relates to uniqueness, to describe exactly why your company is special. Develop that compelling story and keep it out in front of the VC.

MANAGEMENT TEAM

Venture capitalists back management teams more than they back businesses. The most important management characteristic that the venture capitalist will be looking for is honesty. The venture capitalist cannot determine your honesty from your business proposal. The VC will determine your honesty during the meetings with you. The VC will be looking at the management team and trying to determine how honest they are. No venture capitalist expects an entrepreneur to be honest to a fault, but every venture capitalist wants an honorable entrepreneur.

If the venture capitalist thinks that the management team is dishonest, such a suspicion is the kiss of death. There will be no possibility of receiving financial support if the venture capitalist thinks the entrepreneur is dishonorable.

The venture capitalist's first questions about management will relate to their backgrounds. What is the business experience of the management team? What motivates the entrepreneur? Is the entrepreneur an achiever? Can the management team accomplish the job covered in the business proposal? These are the types of questions the venture capitalist will be asking about management in order to find out if the management team is competent.

Next the VC will look at the business proposal and determine what skills and characteristics that will be needed by the management team to make the business proposal happen. Then the VC will try to determine if your team has those skills and characteristics.

If the business proposal needs a terrific sales and marketing team to make it happen, that better be the skill set that you and your management team have. If this is a new production technique and your team doesn't have the required skill set in production, you have failed the test. There are certain skills needed to run any business, and there are special skills needed for certain types of businesses. Your team must have the required skills in both areas. You will need to convince the VC that your team has what is needed to implement the business proposal that you prepared.

After reviewing your business proposal and discussing it with you, the venture capitalist, you hope, will use terms such as "good people," "experienced," and "impressive" to describe the management team. If a venture capitalist uses these key words, you can assume it means the VC has accepted the management team as the people to invest in. Conversely, if the venture capitalist is hesitant about the management team, the VC will most likely not finance the company.

PROJECTIONS AND RETURN ON INVESTMENT

A venture capitalist will try to determine how realistic your projections are. The VC will try to determine if the management team can make these projections happen. A related question the venture capitalist will ask is how much money the venture capital fund can make by investing in your company. All these questions are concerned with the projections and the return on investment set out by you in your business proposal. You should be prepared to defend your sales and earnings projections. The projections should have a concrete foundation in reasonable assumptions. They should not be overly optimistic but must be aggressive enough to attract the venture capitalist.

A projected sales growth of 50 to 100 percent in the very early years is common. Sales growth of 25 percent is minimum and may not be attractive enough to elicit funds from an investor in a new small business. On the other hand, if you are buying an existing business, a solid 10 to 20 percent in sales growth may be sufficient to get the LBO fund interested.

EXIT

Finally, the venture capitalist will ask, "How will I ever get out of the deal?" Venture capitalists ask themselves this question both about bad deals and good deals. Obviously, they want to get their money out of bad deals, but they also want to get their money out of good deals. Owning 49 percent of a small business that is growing rapidly is wonderful if somewhere along the way there is an opportunity to sell part or all of that ownership position and realize cash for the investment.

The goal of all venture capitalists is to exchange their investment in your small business that has appreciated in value for cash. It is a natural desire for one simple reason. The compensation system of venture funds is predicated on realizations. That is, venture capitalists get paid their part of the gain when the equity they own in your company turns into cash or marketable securities. So there is no payday for the VC until the investment that was made in your company appreciates and then is sold. It is the overriding quest of the VC. You must be aware of this desire and the questions that will come from the venture capitalist on this subject. Your business proposal must tell the venture capitalist how the venture capital fund will exit from your situation. Cashing in is nirvana for the VC.

BUSINESS PROPOSAL QUESTIONS

We can consider the likely questions for each stage of the business proposal format by following the headings presented in Chapter 3. Under each heading we will look at what the venture capitalist is seeking and the type of questions you are likely to get. In some cases, the information provided will coach you on the information the venture capitalist is seeking.

PART 1: SUMMARY

The summary will not evoke any questions unless it is inconsistent with the business proposal. Make sure the summary and the business proposal coincide. If you say something in the summary that raises a question and it is not answered in the business proposal, you will probably be questioned about it.

PART 2: BUSINESS AND ITS FUTURE

Generally, the venture capitalist looks to this section for information about your industry and your business. Be aware that most entrepreneurs tend to describe the growth of their business in three phases. Why everyone selects three to mark their periods of growth is strange. You may wish to express your growth plan in something other than three phases.

2.01 General. The venture capitalist will have no questions here as long as you provide the name, address, and telephone number of your business and the individual who should be contacted. If possible, put in the Standard Industrial Classification. Remember, do not use a telephone number that is unattended. If you are not there, have an answering service or a friend answer the telephone for you.

Carry a cell phone or a beeper and give them that number, and always give out your e-mail address. You want the VC to be able to contact you easily. You can play hard to get if you have many VCs that want to invest, but don't play hard to get in person. You are selling them.

2.02 Nature of the Business. Here you will try to describe in a small paragraph the nature of the business. It is important to be succinct and to give the venture capitalist a short phrase that he can use to identify your company. If you are in the computer terminal industry, that information should be in your opening sentence so that the venture capitalist can identify your company by an industry classification. If you are not succinct, the venture capitalist will probably ask you to explain in two or three words what business you are in.

2.03 Business History. In this section the venture capitalist is seeking a synopsis. Even though the venture capitalist has read the business history section he will probably ask you to describe the history of the business. He is seeking the details of what happened in the past. This section is not likely to spark any general questions, but there will be specific questions about events in the history of the business. A typical question might take the form of, "Why have you done such and such?" Other likely questions are: "What are the major milestones your company has achieved? Why has your business been able to achieve these milestones?"

2.04 Business of the Future. Here, too, the venture capitalist is looking for general information about the milestones to be accomplished in the future. The VC will have particular questions about each stage of development that you intend to go through. The basic question will be, "How will you be able to achieve the milestones you have set out in the business proposal?"

2.05 Uniqueness and Compelling Story. The basic question you must answer is, "What makes this business unique?" Or "What is the compelling story for this investment opportunity?" These questions might be phrased in another way: "Given all the small businesses there are in the world, what will make this one succeed?" Remember that most investors believe that in the general area of business, big business usually wins when it competes with small business. Given that axiom, why will your business succeed when it must compete with big business? In order to satisfy the venture capitalist, you must point to something out of the ordinary that makes your company a winner. If you will be just another "me, too" company, the venture capitalist will soon fall asleep.

2.06 Product or Service. Here the venture capitalist wants to find out what you sell and what need the product or service satisfies in the marketplace. The VC will be trying to determine whether your product or service is a commodity or has some originality.

The VC is also interested in the maturity of the product, and the general life cycle of products like this. The questions will be, "Why is this product or service useful? What does it do for the user? Why does the user buy it? What is the expected life cycle of the product and when will another product have to be introduced? Is there a new product planned or on the market now that will help or hurt the company? What product liability is there? That is, if the user buys it and is hurt, what liability will the company have? What price can be charged for the product? How elastic is the price of the product? How durable is the product? How technologically sophisticated is the product? How mature is the product in the life cycle of such a product?"

2.07 Customers or Purchasers of the Product. The venture capitalist wants to know who buys the product or service and why. The VC questions concerning this topic will be, "Does this product meet a real need of the consumer, or does it meet a perceived need that is not necessarily a real need? How does your consumer recognize your product among all the others? Does it have brand name recognition? Is there only one type of buyer for the product? Are you selling to one large company or to the government? Are there repeat users or does the customer need to buy the product only once? Is it a high-quality or low-quality product? Is it a high-styled or low-styled item? Is it a fad or a staple?"

In addition, the venture capitalist will ask you to list each major purchaser of the product or perhaps the top 10 or 20 purchasers of the product by dollar volume. The VC may also ask you to classify the purchasers by type and perhaps by demographic characteristics. The VC will want you to produce a list of names, addresses, and telephone numbers of the top ten users of your product. The VC will want to call the major purchasers and determine how satisfied they are with your product. You should prepare this list in advance, because it is something the venture capitalist will ask for at some point in his investigations. If you don't have a list of users now, you need to prepare a list of potential users of the product or service and describe what marketing research you have performed that makes you believe that these potential customers will buy your product or service. In all of these discussion the VC will be trying to determine how well you know your customer (or potential customer). It is a defining moment. You either know to whom you are selling and why they buy or you don't.

2.08 Backlog. The venture capitalist needs to know what kind of backlog exists both in terms of dollars and in terms of units for each one of your products or services. The typical questions are: "Who are the orders from? How firm are the orders? Can the orders be canceled? Do orders depend on a specific price? Do they depend on performance of prototypes? What is the nature of the backlog and how easily can it evaporate?"

The venture capitalist will want to know how much of the backlog is for orders that cannot be filled and why they cannot be filled. The VC will want to know how firm the unfilled backlog is and if the unfilled backlog can be canceled or modified. For example, you may have indicated that the U.S. government has purchased $1 million worth of your products subject to your shipping them. This would be part of your backlog. As everyone who deals with the government knows, the federal government can cancel an order at any time. Thus, your backlog could drop by $1 million with one registered letter from dear old Uncle Sam. It is important to be able to justify the various orders in a backlog and to show that the purchaser will be able to pay for the product once it is shipped.

2.09 Industry or Market. Here the venture capitalist will be trying to understand your industry. The questions will be, "What are the keys to success in your industry? How do your company and its products fit into the industry?" Some additional basic questions are, "How did you determine the total sales of the industry and its growth rate? What are the basic trends of the industry? What industry changes affect profits most in your company? What barriers to entry are there in this industry? That is, how easy or hard is it for someone to get started in the same business you will be in? Why is your product novel or better when compared with others in the industry? What seasonality is there to sales in the industry? Will you sell on a local, regional, national, or international basis?"

A word of warning: when you use the term total sales in talking about an industry, you must be careful not to include sales that are not addressed by your product. For example, one would not use total computer sales in the United States if one was planning to be a manufacturer of laptop personal computers. The laptop personal computer market is only one segment of the total computer market. The industry your company and product is in is the laptop personal computer market, not the total computer market. As a matter of fact, the laptop personal computer market itself is segmented now.

2.10 Competition. Here the venture capitalist will want to know who the competition is, how strong it is, what advantages it has, and what advantages you have. Typical questions are, "What advantages do you have over your competitor? In terms of price, performance, services, and warranties, how do you compare with your competition? What advantages do your competitors have over you? Who, specifically, is your competition? Who are you similar to in your industry? Who do you compete with on a head-to-head basis? Are there substitutes for your product? If so, who makes the substitutes and how often are they substituted for your product? What is the price differential between your product and the product of your competitors? Are any competitors just entering the industry? If you plan to take a market share from the competition, how will you do it? How do you expect the competition to react to your company? Are any of your competitors public companies? Do you have a role model of the type of company you want to be?"

2.11 Marketing. In this section the venture capitalist will focus on your marketing strategy. The VC wants to know how you are moving the product from the production facility into the hands of the ultimate user. Some of the basic questions will be, "Describe the channels of distribution for your product—that is, how does it get from your facility to the consumer? What are the critical elements of your marketing strategy? Is this primarily a retail or an industrial marketing strategy? How important is advertising in your marketing plan? What is your basic advertising program and how much does it cost? How sensitive are your sales to advertising expenditures? What market penetration have you had in the past? What degree of market penetration have you projected? What will be your marketing strategy when the product or industry matures? How difficult is the sale? Is direct selling necessary—that is, does the salesperson call directly on the customer? Is the sale complex and long or is it relatively simple and straightforward? Is the purchase of the product a large cost item for the buyer or a small-budget item? Is it meaningful in terms of the consumer's budget when the consumer buys the product? What is the time lag between the time the buyer is contacted and the actual sale? Does the government regulate the marketing approach?"

2.12 Production. In this section the venture capitalist will try to understand how the product is produced. Some typical questions are, "What is the capacity of your facility? What are the key weaknesses of its capacity for manufacturing—that is, what component (such as quality control) is the main bottleneck in the operation? How important is quality control? What type of backlog exists now? Is this a standard product that goes through the production process or is it a job-shop operation in which each product is different? What type of health and safety problems are involved in this production process? Are there any revolutionary production processes on the horizon that would help or hurt the company?" If your service has a production cycle, you will also be asked to discuss how the service is rendered.

2.13 Production Characteristics. Here the venture capitalist will zero in on the critical factors in the production process. The questions will be, "Is it a sophisticated product that is difficult to produce? Are there a large number of components? How much of the basic product is purchased from others in the form of subassembled parts? How much value does the company add to the production process? What components are crucial to the product? What liabilities are incurred by workers who must produce the product? Is the production process dangerous in any way?"

2.14 Labor Force and Employees. The venture capitalist wants to know the source and status of the labor force and the type of employees needed to produce and sell the product. His questions are, "Where does the labor supply come from? Is there an adequate supply of quality labor force or must they be trained? What is the relative cost of labor in this area versus other areas of the country for similar labor forces? How hard is it to find good workers in this area? What do you do to attract the best workers? What incentives do you have to keep good workers? Is there a particular type of skilled employee that is essential for this business? If so, how will you attract and keep them at your company? What does your competition pay similar employees to the ones you have or will try to recruit? Do you use an employment agency or headhunter to find employees? What fees do they charge? How successful have they been? What kind of union does the company have? What is the union's relationship with the management? Does the contract come up for renegotiation soon? Exactly how many employees are there, including full-time, part-time, white-collar, blue-collar, technical, nontechnical, degreed and non-degreed? What type of retirement plan is set up for the labor pool? Are there any liabilities in the form of unfunded pension or profit-sharing plans?"

In addition, the VC will want to know if the employees are covered by employment agreements or confidentiality agreements. It is quite common for employees to be made to sign confidentiality agreements as a condition of employment. The VC will want to know how you are handling this area.

In some segments such as the high-tech market, employees are very difficult to recruit. If you are in an area that has a scarce labor market you will have to do some tall selling to convince the VC that you can attract enough good employees to implement your plan.

2.15 Suppliers. Here the venture capitalist will try to determine the source of raw materials. The main questions will be, "Who are the suppliers of the raw materials used in the production process? Is there a single source for any components, especially key components? Are there shortages of some of the required components?"

You should prepare a list of suppliers that includes their names, addresses, telephone numbers, and names of individuals who may be contacted. You should list the largest dollar-volume suppliers first and the terms on which you purchase items from that supplier. You should also list any key suppliers and sole-source suppliers. You should prepare this list in advance for the venture capitalist.

Further, if you are a young company, you must explain how you will get your hands on enough components to build your product. In a time when some components are in short supply and your competition already has first claim on the production of some critical components, you need to be able to explain why you will be able to buy what you need to make your company successful.

2.16 Subcontractors. In this section you must describe any material relationship you have with any subcontractors. What role do they play in your business? How key is their operation? Can they be replaced? Give their names, addresses, telephone numbers, and the individual to contact at the subcontractor's for reference purposes. This is another exhibit you should have available for the venture capitalist.

2.17 Equipment. In this section the venture capitalist will want to find out what type of equipment is available and what type is needed. The questions will be, "What type of equipment is absolutely necessary for the production of your product? Is special-purpose or general-purpose equipment used to produce your product? Is the equipment you need in short supply? How long does it take to get parts for the equipment you have? Is it difficult to order a new piece of equipment? How long does it take to arrive? How old is your company's equipment? How much does it cost to repair each year? What is the dollar value of the capital requirements for equipment over the next five years? Is used equipment available? Will the equipment that you currently use be made obsolete by technological changes or by current items in the marketplace? What kind of equipment does the competition have? Do your competitors have an advantage because of their equipment? Do you have an advantage?"

2.18 Property and Facilities. Here you need to explain what facilities you are currently using and what you will need in the future. The venture capitalist will ask, "What are the terms of the lease? If you own the property, what did you pay for it and what is the balance owed on any mortgage due? What is the current value of the property? Are the facilities adequate for future production as envisioned under the projections? What is the total dollar volume that can be accomplished by using the facilities that you are in now?"

You should have available for the venture capitalist a copy of the lease on the property that you currently use if it is leased. If you own the property, it is appropriate to have on hand an appraisal of the property and a listing of the basic details such as acreage, square footage, and a description of the building in terms of the type of construction.

2.19 Patents and Trademarks. The venture capitalist will want to know what patents or trademarks the company has and in what countries you have filed. Typical questions are, "Is the patent issued? Is the patent in your name or the company's? If it is in the name of the entrepreneur, has it been fully assigned with all rights to the corporation? Have any licensing arrangements been entered into to give others the benefit of the patent? If so, what are the details of any licensing arrangements?" And there are similar questions for trademarks.

2.20 Research and Development. The venture capitalist will want to know how much research and development has been completed in terms of dollars and time and how much will be needed in the future. Typical questions are, "What research and development are going on today? What dollars were expended in the past on research and development, and what sales have resulted from those expenditures? Has the research and development been written off or capitalized? What are the projected expenditures in the coming years and what do you expect to develop from the money spent on research and development?" Venture capitalists are not fond of funding research and development firms. They want companies to exploit new ideas.

2.21 Litigation. The venture capitalist wants to be informed of any legal actions that are in existence or that are being contemplated. Typical questions are, "What suits have been filed against the company? What suits has the company filed against others? Have suits been filed by trade creditors, customers, or users? Are patents being contested? Are there any sexual harassment suits or discrimination suits?"

You should be ready to give full details of any legal situations. If you have suits against your company you should have your lawyer write a letter explaining each legal action in legal terms. Unfortunately for business people in the United States, lawsuits have become a way of life. Don't be afraid to talk about lawsuits to your potential VC partner, because they have heard about almost every kind of suit.

2.22 Government Regulations. Here the venture capitalist wants to know how the various layers of government might influence the growth of your company. His questions will be, "What are the state, local, and federal regulations affecting the operations of the company? Do any FTC, fair trade practice, OSHA, special IRS, SEC, or other government regulations affect the company? How can the company be helped or hindered by these government regulations?" For example, if you are in the drug business, you must have Federal Drug Administration (FDA) approval. Once your company receives FDA approval on a new drug, it has a monopoly on the use of the drug until another company can meet FDA approval.

The federal government plays a role in most business operations. State and local governments are getting in on the act. Every venture capitalist knows this, and you need to know how government rules and regulations will help and hinder the growth of your business.

2.23 Conflicts of Interest. The venture capitalist will be interested in any conflicts of interest. Examples of questions are, "Does the company buy from a supplier whose officer sits on your board of directors? Is there some relationship between a company in which you have a personal investment, and the company that is seeking financing? Are any of the employees of the company relatives of the owners and mangers?" You need to describe any conflicts of interest or potential conflicts of interest between your company and boards of directors, management, key employees, large stockholders, and so on. If there is a potential conflict, describe how it is being solved.

2.24 Insurance. Here the venture capitalist wants to be assured that you have adequate insurance to cover your company in a multitude of areas. The VC will pay attention to fidelity insurance, product liability insurance, the old standby of fire and casualty, and business interruption insurance. Most VCs will require life insurance on key employees. Basic questions will be, "What happens if you are hit by a truck? What happens if the building burns down?" A good answer to each question is, "The insurance company will pay our company millions."

In this era of plentiful litigation, the VC will want to know that you have Officers and Directors insurance, especially if the VC plans to sit on your board of directors. Some VC firms avoid this problem by having their own Officers and Directors insurance that protects them if they are sued while setting on your board of directors. It will be necessary for the company to have this insurance if it is going to attract a strong board of directors.

2.25 Taxes. Here the venture capitalist will want to understand the type of taxes being paid by the company. Questions are, "Are any special taxes levied against the company? Can the company expect any special tax breaks? Are there any outstanding taxes today, such as payroll or income taxes? How can the company shelter some of its income from taxes?"

The United States and each state levy such high taxes on businesses today that a good tax plan is almost as essential as a good business plan. You should work with your accounting firm to make sure you are in the best possible tax situation.

2.26 Corporate Structure. In this area the venture capitalist will want to understand the corporate structure. The VC will ask, "Is it a partnership or is it a corporation? Is the corporation a specialty such as a Subchapter S corporation?" Incidentally, if you are incorporated in one state but are a resident in another, the venture capitalist will want to know why.

And the very popular Limited Liability Company or LLC has tax advantages that make it a more popular selection. All of these corporate entities have consequences for investors. Make sure you have selected the one that will be best for your business.

2.27 Publications and Associations. List the primary publications that cover your industry. The names of the industry magazine and the industry newspaper or newsletter are needed. Also give the venture capitalist the name of the person at your trade association who can be contacted to discuss the industry.

PART 3: MANAGEMENT

In this section the venture capitalist will want to evaluate the management team, their background, experience, and so on. Sometime during a relaxed period in the discussions you may be asked some "silly" questions. Be prepared for a wide variety of such questions: "What did you think of Physics 101 in college? What was your early childhood like? What has been your greatest accomplishment?" Most venture capitalists fancy themselves amateur psychologists. They hope to understand the individuals seeking funds and their motivations. You may receive some unusual questions in this section. Don't be worried that you will answer them wrong. Just be yourself and tell the VC what you think, and everything should be fine.

3.01 Directors and Officers. The venture capitalist may ask you questions about the individuals listed as directors or officers. The VC will want to know why certain people are directors if they have no obvious connection with the company. If the venture capitalist sees your lawyer on the board of directors, the question may be why? When possible, you should have working business people on your board because they will bring their business experience to the boardroom. Except for key directors, the venture capitalist will save most of the questions concerning key employees for the appropriate sections of your proposal, as indicated next.

3.02 Key Employees. Here the venture capitalist will want to know everything possible about the key employees, because the VC will be betting real money on the management team. As at the racetrack, the jockey is just as important as the horse. The VC will want to know the background, experience, age, education, work experience, and marital status of team members, and how many children they have. Most of the more personal questions will come over lunch, or in a friendly get-together somewhere along the way, such as the drive back to the airport in the car with you. Be prepared to provide anecdotes about where you have been and where you are today in terms of your personal life.

What the VC is likely to do in a meeting with you is to ask you to talk about your experience since you went to college. As you describe your experiences you will see where the questions are leading. The VC wants to see that you have achieved in the things you have done in your life. The research into your background will go far beyond any review of your resume. Many VCs will want to know about everything you have done in life.

Formal questions about key employees include, "What profit-and-loss responsibility have the key people had? What experience has the management team had in the industry? Do the key people have the technical knowledge necessary to operate this company in this industry? How dedicated are the key employees to this company? Can this management team make the projections happen? What functional responsibilities does each key employee have? How financially committed are the key employees to the company—that is, how much money has each of them invested? What other business affiliations do they have? What other businesses are they involved in? What ownership positions do they have in other businesses?"

3.03 Management Fidelity. Venture capitalists are regularly approached by swindlers. You should not take offense at the questions that cast doubt on your honesty. Because all venture capitalists have been swindled at least once, they feel they have to be on their guard. Most venture capitalists are slightly paranoid. Be kind and indulge their questions.

Most venture capitalists spend days trying to fathom the fidelity of management. You can help by letting the venture capitalist know your position on fidelity. You should forewarn the VC of any suits against individuals or any credit problems you have had. You may want to obtain a complimentary credit check from a local credit company to determine what your credit will look like to the venture capitalist when the VC runs a credit check. The VC will look for suits against the management team and their credit rating. The venture capitalist will want a list of references on the management. You should prepare an addendum to your resumes that provides a list of references, all of which should be business references. The venture capitalist will call these people in order to verify your fidelity and your business experience.

Many venture capitalists employ private agencies (and some accounting firms will do this work) to develop a complete background check of the individuals that make up the management team. These private agencies are not the same as a private detective, but they are similar. These agencies take the information about you and verify it. They may look in the various courthouse files where you have lived to see if you have had any problems, even driving record problems. For sure, all of your references will be called and each university you say that you graduated from will be contacted. Some of these agencies do an excellent job of verifying information about you and even "digging up dirt" on the members of the management team. When the VC ask you to sign a waiver that permits the firm to look into your background, you can feel good, because it means they are very serious about investing in your company. On the other hand if you have some "stuff" in your background, it may not be a good day.

Some venture capitalists are studying the possibility of giving potential entrepreneurs tests that can be used to determine both their entrepreneurial ability and their honesty. I have not seen the merit in, or accuracy of, such tests. It is rumored that one venture capital company employs a graphologist to examine the handwriting of entrepreneurs in order to determine their entrepreneurial ability and their fidelity. I have not been able to verify this rumor. Who knows, maybe the technique works!

One venture capitalist has his own method of evaluating entrepreneurs. After his junior people have investigated the situation and have asked the entrepreneur every conceivable business question, the senior venture capitalist takes the entrepreneur into his office for a one-to-one discussion. For one or two hours the entrepreneur answers questions about everything conceivable except business. If at the end of that time the venture capitalist has a "good impression," then the entrepreneur has passed the final test.

Most venture capitalists have a gut feeling about entrepreneurs. Unfortunately, even in this book it is impossible to define that feeling. It is a reaction that develops almost automatically as a result of interviewing, talking, and working with entrepreneurs over many years. The subject of passing the personality test of the venture capitalist is discussed also in Chapter 5.

3.04 Remuneration. Here the venture capitalist is trying to determine how well you are paid now and how much you intend to pay yourself in the future. How much will you pay each member of the management team. A simple chart with the proposed compensation and any other forms of compensation can be put in a small list for the VC. The main question in this section will be, "Why are you paying such a high salary to your employees and to yourself?"

3.05 Stock Options. Here, too, the venture capitalist is trying to determine the management team's compensation. You should let the VC know precisely what you are thinking about in terms of ownership of stock and stock options for current management and for any new people coming into the company. You should provide a copy of the stock option plan to the venture capitalist. If you do not have one but intend to have one in the future, you should provide an outline of what you intend to do. The question is, "Why are you giving each person the number of options you have indicated?"

3.06 Stock Option Plan. The plan should be the standard plan or the venture capitalist will raise questions. If you have other deferred compensation plans, tell the venture capitalist about them. A plan is usually put in place to reward those member of the team that have not been hired yet. So here you are setting aside stock options that will be awarded to future executives of the company. Be prepared to defend how many shares you are setting aside to recruit new mangers. And it will be important to state the price you think the options might be granted at.

3.07 Principal Shareholders. In this section the venture capitalist will want to know who owns stock in the company and how much each owner paid for it. If the price is low or the number of shares is large, you need to explain why they received low-priced stock. Anyone owning 5 percent or more of the company should be listed, and you should be prepared to discuss each of them.

3.08 Employment Agreements. You should explain in detail any employment agreements and have copies available for the venture capitalist. The question here is, "Why do you have an employment agreement?" Be aware that venture capitalists disapprove of employment agreements unless they are one-way agreements, somewhat like the indentured servant's contract of old, that require you to work for the company but without a large salary. That is a mild overstatement, but if the employment agreements are slanted too far toward giving you and your team contracts for life, the VC will not invest. There is a lot of room for give and take in employment agreements, but there is a lot of "take" in the eyes of the VC when looking at this problem.

3.09 Conflicts of Interest. Any conflict of interest between an employee and the company should be set out in detail. You might be asked which employees have any connection with other firms that the company does business with. For example, does an employee's father work for a company that sells products to your company? Is there any kind of financial relationship? For example, did his father's company lend your company $50,000? Does one of the employees own the computer that the company leases? Such conflicts of interest should be revealed. The venture capitalist may uncover them, so it is better for you to reveal them at the outset.

3.10 Consultants, Accountants, Lawyers, Bankers, and Others. You should prepare a list with the names, addresses, and telephone numbers of your lawyers, accountants, bankers, and consultants, along with the names of persons to contact. The stronger these professionals are, the better your VC will feel. VCs know that a top accounting firm is not going to let you make false statements on your financials, so they like having the big accounting firms work with you.

PART 4: DESCRIPTION OF THE FINANCING

In this section the venture capitalist will try to establish and negotiate with you the type of financing that is acceptable to both you and the VC. The questions the VC will ask you in the meeting and the questions you should ask yourself beforehand are set out under each heading as follows:

4.01 Proposed Financing. If you are proposing a loan from a mezzanine fund, what interest rate will it be? Why is the interest rate so low? Can the rate be increased? On what terms will the loan be made? Why do you need the money for such a long time? Why is there a need for an interest-only period? When can you begin repayment? Can repayment begin sooner? Will the interest rate be variable or fixed? Will the loan be convertible into common or preferred stock? Can the conversion rate be lower?

If it is preferred stock you are proposing the VC buy, what will the coupon or dividend be? And can the dividend be raised? Will the preferred stock coupon be cumulative in case you do not pay it for a calendar quarter? What redemption will there be and can it be sooner? Is it convertible into common stock? If so, what is the conversion price? Can the conversion price be reduced? What restrictions are there on the shares? Does the preferred stock have voting rights?

If you are selling common stock, the key question is price. What is the price of the stock? Will you be required to redeem the common stock in case you miss your projectionist? Will you be required to redeem the common stock required in order to give the investor's money back? Will there be restrictions on the shares? What voting rights will holders of common stock have? What registration rights will they have? That is, can the venture capitalist make you register the stock so it will be a public company?

If you offer options with any of the foregoing, you need to consider the price of the option and why you selected a certain price. What is the exercise price that one must pay once the option is exercised into common stock? How many shares will it exercise into? What is the expiration period of the option?

All of these methods of financing your business will have an impact on the return on investment for the Venture Capitalist. Each decision that is made on each of the securities that you are trying to sell will impact one calculation that the VC will do called "valuation of the business." When you propose the terms, the VC will determine from that offer what you value the business at—that is, if you were going to sell the business today, what would be the value. Some VCs use a "pre-money valuation" and others use a "post-money valuation." The first analysis says what the value of the business is before the money that you are trying to raise goes into the company, and the second tells what the business is worth after the money goes in. In either case, a value has been placed on the business by the proposed transaction. For example, if you want to sell 50 percent of the stock of your company for $5 million, it means the entire business is worth $10 million. To get ready for this discussion, think how much you would sell the business for and let that be your guide as you try to sell the VC on the same value.

4.02 Capital Structure. The venture capitalist will want to see a list of all the money you have raised and any long-term debt that you have borrowed. It is typical for you to provide a list of the capital (both debt and equity) that has been raised for the business. If you have a lot of debt that needs repaying soon, it will be of concern to the VC. You will have to specify all the loans and list all the collateral for each of the term financings and to give specific terms, conditions, and interest rates on each debt item.

On the other hand, you may have raised successive rounds of preferred stock. This is usually shown in an alphabetic listing of each round such as series A preferred stock, series B preferred stock, etc. After each one list the amount raised and the price paid per share of preferred and the price for conversion into common stock.

4.03 Collateral for the Financing. If you are seeking a mezzanine round of debt, the question will be what collateral can you offer the venture capitalist as security for his loan/investment in your firm? What value does the collateral have, and why have you placed such a value on the collateral? Do you have an appraisal or something to show there is value?

4.04 Guarantees. In debt financings it is common for the mezzanine fund to ask for collateral for the loan. So the VC will ask, "What personal or corporate guarantees will be given on the investment?" If you provide a personal guarantee accompanied by a personal financial statement, the venture capitalist will ask questions about the personal financial statement. The VC will want to know why you have put a high value on certain assets. If a separate company will guarantee the loan, its financial statement will also have to be examined by the venture capitalist, because he will want to know the financial strengths of the company.

4.05 Conditions. If the venture capitalist has invested in your company through a debt mezzanine instrument, the VC may want your company to maintain certain ratios. If you select the ratios, the VC will want to know why you selected ratios that are easy to meet. When it comes to disbursing funds, the venture capitalist may make the disbursement conditional on certain milestones reached by the company. If you identify these milestones, the venture capitalist will want to know why these are significant, and why reaching them makes the company more valuable.

4.06 Reporting. This is a very key point for every VC. They all want to know that you will provide the venture capitalist a monthly financial statement. If this is an early-stage company, there may be less need for this since the VC will be around the company more often. But you should be prepared to provide such statements. The VC will want to know that you will provide updated projections at least once or twice a year. And VCs will ask, "What special information will you give us so that we can follow the company's progress?" Sometimes these are monthly operating reports that state in a few pages what achievements have been made and what setbacks have been experienced.

4.07 Use of Proceeds. When you spell out the use of proceeds, the venture capitalist will want to know precisely why you want to spend so much money on certain items. By spending money on these items, what specifically do you accomplish for the company? You will need to be specific in the use of proceeds and the justification for each expenditure.

4.08 Ownership. The venture capitalist will want to know exactly how much of the company the VC fund will own if the fund invests. The VC will want to know how much others own, primarily key management. No VC will accept the idea of a small ownership for key management because the incentive will be too low. Key management must have a substantial stake in the ownership of the company or they will not be motivated to make a lot of money and raise the value of the stock.

One of the little games a VC will play at this point is to ask you what you think your stock will be worth in five years. It is a good idea for you to do this anyway so you know what you are working for, but you should also be ready to answer this for the VC. And remember the projections you gave the VC? This calculation of what you think your shares are worth better match closely to that projection.

4.09 Dilution. This area will involve questions about the value of the company. Why, for example, should a venture capitalist pay a high price for his small ownership in a company when others have paid much less? You will need to justify why the venture capitalist is being asked to pay such a premium. One justification acceptable to the venture capitalist in a start-up is that you have put together the team and the idea and these have given the company value. If you have an existing company, then you should have reached some milestones that have increased the value.

Be aware that there are few professional managers of VC funds that value start-up companies at greater than $10 million. There are just too few ideas that are worth over $10 million. So if you have an idea and want to start a company, it will be hard to get a VC to pay more than $3 million for 30 percent ownership.

4.10 Fees Paid. There are many good brokers that can help you raise venture capital, and if you use one, the VC will want you to answer some questions. Is a broker's fee being paid for this financing? Why? What did the broker do to deserve the fee? If the broker performed a service, he deserves a fee. If the broker performed little service, he deserves a small fee.

4.11 Investor Involvement. Most VCs will expect you to offer them a seat on the board of directors. So you need to answer these questions: Will you give the venture capitalist a seat on the board of directors? Will you give the VC fund veto power over certain transactions? Will you give the VC fund a consulting contract? Will the VC fund have veto over certain transactions such as the sale of additional shares? You need to offer a board seat as a minimum.

Sometimes in high-risk situations, the VC will ask that all of your shares be put in a voting trust so that if the company does not meet its projections or milestones, the VC fund can vote the shares in the trust. In voting the shares they may vote you out of a job, vote you off the board, and even vote to sell the company. So fight like hell to avoid the voting trust, but if you have to give in, try to limit when the trust can be used.

PART 5: RISK FACTORS

Just when you thought it couldn't get worse, it does. This section is a kind of catchall part of the process. The venture capitalist will ask you certain questions that will help determine the amount of risk your business poses. These questions will tend to be negative, so don't be offended. The questions may downgrade your company, and you will need to be positive and upbeat in conversations on this subject with the venture capitalist. In essence, the VC takes off the white hat and puts on the black hat and is now trying to poke holes in everything you have written or said. Just look at it as a game and you are defending your business against hostile attacks. Be ready by looking at the list of typical risk factors that everyone looks at. Eat a lot of red meat and drink a lot of caffeine and respond to each question with a brilliant defense answer.

5.01 Limited Operating History. The door is likely to be opened with some of these. What makes you think you can start a new company? Have you ever started a new company before? What problems do you expect to run into starting a new company? How are you going to solve all the problems of a new company? What people on your management team will help you in this? The questions will not be so aggressive, but they will be there.

5.02 Limited Resources. If you do not have enough money to break even, what will you do for the next round of financing? Precisely, how much money is needed to carry this company to the point of cash flow break-even? What will you do if positive cash flow is not achieved?

5.03 Limited Management Experience. How many of your key managers are skilled in this industry? What have they been doing for the last ten years that makes their experience valuable in this industry? What outside help will enable them to overcome their lack of experience or ability?

5.04 Market Uncertainties. What could go wrong with the marketing plan? What is going on in the market that could destroy this company? What new inventions are around the corner that would make your product obsolete? What strategy might the competition use in the marketplace?

Often the best-laid plans for marketing are destroyed by items that have never been thought of. Consider the venture capital company that financed the acquisition of a yacht club. The idea was to sell boat slips in somewhat the same way that condominiums are sold—that is, people would buy the boat slips and pay an annual fee to belong to the club. The proposal projected that 50 percent of the existing boat slip renters would convert to owners. Unknown to the entrepreneurs was the fact that the boat slip renters at this yacht club were extremely clannish. After it was announced that the slips would be sold, the renters banded together and boycotted the sale. They scared away many potential outside buyers by acting as a group. As a result, sales were not even close to projected sales and the conversion never took place. The entrepreneur and venture capitalist lost out.

Venture capitalists may have a number of such war stories engraved in their minds. They may be able to come up with more market uncertainties than you will be able to explore in your business proposal. Be prepared for the questions that will be based on their bad experiences. You know you are going to get a difficult question when the VC begins with "I once lost money when I invested in...."

5.05 Production Uncertainties. If your product has never been produced before, why do you think you can produce it at the price you have projected? Have you ever run a production facility? Has anyone else on your staff done so? Has that person ever started a new production facility?

New production facilities are difficult to start. It seems that Murphy's law finds its true environment in a new production facility. There is the story of a venture capitalist who looked into financing a new yeast facility by asking several of the existing yeast facilities what problems a new yeast plant might have. He ran into a fellow who had actually started one 20 years before. According to this experienced fellow, when the yeast operations were moved from the old plant to the new plant, the yeast failed to grow at the rate it had grown before. The fellow went back to the old plant to find out why the yeast would grow there without difficulty. It was then he realized that the walls, the floor, and the roof were permeated with the yeast culture. This "cultured environment" was obviously conducive to growing a tremendous amount of yeast. The fellow reported that it took the new facility over a year to reach the same environmental state.

The venture capitalist declined to invest in the venture for this and other reasons. Others invested and, sure enough, it took an extra year and an extra few million dollars in working capital to break even. You can be sure that every seasoned venture capitalist has experienced starting a new production facility a number of times. The VC will be keenly aware of many of the problems that can occur in a new production environment.

5.06 Liquidation. Liquidation questions will be along the following lines. If the company had to be liquidated after the venture capitalist investment but some progress had been made, how much would an investor get back? Why do you say that you could liquidate the assets for those values? Have you ever liquidated a company before?

If you have had no experience in liquidating a company or do not know how it is done, the venture capitalist will be delighted to tell you about one of the liquidations that his fund has experienced. There was the venture capitalist who liquidated a knitting mill during one of the past recessions. Most of the collateralized lenders thought they had sufficient collateral to recover all their money on liquidation. The only problem was that many knitting mills had been liquidated during the year, and now all the usual buyers of used knitting equipment had their warehouses packed full. They were certainly not interested in buying additional knitting equipment. Before long, bidders on pieces of knitting equipment were asking whether they could just take off the parts they needed and leave the machine to be thrown away. In that environment, you know that you are going to lose. The venture capitalist and the bank lost a bundle.

Liquidating a service company is a complete nightmare, because there are few assets. Desk, chairs, personal computers, cubicles, and other office furniture and machinery are worth about 10 percent of their original value. One can only hope that any patents or trademarks will be worth something to someone.

Most VCs do not rely on liquidation value. Instead, when the going gets rough the VCs look for buyers for the company. They try to merge the business with a strategic buyer or sell it for something. They realize that the value of a "going concern" is usually worth more than the sale value of its assets.

5.07 Dependence on Key Management. If key management dies, how will the company survive? If key management dies, how can the company grow and prosper without the driving force of the key management? How would the venture capitalist be protected if a key manager died? How hard would it be to replace that key person? These are the types of questions that the venture capitalist will be pushing at you regarding the loss of key management personnel.

5.08 What Could Go Wrong? The question that is uppermost in every venture capitalist's mind is, "What factors could make the company a disaster situation?" The venture capitalist is almost certain to ask the entrepreneur, "What could go wrong?" Or the VC might say: "What do you worry about most?" In answering this question, you need to lay out several scenarios indicating the aspect of the business that could be fouled up and how you would react and solve such a problem.

This is normally not a large section in the business proposal, but it will be a key point in the questions asked by the venture capitalist. If you don't worry about anything, either you are lying or you're a fruitcake. Running a small business is the biggest headache in the world. So write out your answer to this question, because it is coming.

5.09 Other Items. Other questions may be quite random ones that are seeking general information. What financial reserves do you consider the company needs? Does a noninvestor employee control the company because he is key to the operation? What is your greatest achievement with this business?

Part 6: Return on Investment and Exit

In this section the venture capitalist will ask you how much money the venture capital fund can make, and when do you think the fund will be able to make an exit, meaning sell for cash. This is normally not a large section in the proposal, but it will be a key point in the questions asked by the venture capitalist. Remember they don't hit pay dirt in their personal compensation until they are able to sell their investment in your company for cash.

6.01 Public Offering. Have you talked to a brokerage firm about a public offering? When do you think you might be able to go public? What multiple do you think the stock would sell for in a public offering? How did you arrive at this estimate of the multiple? What public company resembles your company most? What multiple are they trading at? Who took them public?

This is not going to be a big item for the VCs; they have more contacts than you do in the brokerage community. Especially if your company is a high-tech firm, there will be significant knowledge about public companies in the space you are trying to build your business. But try to get enough information on this subject so you do not look like a clod who is not knowledgeable about the public offering area.

6.02 Sale. This is another set of exit question, this time about selling your business. What other companies would be interested in buying your company if your business made its projections? Why is the technology or product desired by other companies? If so, name the companies that might want to buy your company. Have you contacted any investment bankers about selling the business or parts of the business? If so, what interest level have they shown?

Oh by the way, investment banker is a nice term for various types of brokers. An investment banker in the mergers and acquisition department of a large stock brokerage firm is a person who helps companies that want to get sold and helps companies that want to be purchased. Investment bankers can give you an idea who might be a buyer for your company.

6.03 Buyback. The final exit question involves your company's buying back the stock you sell to the venture capitalist in future years once your business is successful. The questions usually go like this: If your company is to buy back the shares owned by the venture capitalist, what method could be used to value the shares? What basis has been used to place a value on companies that have been sold in your industry? How would you finance the purchase?

6.04 Return on Investment. Here the VC is asking you to play a little game. The VC says, "If a public offering of the stock of your company was made three years from today, and the venture capitalist was able to sell all of the shares the VC fund has purchased in this financing in say two years after that public offering date, then what would be the return on investment to the venture capitalist?"

Then take a less successful future and the question is, "How much money would the VC make if you made only half of your projected sales?" These little games get back to return on investment, or ROI. The VC is just letting you help do the math on how much money they will make. Help the VC with the math, and make sure it shows that the fund will make a ton of money.

PART 7: ANALYSIS OF OPERATIONS AND PROJECTIONS

The venture capitalist will spend a great deal of time asking you about the numbers and assumptions in your projections. Some general questions are set out under the headings below, but you can also expect many more specific questions about the assumptions and calculations behind the financial projections.

7.01 General. Many general questions will be asked about your assumptions, such as, "What makes you think the gross margin will be as set out in the projections? What return on investment do other companies in your industry have? Why will your ROI be higher?" In general, you will be expected to defend every single number in the spreadsheet.

7.02 Ratio Analysis. If the ratios you presented for each year seem to be different, the venture capitalist will want you to explain why they are not the same each year. For example, if your gross margin changes every year, going up and down, or steadily upward, the venture capitalist will want you to explain why this is happening. If payroll or other items go up drastically, the venture capitalist will want to know why the salary levels, as a percentage, increased so rapidly.

7.03 Results of Operation. The venture capitalist will be particularly interested in any past performance. Questions about the numbers will center on profits and projected profits. Normally, the venture capitalist will not be upset by losses in the early years as long as the company shows some progress toward losing less money on a monthly basis. If you have increased losses, the venture capitalist will look at the situation as a turnaround if you are an existing business. If you are a new business, the venture capitalist will expect your profit and loss projections to track the now famous "J" curve. That is, if you plotted the losses and then profits of a new business, there would be slight losses in the beginning, greater losses in the next few years, and then zooming to very high profits in the out years. As long as the out years are not too far out, the J curve will be acceptable and expected by the venture capitalist.

7.04 Financial Conditions. The balance sheet will not be of primary importance to the venture capitalist unless the VC fund you have approached is a lender. If that is the case, the VC will look through the balance sheet seeking some collateral for the loan. Balance sheets showing large amounts of research and development that have been capitalized or a balance sheet that has a large slug of goodwill will require special explanations to the venture capitalist. In a review of the balance sheet the venture capitalist will subtract all goodwill and capitalized research and development in order to arrive at a tangible book value closer to liquidation value of the company.

Avoiding goodwill in buyouts has become an art form practiced by the best accounting and legal firms. If you are buying a company, make sure you get some excellent advice to avoid creating goodwill.

7.05 Contingent Liabilities. Most venture capitalists are greatly concerned about contingent liabilities. They will ask many questions as they look for contingent liabilities. Have you guaranteed loans or other debts for some other business? Have you agreed to purchase a specific quantity of goods from some supplier? Have you signed a lease that escalates in rental prices? Is there some contract with an employee or customer that creates an unknown amount of liability?

Many VC's are obsessed with finding the boogeyman known as contingent liabilities, particularly undisclosed ones. Just go with the flow and endure their questions.

PART 8: FINANCIAL STATEMENTS

The venture capitalist will spend a lot of time analyzing your financial statements. The VC will ask you questions about profitability. He or she will ask you about the auditor. The VC will ask you about any subsidiaries and how they are consolidated. Above all, the VC will want to know why certain things appear on your financial statements.

PART 9: FINANCIAL PROJECTIONS

In this section the venture capitalist will want to know how your projections have been constructed. That is, why do your projections go up so dramatically? What are the basic assumptions in your projections? What are the sensitive items in your cash flow projections? The venture capitalist will perform a type of sensitivity analysis on your financial projections. Most VCs will adjust certain items in the projections in order to see what other items change drastically. They want to see to what extent increased sales will demand an increased amount of working capital. The venture capitalist will spend a great deal of time asking you questions about the financial projections, and you should know your projections very well in order to answer these questions easily.

By far the best thing to do for VCs is to give them a copy of your spreadsheet and let them manipulate the numbers. They can stress the financials for all types of conditions. Most VCs will use their own spreadsheet and plug in your numbers. You may find yourself reviewing their spreadsheet to answer questions about how the business will perform under certain assumptions. If you can get the VC to work off your spreadsheet, you have a chance to avoid some confusion, but nine times out of ten you will end up working off their spreadsheet.

In building the spreadsheet it is important to build a monthly spreadsheet for the first few years if you have any seasonality in the business. If there is no seasonality, you may be able to use only annual projections.

PART 10: PRODUCT LITERATURE, BROCHURES, ARTICLES, AND PICTURES

The venture capitalist will look at the pictures and product/services brochures and try to determine how your product fits into the venture capitalists way of looking at the world. Be ready for any offhand questions about the product. For example, why did you use plastic in the handle of the product? What colors does it come in? Why did you write the code in that computer language?

OTHER INFORMATION THE VENTURE CAPITALIST WILL NEED

You should have answers for the questions previously set out regarding your business proposal. You should also have ready answers for the questions that are not directly concerned with the business proposal but that we have covered so that you will be prepared on all fronts. If you can answer the questions in this chapter, you will be prepared for most questions from the venture capitalist. Many of these questions require you to give the venture capitalist additional items besides the business proposal. Listed below are the other papers you should have ready for the venture capitalist as the due diligence process drags on.

REFERENCES ON THE BUSINESS

Give the name, address, and telephone number of people who are familiar with your business and can give you a good reference. (Chapter 6 covers the questions the venture capitalist may ask your references.)

REFERENCES ON KEY EMPLOYEES

In this instance, you need the name, address, and telephone number of the person who is familiar with the key employees of the business and who can vouch for the reliability of each of the key employees. It is usually better to have each of the key employees draw up their own reference list.

BANKERS, LAWYERS, ACCOUNTANTS, AND CONSULTANTS

Make a list of all the people who are key to your business such as your bankers, lawyers, accountants, and consultants. List their names, addresses, telephone numbers, and the person to contact at that reference.

LARGEST SUPPLIERS

Here, enumerate your ten largest suppliers and give names, addresses, telephone numbers, and persons to contact at each supplier. List the dollar volume that you have purchased from each supplier or that you expect to purchase in the coming years.

If you don't have any suppliers yet because you are a start-up, you need to put down the suppliers that you have talked to about supplying to your company. In times of shortages, this is a key list.

LARGEST PURCHASERS

In this list give the names, addresses, telephone numbers, and the key persons to contact for the largest purchasers of your product. Give the dollar volume that has been purchased in the past and the amount you expect to be purchased in the future.

And if you are a new business, give the names of some of your proposed customers. Obviously, if you are selling retail or over the Web, there isn't much you can do here.

BACKLOG

The venture capitalist will ask you many questions about your backlog. Everyone always wants to know how firm the orders really are. The VC will want to call a number of the purchasers and confirm their order backlog. The VC will want to know the history of backlog orders. How many of them were actually fulfilled? For example, if you have converted your backlogs into actual sales 99 percent of the time, the venture capitalist will be pleased. If the conversion is only 50 percent, then your backlog should be cut in half.

Prepare a list of the customers in the backlog, listing the person that the venture capitalist can talk to in order to verify the order. Give the person's name, address, and telephone number, plus a description of the order. However, if you are a new business or you are selling retail or on the Web, this section is not necessary.

AGING OF ACCOUNTS RECEIVABLE

Here you should provide all your accounts receivable and arrange them in columns by age. The first column should contain the amounts of those accounts under 30 days, the second column over 30 days, the third column over 60 days, and the fourth column over 90 days. The venture capitalist will be trying to determine the quality of your accounts receivable.

In one venture capital situation the entrepreneur indicated to the mezzanine lender that the company had $2 million worth of accounts receivable to pledge as collateral. But the company had only $100,000 in sales. Needless to say, this looked unusual. Further investigation revealed that the entrepreneur had agreed to sell his product, a specialty type of copier, if the buyer would sign a note to pay for it over the next 12 months. These notes were conditioned upon delivery of the product. The entrepreneur tried to suggest these notes were accounts receivable. He wanted to use them as collateral for loans from banks and for a long-term note from the mezzanine venture capitalists. Needless to say, he never received any financing.

AGING OF ACCOUNTS PAYABLE

In this tabulation give the age of the accounts payable just as you did for receivables above.

DEBTS AND TERMS SUMMARIZED

Here, enter each major debt that you have, including personal loans in the business. Give the terms of the debt, such as interest rate, repayment terms, and final due date. List the collateral for the loan and personal guarantees of the loan. Be prepared to give the venture capitalist a copy of the actual loan documents.

LEASES

Summarize information about each lease that you have, and have a copy of the lease on hand in case the venture capitalist asks for it.

TAX RETURNS

Be prepared to give the venture capitalist a copy of the tax returns for the last three years.

OTHER GOVERNMENT DATA

Be prepared to give the venture capitalist a copy of any OSHA reports, EPA reports, SEC reports, and so on.

UNION CONTRACT

Summarize on one page the union contract, and be sure to have a copy of the contract for the venture capitalist if he or she asks for it.

PERSONAL FINANCIAL STATEMENTS

Prepare a personal financial statement for each key employee, listing his/her assets, liabilities, net worth, any contingent liabilities, and the employee's annual income. You may want to use a standard bank form for the personal financial statement. The personal financial statement is usually supplied only if the venture capitalist is a mezzanine lender and requires a personal guarantee of the loan by key employees.

LONG RESUME

Have each of the key employees complete a two- to three-page detailed resume showing where he or she has worked during the past ten years (minimum) and the dates, the specific job titles, and names of people who can be contacted at these various places. This information should be arranged chronologically so the key person's progress can be seen. Any other materials, such as published articles or other achievements, should be included in this long resume. It is important to bring out all achievements.

You can expect the venture capitalist to review this in detail, and it may be the starting point for the background check on you and your team.

WILL THE VENTURE CAPITALIST ASK ALL THESE QUESTIONS?

The venture capitalist will not ask anywhere near the number of questions listed in this chapter. You will likely meet with a number of people from the VC firm and they will be doing well if they ask one-third of the questions listed here. The point is that you must be ready for all of the questions, because you don't know which third they will ask. Many of the questions do not have a "right" answer. In some situations the answer could be completely different than it is in others. It is important that you practice answering these questions and that you have a reasonable answer for the venture capitalist. One thing is for sure: some of the questions the venture capitalist will ask are listed in this chapter. You are practicing for an oral exam from the VC. Practice makes perfect.

OBJECTIVE

Your objective in this chapter has been to understand your own business proposal, and to be ready for every conceivable question that the venture capitalist can throw at you. Your motto must be, "Be prepared!" Be prepared for all the questions about your business. And if you don't know the answer to the questions, just say I don't know but I will get that information and get back to you. Now let us turn to Chapter 5, which tells you what to expect in your first meeting with the venture capitalist.

5 MEETINGS AND NEGOTIATIONS

CAN YOU HAVE IT YOUR WAY?

WHAT YOU NEED TO KNOW TO GET
THE BEST DEAL.

After reading the summary and business proposal, the venture capitalist will normally telephone you to ask some basic questions about your business. The venture capitalist will determine what kind of deal you are seeking. If all signs are "go," the venture capitalist will probably request a meeting in his office. If you are an existing business, then most venture capitalists will make a trip to your office to discuss your company. Most venture capitalists like to have the initial meeting at their place because it saves time. It reduces their travel, which is heavy in the venture capital business. Also, from the standpoint of negotiations, they are in slightly better negotiating position on their own turf. Or at least that is what they think.

THE OFFICE OF THE VENTURE CAPITALIST

The location and surroundings of a venture capitalist range from modest to opulent. The venture capitalist who interviews you in opulent surroundings should be no more believable than one in modest surroundings. After all, jerks can rent expensive furniture too. The surroundings you visit probably are not related to the personality of the person you are meeting. It may be fairly difficult for you to gauge how you should act by the surroundings of the venture capitalist. For example, you might think that ultramodern surroundings reflect an interest in ultramodern investments. However, it could just mean that the venture capitalist's decorator or space planner likes modern furniture.

The meeting place may indicate the venture capitalist's approach to your deal. Some like to conduct business in their offices, others in a conference room. From my experience, venture capitalists who receive people and conduct their business in a conference room are more corporate in nature. They may take a more formal view of your business. Venture capitalists who receive you in the office, and who conduct discussions and negotiations there are generally receptive and open to your approach to life and to making a creative decision. These observations, it should be remembered, are based on my own limited survey.

And there is another visual cue for you. If the office or conference room has a chalkboard for putting things up for all to see, it is a good sign that there is an open atmosphere in the office. Be prepared to step up to the board and put down key points or illustrate points and numbers.

WHAT DO VENTURE CAPITALISTS LOOK LIKE?

Venture capitalists look like everybody else. They are part of the great American middle class. Most venture capitalists act and dress like investment bankers on Wall Street. Some of them dress and act like bankers in any major metropolitan bank. In some of the smaller venture firms in small towns, they act and dress much as you would expect any small town banker to act and dress. Many men in the field are fairly conservative in their dress and wear white shirts and dark suits. There are some notable exceptions. A number of venture capitalists have full beards. In a room full of venture capitalists these fellows stand out.

Despite some regional differences, all in all, you will find VC's fairly similar in their appearance and in their approach to investing in companies. Even if they have a coat and tie on, they usually can be expected to take their coat off during the meetings with you.

As you move down the chain of command in the VC firm, you will find the associates. Most of them dress casually; you will not see many "suits." What will they look and dress like, however, when they become the general partners?

How Long Will the Meeting Last?

The initial meeting in the venture capitalist's office usually lasts from one to five hours, depending on the depth of the discussions. You should expect at least two and as many as five people in the meeting, including you and your team. On the average, you should expect to be in the meeting approximately two hours. During the meeting the venture capitalist will attempt to "read" your personality and the makeup of your team. The VC will want to obtain a good impression of you as an individual. The VC team will be analyzing your character and judging your ability as an entrepreneur. And they will be looking at your team the same way. Most venture capitalists believe that first impressions are meaningful. If it is a poor one, most likely the deal will never go further. Needless to say, the initial meeting is a critical one for you.

In this meeting you should dress appropriately in your most conservative attire. You should probably act reserved but at the same time show entrepreneurial energy. In your meeting with the venture capitalist you should be straightforward. Present yourself as the person who can get the job done.

This is a moment of "personal selling." You are selling yourself, your team, and your company. Get up for the game and be rested and ready to give a great performance.

WHAT IS THE OBJECT OF THE MEETING?

The venture capitalist holds a meeting with you to accomplish three basic objectives:

1. They want more information about the business and how it will make money.
2. The meeting provides an opportunity to evaluate you, the management, in a face-to-face situation.
3. The venture capitalist wants to "cut the deal," meaning structure the investment, which is the ultimate goal of the meeting.

The deal may not be completely structured in this initial meeting. If, however, you leave an initial meeting without having discussed even a preliminary structure of the investment to be made by the venture capitalist, you've probably lost the investment. The VC is not interested unless the deal is discussed, at least on a preliminary basis.

This little event is called "cutting a deal." If it sounds painful for you, you are right. But this is why you came to the meeting, to see if there is a deal. Don't be shy about "asking for the check." If the VC does not bring up cutting a deal, then you should press for it. In the interest of finding out if the VC is interested, you should ask the VC what type of deal he or she thinks is reasonable. Your brightest moment in the meeting will be when the VC starts talking about a deal. It means there is an interest in your company.

If you are able to arrive at a preliminary understanding of what the deal may look like, you must remember that the preliminary deal is contingent upon the venture capitalist's final review of you, your business, and your industry. If the original perception changes for any reason, then they will want to change the preliminary deal, or even worse, not go through with it. As the venture capitalists compare your business proposal with the findings of their due diligence, the original impression should be confirmed. If there is a difference, then the deal you have struck during your meeting will be void.

WHAT HAPPENS IN A TYPICAL MEETING WITH A VENTURE CAPITALIST?

In a typical session, the entrepreneur enters the office and a few pleasantries are exchanged. The venture capitalist usually begins the conversation with, "What can I do for you?" or some other open-ended question. It is surprising how many directions a conversation can take from that question. What most venture capitalists want to hear from entrepreneurs is a verbal presentation of what the business is all about, how much money they need, and what they plan to do with the money. You need not be detailed and long-winded unless asked specific questions. Your presentation should be energizing, not dull.

It is important to appear energetic. Starting and running a small business and developing it into a medium-sized business takes a tremendous amount of energy. If you seem to be slow and methodical, you will probably not get backing. After all, it is your energy, your creativeness, your organization, and your leadership that will make it all happen. Also, you need to appear cheerful. If you come across as an unhappy soul, it is very unlikely that anyone will want to put money behind you. So, besides looking for innate intelligence and knowledge of the business, the venture capitalist will be looking for an energetic and cheerful entrepreneur.

Personally, I also look for a good sense of humor. Two people whom I backed and who failed both lacked a sense of humor, and that experience may account for my interest in this quality in an entrepreneur. I have worked with other venture capitalists who say they have backed humorless, boring people who made a lot of money. The basic qualities venture capitalists look for seem to be energy and a will to succeed. Remember, throughout your meeting you are selling your business proposal and you are also selling yourself as the one person the venture capitalist should back. Show them you are a fireball!

WHAT TYPE OF PRESENTATION SHOULD BE MADE?

In most of your meetings with the venture capitalist you will both be working from the business proposal that you have previously sent to the venture capitalist. Many entrepreneurs think they should show slides or large flip charts. Neither of these props is necessary. Most venture capitalists do not want to see a professional presentation.

Slides are seldom as good as a set of pictures that you can pass across the table to the venture capitalist. Pictures will show the VC what your product looks like. You do not need to leave the pictures with the venture capitalist, although a plain paper copy of several of the pictures could be included in case the venture capitalist wants to keep pictures. If you have a model or sample of the product you are manufacturing, bring it along. An individual once gave a demonstration of a new surgical technique in my office using a cushion to represent a person's stomach. It was very effective in illustrating the proprietary method used for holding a patient's stomach open during surgery. My sofa cushion didn't look too good afterwards.

A computer-driven slide show with animations is a wonderful tool, and it seems to be the universal stock and trade of most presentations today, but it can be time-consuming and tedious. And a long-winded recitation along with it is a good way to put your VC to sleep. This type of show is good for large groups but not for a small group of venture capitalists. If you feel you must use it, then keep it to a small number of slides, no more than 15, and the show should be over in 20 minutes. Handing out the slides is much preferable. Then the slides look more like an outline that you want to use as your presentation. But even if you have hand-out slides, keep their number to 15 or less and the formal presentation to 20 minutes. And don't be surprised if the VC doesn't want to hear the presentation. It is a good sign, because it means that the VC wants to get to discussions about your plan and may have actually read the plan with some attention to detail.

Another effective mechanism is a book of pictures. This method, akin to a scrapbook, shows prototypes as well as operating units and can effectively illustrate how a new technology operates. You do not need to leave the book with the venture capitalist. Once the VC has an understanding of the process, the pictures will not be necessary for presentation purposes.

WHAT IS THE PRIMARY CHARACTERISTIC THE VENTURE CAPITALIST IS SEEKING IN AN ENTREPRENEUR?

The general consensus among venture capitalists is that entrepreneurs should be achievers. They have a positive and optimistic approach to life. In your meeting with the venture capitalist, you want to project yourself as an achiever—a person who has achieved things already, which you should stress, and a person who will achieve in the future. In essence, you should adopt a positive mental attitude when making your presentation to the venture capitalist.

Various analyses indicate that certain attributes correlate positively or negatively with the achieving personality. For example, a high positive correlation has been found in individuals who have been Eagle Scouts. The lowest correlation has been found among pipe smokers. Venture capitalists do not take to heart such generalizations. In the meeting, you should be yourself; do not try to act like someone's stereotype of an entrepreneur. Display a positive attitude and an intelligent, inquiring mind and have answers for the questions being asked. Be pleasantly aggressive in the meeting and sell, sell, sell. You should convey your concept with as much positive verbiage as possible.

Unfortunately, a few venture capitalists do make investments on a phyletic basis. Others are prejudice or sexist in their decision making. If you happen to encounter one of those poor souls, go on to the next venture capitalist. Do not waste your time trying to change emotional prejudices.

WHAT ARE THE OTHER CHARACTERISTICS OF THE ENTREPRENEUR?

The venture capitalist will be looking for seven basic characteristics. This doesn't mean the VC is looking for an ideal human being, but merely that the VC would like to see a number of these qualities. Thus, your lack of strength in one area or another may be acceptable. Different venture capitalists will emphasize different items in the list, and some industries will require more strength in some areas than will other industries. You should keep in mind that this is a laundry list of the qualities of the ideal entrepreneur. No one is expected to have them all. People will differ in their qualities, but we can examine these seven according to the way they are ranked by venture capitalists, most of whom put honesty at the top of the list.

HONESTY

Every venture capitalist wants an honest entrepreneur. Some venture capitalists believe that a dishonest entrepreneur can still make money for them. That may be true as long as the dishonest entrepreneur cheats only other people and not the venture capitalist. Most venture capitalists will work only with an honest entrepreneur because they realize a dishonest one might someday turn on them. Honesty is made up of a number of components:

1. Integrity, in that the entrepreneur tells the truth and is honest to the venture capitalist.
2. Fidelity, meaning that the entrepreneur is trustworthy in the entrepreneur's dealings with the venture capitalist and with others.
3. Loyalty, meaning that the entrepreneur stands by commitments made.
4. Equitability, meaning that the entrepreneur believes in fair play.

In your relationship with the venture capitalist, remember honesty and its components. Build your credibility with the venture capitalist by demonstrating whenever possible that you are an honest entrepreneur.

Desire to Win

Venture capitalists want to believe that you have a strong desire to win, that you want to accomplish your goals. They need to know that you use money as a measure of performance in your activities. Building the best computer in the world may be a tremendous achievement, but it means nothing to the venture capitalist unless it can be sold at a profit. You must translate your feelings and your drive into goals that are measured in terms of money. You must demonstrate that you have a desire to make money, not so much because of greed, but because money is the ruler by which you measure your performance. The venture capitalist must understand that you are an achiever, or your venture will not get backing from the fund.

Energy

This quality comes in many forms. First, you must have physical and mental energy to accomplish the tasks that have been set out. You must have the strength to complete the years of effort that will be needed to bring about your financial plan.

You must demonstrate to the venture capitalist your capacity for hard work. You must demonstrate that you have drive, enthusiasm, and initiative. The venture capitalist must know that you are tenacious in your desire to achieve goals and that you have a long-term commitment to achieve them.

The VC does not want to back a stubborn person, but one who has the commitment and the energy to make it all happen. Being an entrepreneur will consume large amounts of energy. Without a large amount of physical and mental energy, most business proposals cannot be realized.

INTELLIGENCE

The venture capitalist will want to know that you are an intelligent individual. There are many components to intelligence. It is certainly demonstrated by advanced degrees from recognized universities. But many intelligent people have not attended college. By intelligence, the venture capitalist means a rational human being, one who is logical in his thinking, one who has the ability to understand complex situations and the reasoning power to analyze those complex situations. The VC will want to know that you have good judgment and that after analyzing a problem you have the ability to select the right solution.

You must be able to take the appropriate amount of risk for the reward at hand. There is no way that the venture capitalist or anyone else can measure the type of intelligence that is needed in entrepreneurial activity. Your intelligence will be judged by your response to the questions and the solutions you have provided in your business proposal. Your entrepreneurial ability will be judged on the basis of the venture capitalist's experience in dealing with other entrepreneurs.

KNOWLEDGE

Knowledge also comes in many forms. Certainly an education at a good university indicates a knowledge of basic subjects. But the venture capitalist is more interested in your experience. What lessons did you learn from past failures? How much experience do you have in the industry you are about to enter? Do you have within your brain the information about the industry that is necessary for success? Have you analyzed the industry and determined the keys to success in your business? Can you accept criticism and profit from it? The venture capitalist will want to determine what knowledge you have about this particular situation that makes you able to make money at it.

LEADERSHIP

Leadership has been studied almost to excess in business schools, yet it has seldom been studied from the perspective of entrepreneurship. The venture capitalist must understand that you have the leadership qualities necessary to be the center of attraction in a small growth-oriented company. You must have the courage to take personal responsibility for an entire corporation. You must have the courage to take risks and to tolerate these risks during adversity as you go in the direction others have not tread.

With respect to personality, leadership involves self-confidence, a positive attitude, and some degree of self-centeredness. The venture capitalist will be trying to determine if you have those leadership qualities. Can you set the standards for yourself and for others and carry them out? Do you have the leadership capability to see the problems at hand and to change the strategic plan if necessary in order to ensure profitability? You must not be so self-confident or egocentric that you refuse to do a menial task or solve a problem that is "beneath you." Leadership in many ways means getting the job done, either by doing it yourself, or, most often, by doing it through other people.

CREATIVITY

Although it is important for an entrepreneur to be creative, too often the creative side of entrepreneurship has been emphasized to the exclusion of many other necessary traits. The venture capitalist will want to know that you are resourceful and that you are a problem solver. The VC wants to see that you have a new or unique approach in this business situation and you have applied it to your business.

All seven of these characteristics are important. You should review them in detail and try to see where your own personality fits into these categories. If you are weak in an area such as knowledge, you may want to bring along a team member in your organization who has extensive knowledge of the industry. Your team member can answer the questions about the industry that you may not be entirely familiar with. If you are not the creative genius in the group, you may wish to bring along the person in your team who has created the idea. Again, you personally do not have to embody all of these qualities, but you must show achievement and honesty. Your team should have all of them well covered.

KNOW YOUR STUFF

During this meeting with the venture capitalist, you will be asked a thousand questions about your business. Many of these questions were covered in Chapter 4. Often, two or three venture capitalists will be in the room, firing questions at you from every direction. There will be marketing questions, production questions, financial questions, and a number of questions about your projections. You need to know every part of your business proposal in detail. You must know your business inside and out or the venture capitalist will think that you are not knowledgeable about your business, your industry, or the people.

If you are a heavyweight in marketing but a lightweight in finance, you may wish to bring along a team member who is a strong financial person. If you do not have a controller who can stand up to the questioning, your accountant may be willing to play this role. If you are not a heavyweight in the production side or some other segment of your business, you may wish to bring along the person on your team who is strong in this area. It is not unusual for the entrepreneur and one or two others in the management team to be at the meeting and participate in the discussions. If these people are not part owners in the business and you do not want them to know what kind of deal you are negotiating, you may wish to tell the venture capitalist ahead of time. Tell the VC that you would like to discuss your management team, the financial details, and projections, and after those discussions, you would like to dismiss the other people before you negotiate a deal. The VC will be receptive to this type of situation and will be sympathetic to confidential discussions.

Things You Do Not Say to the Venture Capitalist

Your conversation may run for hours. Make sure you get to the point of the meeting, which is to get a deal from the VC. During this meeting with the VC you do not want to relax and become overly talkative. You may say some things you should not be saying at this point in your relationship with the venture capitalist. Here are some things to avoid.

Big Plans

During the discussion you should concentrate on your business proposal. You should avoid certain topics. Leave out all the grandiose plans you have for the future. The idea that your company might someday have 13 divisions in 47 states and might approach $1 billion in sales is not relevant to the venture capitalist's analysis of your business proposal over the next three years. In fact, such grandiose plans will probably scare the hell out of the VC and make him or her think of you as a dreamer.

If somewhere in the back of your mind you have an idea for another product, or for additional bells and whistles on your existing product, or the hope of acquiring another business, or other things that are not part of the business proposal, do not bring them up during the meeting. To do so will only sidetrack the venture capitalist from the written business proposal and reduce your chances of obtaining financing. Don't give the VC a chance to question your business judgment. The conclusion may be that you are spreading yourself too thin.

MAKE MONEY

One of the things venture capitalists like to ask an entrepreneur after the in-depth discussion of his or her business proposal usually goes something like this:

Venture Capitalist: After discussing this business proposal in detail with you, I think it is going to take a tremendous effort on your part. It is going to take a great deal of work and may involve many long hours. It will mean a sacrifice. It's going to be a grind for the next four to five years. Why in the world would someone like you want to do something like this?

Entrepreneur #1 (wrong answer): I have always wanted to own my own business. I just don't like working for someone else. Where I am now, I have to report to people who just don't understand how to get something done. There is just too much bureaucracy, and there just isn't enough opportunity for me to express myself. My boss doesn't understand me. I want to be my own boss so that I don't have to answer to anyone.

Entrepreneur #2 (right answer): I have always wanted to own my own business, but that is only part of this whole plan. What I really want to do is make a lot of money. I see this as a unique opportunity for you and me. We'll put together my ideas and your money and have a winner. It's a golden opportunity for us both.

As you can see, the two answers above are quite different. The first entrepreneur seems to think that by owning his own business he will not have to answer to anyone. Nothing could be further from the truth. An entrepreneur must answer to investors, bankers, accounts payable when they have not been paid promptly, the Internal Revenue Service when they have not been paid the taxes due, and the state sales tax collection agency and payroll taxes. And more than anything, an entrepreneur has to answer to the customer. The customer rules the daily lives of entrepreneurs.

The list is far greater than most entrepreneurs ever imagine. I remember asking a friend of mine who had finally obtained his own business how it felt to be president. He responded, "I think about it every night when I sweep out the place." Being an entrepreneur with your own business does not mean riding around in a big car while making decisions. It means hard work that involves scrimping and saving, and it is a tough life. When something goes wrong, you have to fix it.

In the conversation above, the second entrepreneur said the right things as far as the venture capitalist is concerned. That is, the entrepreneur focused on making money. Keep in mind that the venture capitalist is not interested in your psychological or sociological need to be independent. The VC has no interest in solving your personal problems. The VC is interested in making money.

HONESTY

As we discussed previously, honesty is the most important characteristic of an entrepreneur. Honesty is probably the most difficult characteristic to evaluate. Most venture capitalists recognize that there are two levels of dishonesty.

First there are con artists. They tell you how much they will make money by cheating others, and at the same time tell you how they will share it all with you. They describe the method by which they are going to cheat the government, how much money they are going to cut out of suppliers through negotiations, how they will lie to lending institutions to gain credit, and, in short, do anything to make money. Then they look straight across the table and tell the venture capitalist how much the VC will get by being a partner. The con artists are seeking to gain the confidence of the VC. Once confidence is gained, the con artist will take the money and be gone. This type of dishonesty is not too difficult to spot even if it does not come out in the meeting. It usually sticks out like a sore thumb when checking the background of the individual.

The second kind of dishonesty is known in business school parlance as "constructive deception," or, more commonly, as telling white lies. An example of a constructive deception is the statement, "My board of directors will never agree to that proposal." Since the board usually follows the lead of the management, the statement is a disguise for the real response, "I don't like your proposal." The statement is a way for management to hide behind the board of directors in order to give the answer, no.

Another form of constructive deception used by venture capitalists can be illustrated by the comment, "Your type of investment just doesn't fit into our investment strategy." What the venture capitalist may mean by this response is that the deal is not to the VC's liking. The VC is using a neutral excuse to turn down the proposal, rather than give a direct rejection. I have used both of these constructive deceptions in order to negotiate or turn down a deal. That type of constructive deception is acceptable in business.

Constructive deception is not the same as evading answers, nor does it mean not doing what one says one will do. For example, constructive deception cannot be equated with not answering a question when directly asked about it. When someone tries to avoid an issue or a question, that behavior is like a con artist. Similar to the con artist is the entrepreneur who does not take the action that was agreed to be taken. This type of behavior, too, casts doubt on a person's honesty. In other words, it is all right to tell a white lie to a venture capitalist but not to tell big lies. Such behavior will kill the deal. A venture capitalist looking at you for the first time will be trying to determine the degree of your honesty. If you tell him a lie and you are caught, you can wave goodbye to your financing. Be sensitive to the fact that venture capitalists will not back dishonest people.

THINGS NOT TO DO IN THE MEETING

Because the venture capitalist has to see people all day long and talk to them about their business plans, most venture capitalist develop certain pet peeves. Here are a few of them.

Do Not Avoid Answering Questions and Do Not Give Vague Answers

The venture capitalist does not have the time to tolerate coyness, so avoid answering questions in a circuitous way that forces the VC to repeat questions. If you are handing out vague answers, the venture capitalist will in turn give you an un-vague answer when you ask if the VC wants to invest in your company. Play it simple, and play it straight. Give a direct answer to a direct question. If you do not understand the question, do not give vague or meandering answers. Ask specifically what the venture capitalist is looking for and then answer directly. Most venture capitalists spend their days asking questions. They have become highly skilled in interrogating people. If they find you leading them around in a circle, you can bet you will not be getting any money from them.

Do Not Hide Significant Problems

If your company has had significant problems such as lawsuits, or large thefts in the past, especially in the immediate past, do not hide them from the venture capitalist. Assume that the VC will eventually find out about them and that when that happens, the VC will be quite upset that you have not revealed them. If the venture capitalist asks the rather vague question, "Are there any other significant problems that I haven't asked about?" go ahead and state the significant problems you see.

Many times a venture capitalist asks, "What can go wrong and how can this entire situation fail?" In this instance you should give a solid answer. The answer should not be, "Nothing can go wrong." Obviously things can go wrong and there are probabilities that certain things can go wrong. You should answer in that vein, perhaps by saying, "It is possible that a new competitor will enter the marketplace." Then you should respond to that probability by indicating how your company would react. Do not hide significant problems from the venture capitalist. To do so can only buy you trouble.

Do Not Bring Your Lawyer to the Negotiations

Lawyers are by nature combative. They spend three years in law school arguing with one another. Then they join a profession that is argumentative. Many lawyers spend the entire day writing legal documents that try to cover every conceivable possibility. They are constantly thinking about what can go wrong, and how their clients can be hurt. This is what they should be doing. As a result, however, when lawyers come to negotiating sessions they tend to be long-winded and eloquent. They tend to be combative on minor issues and argumentative about probabilities. If you want to make a deal with the venture capitalist, leave your lawyer at his or her office. It will be cheaper for you, and you will negotiate a business deal that the lawyer can put in legal language later.

Do Not Press for an Immediate Decision

Asking the venture capitalist for an immediate decision will only make the VC nervous. The best approach is to ask the venture capitalist, "If we assume that what I have presented in the business proposal is correct, can you please outline in general terms what you might be thinking of?" If the VC is unwilling to outline the terms, you may wish to coax the VC along by suggesting certain terms. By doing this you can observe the reaction of the VCs in the room. The idea is not to get the venture capitalist to shake your hand and say, "We have a deal." After all, this is your first meeting and the VC has just read the business proposal. Do not expect the VC to conclude the transaction at that meeting. However, you should expect the VC to give you an indication of whether the VC is interested in the deal and if so, to give you the general parameters of the type of deal the VC believes would best fit the situation.

DO NOT BE RIGID IN PRICING

If you have structured your deal to sell only common stock at a certain price per share for a certain percentage of the company, and if you are unwilling to move from that position, you may not receive financing from any venture capital firm. It would be a rare coincidence if the terms you set for an investment in your business proposal fit precisely those offered by a venture capitalist. Do not enter into negotiations with the idea that you can obtain only one deal. Negotiate with the venture capitalist. To negotiate means to give and take. After the negotiations are over and you have reached some conclusions, you can still change your mind. A discussion does not require you to live with the conclusions. At the end of the day you can say, "I understand what the proposed deal is. I want several days to think about it before I firmly agree to what we have discussed." This is a perfectly acceptable position to take. You should always negotiate with the venture capitalist, because in the negotiations you may arrive at a position that is more advantageous than your original position.

HOW TO NEGOTIATE IN THE FIRST OR SUBSEQUENT MEETINGS

Negotiating is the subject of numerous books, each author professing to have the right technique. The method you use will be a reflection of your approach to business. In addition, negotiating techniques depend primarily upon the situation, the personalities, and the relative strengths of both parties. In negotiations between individuals of high education, calm personalities, and similar strengths, the technique that usually works best is logical persuasion. That is, each party has a point to sell and each one attempts to sell it to the best advantage. There is give and take. Both parties have needs and each is seeking a solution. The best salesperson usually wins the most points, but both parties win because there is a successful deal.

Another technique is touted in many seminars and highly publicized books. It focuses on the overbearing personality with little education, dissimilar positions and strengths, and communication in the form of grunts and demands. Some of the "peace" negotiations among waring nations seem to resemble this approach.

A number of other books concentrate on "hard" negotiating techniques, and—describe how you can browbeat anyone into submission. There is a good lesson to be learned from these outrageous negotiating techniques. If, after the negotiations are completed, each party goes its separate way, then this technique can be used successfully. However, if the two parties must "live" with one another after the negotiations are completed, as must be done after a venture capital investment, then any technique that injures the other party cannot be employed. It will impair the relationship for the duration of the investment. So in any negotiations you need to keep in mind that after the negotiations are over and you have to work together, it is not going to be a good working relationship if it starts with difficult negotiations.

There is a saying in the investment business that "the Golden Rule prevails." The Golden Rule is, "He or she who has the gold makes the rule." However, if a venture capitalist uses this axiom exclusively the VC will have problems with his or her investments. After the investment is made, the entrepreneur will have the gold and the entrepreneur will make the rules. In reality, each party has something to give. You have your company, the proposal that you have put together, and an idea of what you can do in the future. The venture capital investor has money, experience in the business world, and financial contacts. Each has a position to protect, and each must give good value to the other party or the relationship will not work. Remember this in your dealings with venture capitalists, and if you find yourself negotiating with a hard, uncompromising venture capitalist, walk out of the office. Things will not get better after the negotiations.

In negotiating with the venture capitalist, you should keep in mind that if you both can agree on the terms, you will be living with each other for a considerable amount of time. Therefore, during the negotiations it is appropriate for you to conduct yourself in a manner that is conducive to a long-term relationship rather than a short-term one. If it takes a struggle to obtain the commitment, you will only be hampered in your long-term relationship. In the negotiations you should listen to the needs of the venture capitalist but you should not forget your own needs. Do not be afraid to ask for anything you think is meaningful, and try to negotiate a deal that you both can live with.

How to Cut the Deal

Once the venture capitalist has heard the entrepreneur's presentation and has asked questions about the business, the next logical step is to negotiate the terms of the investment. If the venture capitalist gives a weak answer to an entrepreneur such as, "Well, we'll have to study your proposal some more and get back to you in a few days," you have failed to generate enough interest for the venture capitalist to negotiate a deal with you. As a rule, if you leave the venture capitalist's office without having negotiated at least a preliminary deal, chances are you will never obtain a deal.

Many new people in the venture capital field live and die for deal making. Experienced venture capitalists, on the other hand, like reviewing proposals and hearing from entrepreneurs. Cutting the deal is relatively unimportant to their personal satisfaction. By the time they have come to the point of negotiating the investment terms, the experienced venture capitalist usually knows what it will take before the VC fund will invest. If the VC cannot move the entrepreneur close to an acceptable position, then the deal dies. An experienced venture capitalist will never reach for deals nor will the VC try to browbeat the entrepreneur into a position the entrepreneur does not want.

If an entrepreneur must accept terms that the entrepreneur feels are unreasonable, then the VC believes the entrepreneur will be looking for an opportunity to retaliate throughout the investment period. As everyone in the venture capital business knows, if an entrepreneur wants to harm the venture capitalist, the entrepreneur has ample opportunity to do so while running his business.

Fortunately, most venture capitalists do not have to reach for an investment, because a great many excellent investments are available. Perhaps when good investments become scarcer, venture capitalists will have to be more aggressive in seeking deals. In the interim, most are content to sit in their chairs and try to create deals that fit their needs and the needs of the entrepreneur.

OWNERSHIP BY THE VENTURE CAPITALIST

The opening gambit in determining how much equity the venture capitalist will own in a company is usually a question to the entrepreneur. "How much equity are you willing to give up?" a VC might ask. Some entrepreneurs are willing to give up more than the venture capitalist needs to make the deal. Of course this makes "negotiating" quite easy. Some entrepreneurs are stingy when it comes to the ownership they are willing to give up, and this approach usually kills the process for most venture capitalists. Trying to persuade entrepreneurs to give up more than a very small percentage of their company is a waste of good time. When the entrepreneur is unwilling to give up a reasonable portion of the company, no persuasive argument will work.

Entrepreneurs will think of hundreds of persuasive arguments to suggest why a venture capitalist should own a small percentage of the company. Some entrepreneurs start by discussing the return on investment that the venture capitalist will have if the VC fund invests. The discussion usually proceeds as follows:

Entrepreneur: If you invest $3 million and you get 10 percent of the company, you will make a fortune.

Venture Capitalist: But if I get only 10 percent of the company for $3 million, this means that 100 percent of the company is worth $30 million. I don't see how a company at this stage of development is worth $30 million because of an idea.

Entrepreneur: Wait. Let me finish. When we hit the projections that we are shooting for in five years, the company will be earning about $30 million after taxes. Using a price-earnings ratio of 20 to one on after-tax dollars, the company will be worth $600 million. Your 10 percent will be worth $60 million. You will have received a 20-to-one return on your investment in only five years. That seems to be super.

Venture Capitalist: And if your company fails, I lose $3 million and you lose very little. And if the company goes as you say it is going to go, you will have made $540 million and invested a small amount, while I invest $3 million and receive $60 million. This is just not an equitable distribution of the potential return if you consider the risk you are asking me to take on my $3 million.

The foregoing discussion has occurred so many times with venture capitalists that they literally cringe when they see or hear the "return on investment" argument. The fallacy of the entire argument is that the entrepreneur is basing the valuation on future earnings, as though the company was a public company with assured future earnings, when in reality the company is not even in existence or is merely in the formative stages. In addition, the entrepreneur is using earnings that are five years away, when most analyses use the present year's earnings. It is not an appropriate methodology, and using it with the venture capitalist will only set you on the wrong trail.

How Do Venture Capitalists Price Investments?

Venture capitalists think about a company on the basis of pricing. That is, if they are buying a percentage of the company, what does that make the entire company worth? The variables that the venture capitalist uses to determine price are the entrepreneur's investment, upside potential, downside risk, additional funds, and exit vehicle. Each of these is now discussed in turn.

ENTREPRENEUR'S INVESTMENT

How much money is the entrepreneur investing, relative to the total amount of money that is being invested by all investors? If the entrepreneur is investing very little, then the entrepreneur should expect to receive less equity in the company—an idea is worth only so much. To think you can own control of a company because you have the idea or you found the company for sale is unrealistic.

If you do not intend to invest any money, the deal will have to be extremely attractive before any venture capitalist will wish to invest in your company. If you are like most people in the middle-class segment of society, you don't have much money to put into a business. But taking out a second mortgage on your house or borrowing on your personal signature at a bank to raise some money to invest in the company will be a sign of your commitment to the venture capitalist. The venture capitalist realizes that you are putting your sweat and blood into the company. Each VC will know that if the business fails, you will have a black mark on your record and you will be set back for many years of your life. Nevertheless, the VC still wants to know that you cannot walk away from the deal without suffering some economic loss. In the preceding example, where the entrepreneur was seeking $3 million with only a small personal investment, the venture capitalist will want much more of the company. In start-up companies it is very difficult to get a double digit valuation (over $10 million). So if your idea is worth say $6 million and you want to raise $3 million, expect to give up half the company. With an investment of $300,000 (10 percent of the deal), the entrepreneur is probably in a position to negotiate 60 to 70 percent of the equity for her/himself. If you invest one-third, then you can probably retain two-thirds of the equity.

Another way to ensure that you have a large piece of the equity is to give collateral to the venture capital fund. A venture capital fund does not often obtain good collateral for its mezzanine loans and investments in small business. However, if collateral is available—such as machinery and equipment, perhaps a second mortgage on real estate, or other hard assets—you will be in a much better position to negotiate with the venture capitalist. If you are a new business with a patent, the patent may be good collateral value for the VC. By providing collateral for the investment, the downside risk for the venture capitalist will have been curbed to some extent. The more collateral you can provide, the lower the risk to the VC and the greater opportunity you will have to own more of your company.

There is no scientific method of setting the equity ownership. It will be up to discussions and negotiations between you and the venture capitalist. If the VC believes in you and if the VC believes the downside risk is relatively small, then you will come away from the negotiating table with a larger share of equity ownership in your company. By having a strong, straightforward business proposal, by presenting yourself as an aggressive, eager, energetic, intelligent entrepreneur, you can obtain a substantial position in your own company after receiving a substantial amount of venture capital.

UPSIDE POTENTIAL

This section is like the quest for the Holy Grail. Every VC spends a lifetime seeking the upside potential. Expect a lot of questions on the subject. Here are a few: What is the upside potential of the investment? How much money can the venture capitalist make? What kind of profits can the company generate? What is the probability the projections will be achieved on schedule? Any negative factors in this area will mean that the venture capitalist will have to receive more equity ownership and the entrepreneur less, because the upside has been reduced.

In your negotiations with the venture capital firm on the amount of equity that it ought to own, it will generally be looking for return on investment. Most venture capital firms think of return on investment in technical terms known as internal rate of return. Internal rate of return answers the question, "How much interest would I have to receive on my money in order to equal the return on investment I will get from investing in this project?" The venture capitalist is basically saying, "One can invest the money today in a money market fund and have a certain interest as a return on investment. If one invests in your company and at the end of some period of time receives a great deal of money back (a big capital gain), then what interest rate would one have had to receive (on a compound, annual rate of return) in order to equal what one would get from investing in your company?"

Most venture capital companies are thinking in terms of a five-year horizon. You might think that if you could double the venture capitalist's money every five years he would be quite satisfied. Actually, this only computes to an internal rate of return of 15 percent per annum—not very much for taking the amount of risk your business makes the VC take. A triple in five years yields 25 percent per annum, which is no slouch in terms of investment. If all the venture capitalist's investments returned 25 percent, then the VC would be considered a success. However, some investments fail, and, therefore, the venture capitalist must receive a higher return on investment than 25 percent in order to pay for the mistakes. Five times the money invested in five years is 38 percent per annum. Now you have the venture capitalist's attention, and now you see what you are going to have to do. You must give the VC fund a return equal to five times the initial investment in order to attract the capital from the VC fund.

Below is a table that carries the computation of internal rate of return for various periods.

WHEN PROFIT IS RETURNED	IRR
2 times the investment in 5 years	15%
3 times the investment in 5 years	25%
5 times the investment in 5 years	38%
7 times the investment in 5 years	48%
10 times the investment in 5 years	58%

The calculation above suggests that you have to give the venture capitalist about one times the money the VC invested for each year they are invested in the company. This does not address the risk or the stage of investment. This rule of thumb works out fairly well in the initial years. The problem, of course, is that the longer the money stays out, the lower the internal rate of return is because of the time value of money. The time value of money means it is better to have a dollar in one year than to receive the dollar in ten years.

WHEN THE PROFIT IS RETURNED	IRR
3 times the investment in 3 years	44%
4 times the investment in 4 years	41%
5 times the investment in 5 years	38%
7 times the investment in 7 years	32%
10 times the investment in 10 years	26%

Every venture capitalist has a profit target for the investments of his or her fund. It may be as low as 20 percent for investments that are not particularly venturesome, and as high as 50 percent for those VC funds that fund start-ups. The profit target is determined by the type of investment. If there is a lot of collateral, the mezzanine venture capitalist will take a lower return on investment because the risk is less. The rate of return will depend on the stage or type of company that the venture capitalist is investing in. Obviously, start-ups and turnarounds demand a higher return on investment than would a leverage buyout or a third-round financing.

TYPE OF INVESTMENT	EXPECTED IRR
Start-up (the idea on paper)	50+% per year
First stage (prototype product)	40–60%
Second stage (production beginning, few sales)	30–40%
Third stage (sales going but unknown top)	20–30%
Turnaround (in trouble)	50%
Buyouts	30–40%

These figures are only general guidelines. For each investment the venture capitalist makes, the expected return is based on the risk taken. If there is sufficient collateral and a good cash flow, the venture capitalist will take a lower return on investment. The lower the venture capitalist perceives the risk to be, the lower return the VC will take. You should not expect any venture capitalist to accept less than 20 percent return on investment. After all, this 20 percent is calculated before overhead of operating the fund. You should also remember that many venture firms are leveraged. That is, they borrow their money from other institutions. These leveraged funds will calculate their internal rate of return before interest cost but will be looking for more immediate return on investment.

Most venture capitalists invest with the idea of hitting a "big winner," but they also try to avoid any losses. If they think the probability of loss is 50-50, your return on investment figures will have to be spectacular in order to attract them. A 20 percent chance of loss is more in line with the venture capitalist's perception of risk and reward. As that figure goes from 80 percent to 90 percent, and perhaps even close to 97 or 98 percent, the venture capitalist will lower the return on investment expectations.

You might ask yourself why the venture capitalist needs such high returns on investment if there is only a 90 or 95 percent chance that their VC fund will lose money on the investment. Actually, the venture capitalist will not invest in situations in which there is a reasonable chance of losing the investment. No one actually thinks the risk is great when they invest. As all venture capitalists say, "No one invests in a bad deal." All investments look promising when they are first made.

Most venture capital investments turn out to be mediocre investments. That is, the venture capitalist does not lose money, but neither does the VC fund make a great deal of money. Probably seven out of every ten are mediocre investments for venture capitalists and it is the other three that bring in a sufficient return on investment to overshadow the mediocre seven investments. You should understand the venture capitalist's aversion to losing the capital in the fund. The VC is much like a gambler standing at a casino table. The VC can continue to play the game and stand a chance of making a great deal of money as long as the VC doesn't lose all of his or her chips. If each time the VC places a few bets down and can at least get the bet (the principal) back, the VC can continue to play the game. Once the VC begins losing the principal chips, the VC has less and less opportunity to win. In your negotiations with the venture capitalist you should keep in mind the risk-and-reward analysis and be sensitive to it. It is the guiding light for all VCs.

DOWNSIDE RISK

The third principle that venture capitalists follow in pricing investments is the downside risk. They ask, "What is the downside risk?" In other words, how much of the investment made by the venture capitalist would be lost in a liquidation? What is the probability that a liquidation could occur? The higher the downside risk and the lower the liquidation value of the company, the more equity ownership in your company the venture capitalist will have to receive to compensate for the risk; conversely, the less the equity that will be available for the entrepreneur.

After assessing the probability that the company will get in trouble and be liquidated, the VC will assess the probability that the business will get in trouble and have to be sold to salvage part of the investment. This is a little different analysis because while many businesses will not liquidate for much, there may be significant value that a strategic buyer would pay for the business as a going concern. So a second level of analysis is done by the VC to see what the business would be worth if it was sold. This may help you deflect some of the questions about the risk of your business. If you can say: "If our business does not take off, then we will sell it to the XYZ company," that can mitigate some of the risk of the investment and get you a better deal with the VC.

Downside risk is very difficult to evaluate. As an entrepreneur you are probably optimistic about the business and cannot see the downside risk. You do not understand that if the business fails, nothing will be left for the investors. You can reduce the downside risk to the venture capital firm in two basic ways: by means of collateral and by the structure of the deal.

Offering the venture capital company collateral can give the VC more hope of not losing the investment. Obviously, if you have land and a building or machinery and equipment, these can be used to collateralize the investment. Having an appraisal prepared on the machinery and equipment or land and the building to show their true worth will help. Providing the venture capital firm with a second mortgage or a third mortgage on valuable land and the building, or providing a security interest in the machinery and equipment, will help mitigate the venture capitalist's fear of losing the investment. This means that you will have to give up less equity ownership to the venture capitalist.

Other items can be used as collateral. You may have valuable patents for your new product. These patents may be worth a great deal. You may have already received an offer from a large company to purchase the patents. Such an offer would establish the worth of the patents. By giving the patents as collateral, the venture capital company will need less ownership in the company because the downside is protected. You may also have a valuable lease on a retail location for your business. This, too, could be used as collateral through an assignment of the lease to the venture capital firm. If you have some personal net worth or have the ability to earn money as an expert in your business, you may wish to give your personal guarantee to the venture capital firm. Your personal guarantee, of course, could mean that you would have to pay off the investment made by the venture capital firm if the business failed.

There is another way of solving part of the downside risk problem. You can structure the venture capitalist's investment in order to give the VC confidence that the business will not fail. For example, you could purchase common stock in the business with your funds and the venture capitalist could purchase preferred stock. This would give the VC firm a preferred position if the company were to be liquidated. Furthermore, you could give the venture capitalist a debt position in the company—that is, as a debtor of the company the VC fund would have certain rights that stockholders, either preferred or common, would not have.

Finally, you could give a secured position on your assets to the venture capital firm. By moving the venture capitalist from an unsecured to a secured creditor position, you will make the venture capitalist feel that the downside risk is less for the VC's fund, and, therefore, the fund will need less equity because the risk is lower. You should always remember that there is a direct correlation between the amount of risk the venture capitalist believes the VC fund is taking and the amount of return on investment the VC fund is seeking.

However, be warned that if you can reduce the risk, there are some VC funds that cannot look at any opportunity unless it meets their minimum hurdle rate of return. Some VC funds, when they raise funding from their investors, state a minimum return on investment that they will require or they will not invest in the business. So even though you have protected the downside, you will not be able to get some VC funds to invest because you have decreased the return you are offering. This just means you have to find another VC fund that will accept the lower return because the risk is lower.

Additional Funds

How much additional money will be needed in the years ahead to keep the business growing? Obviously, one investment by a venture capital fund will not produce a large conglomerate. It takes successive rounds of financing, either in the public market or in private placements, to bring a company from its early stages to maturity. Each successive requirement for capital will cause dilution of ownership by existing stockholders, unless the venture capitalists are willing to put up their pro rata share each time. Since it is unlikely the venture capitalist will invest every time funds are needed, there will be some dilution in the VC fund's ownership position. The more the dilution, the more equity ownership the venture capitalist will want on the initial investment, so the VC fund will not mind being diluted to a lower percentage position.

There are many great companies that grew to be giants, but the problem is that no one projected correctly how much capital it would take to make a success. So while the company grew, more capital had to be raised, which diluted the earnings per percentage of ownership for the initial investor. So while the business grew, the earnings per percentage of ownership did not and the investment was a poor one.

There are two ways to approach the problem of additional funding. The first is obvious; you could raise enough money to take you from your current position to the stage of public offering and positive cash flow. This may sound ludicrous but it is happening more and more in the venture capital field. In the past, an entrepreneur came to the venture capitalist with an idea. The venture capitalist put out a small amount of money to see if the idea would work. Once it was determined that the idea worked, the venture capitalist invested additional funds. More people would be hired, and the prototype would go into production. During the production process more money would be invested, perhaps for a complete marketing of the product. Each successive round of financing would cause further dilution in the venture capitalist's position if the VC fund did not participate in the next round of financing.

In recent years a more organized approach has appeared. A group of entrepreneurs working as a team have shown up on the doorsteps of venture capitalists. They have raised enormous amounts of money for their business, enough to take it from its initial starting point through sales and break-even. This new approach to venture financing has consumed large quantities of cash and has increased the size of the possible loss by the venture capital firm. On the other hand, when the full management team is in place and there are supposedly enough funds to take the venture to cash flow break-even, the venture capitalist is in a position to quantify many of the risks not quantifiable under the old scenario just described.

At any rate, the venture capitalist will be looking at your cash flow statement to determine how many rounds of financing are going to be needed, and, therefore, how much dilution might occur if the VC fund doesn't participate in successive rounds of financing. You should be aware of this approach and make sure the venture capitalist understands the need for additional funds so that the VC can evaluate the risk of dilution.

PUBLIC OFFERING OR EXIT

As a final measure for pricing an investment, the venture capitalist will ask, "What is the probability that the company can go public so that a price-earnings ratio can be used on the earnings to determine value rather than a private valuation?" This is important both for bringing liquidity to the venture capitalist and for providing a marketplace valuation on the company. The less likelihood there is for the company to go public, the less likely the entrepreneur will own a large share of the stock. This is because the exit for the VC will be a private sale, and a private sale almost always brings a lower price for the stock than if the company were a public company. If there is little chance of a public offering, what other exit is available?

When you are negotiating with the venture capitalist, keep in mind that the VC always wants to sell the VC fund's position in your company. It is just a matter of time and price. Even if the VC ends up with an equity position greater than 51 percent, the VC fund will still need to sell its equity position to you or to someone else. The entrepreneur should not be concerned about the long-term ownership by the venture capitalist's company and the entrepreneur's desire to own a majority of the company. In order to avoid having the company sold to someone, you should insist on having the right of first refusal on the sale of the company's stock owned by the venture capitalist. This will give you the opportunity to buy the stock owned by the venture capitalist if it is being sold at an unreasonably low price.

Also, the entrepreneur should not be worried about the fact that a venture capitalist could own more than 50 percent and control the company. Telling the entrepreneur what to do is not the method of operation for most venture capitalists. Most venture capital companies are not active operators in their investment companies. The only time the VC will become active in management is if the small company gets in trouble. Then the VC will have something to say about the management of the company.

The entrepreneur should not be concerned that the venture capitalist might own more than 50 percent and somehow tell the entrepreneur how to run the business. The venture capitalist physically does not have time to run the companies in which the VC fund has an investment. Most professional venture capitalists would not dream of telling an entrepreneur how to run his or her business on a day-to-day basis, because the venture capitalists do not know enough about the business.

AFTER THE NEGOTIATIONS

When the negotiations are complete, you must feel satisfied with the deal you have negotiated. If you feel you have ruined the negotiations and that the venture capitalist will now own too much of your company for what the VC fund is investing, you are advised not to go forward with the deal. Going forward with a deal that you don't feel satisfied with will only end in a great deal of misery for you and for the venture capitalist.

However, before you throw away the deal by turning down the venture capitalist's offer, you should discuss the offer with as many people as possible: your stockbroker, your lawyer, your banker, and other people you think will have the ability to evaluate what is happening. You may be pleasantly surprised that the offer and deal you have structured are the best that you can expect in the current marketplace.

OBJECTIVE

After the negotiations are over, both parties will have an idea of what they believe they have agreed to. It has been my experience and the experience of many others that these perceptions of the agreement rarely coincide. It is surprising how people can sit in the same room for hours and come away with a different notion of what was agreed to. These misunderstandings are the basic reason behind the simplified commitment letter that is discussed in the next chapter.

Your objective now is to obtain a commitment letter from the venture capital firm evidencing the agreement that resulted from the meetings you have had. Any good venture capital firm should take no longer than 20 days to send a commitment letter. Many venture capital firms have to go to their board of directors for approval, but they can issue a commitment letter subject to board approval.

Any commitment letter at this stage will be subject to the "due diligence" of the venture capitalist, as described in Chapter 7. What this really means is that you have a noncommitment commitment letter, because there are many ways for the VC to get out of the letter. The quicker you can reduce the amount of discussion and obtain a commitment letter, the further you will progress toward obtaining money. If you have not received such a letter within 15 days after your meeting, you should call the venture capitalist and discuss when you might be able to obtain such a letter. In the next chapter we discuss the contents of the commitment letter.

6 THE COMMITMENT LETTER

CAN IT ALL BE PUT INTO WORDS? YOUR AGREEMENTS MUST ALWAYS BE PUT IN WRITING.

Every venture capital company has a different way of making a commitment to you. It may seem hard to believe, but many venture capital companies will not issue a commitment letter. They will tell you about the proposed deal. They may write it down on paper, but they will not sign a letter that is a formal commitment. Once you have reached an oral agreement with them, they will begin to draw up the legal documents and attempt to close on the investment on the basis of the oral understanding you have reached.

Personally, I like a commitment letter. It seems to me there should be an intermediate step between oral understanding and legal documents. This step involves writing down in a commitment letter the bargain struck by each side, so that both can agree to it in a semibinding manner. Obviously, if neither can agree on the terms and conditions of a letter, no legal documents can be drawn. There are, in essence, two types of commitment letters: the one-page commitment letter issued by banks and some venture capital companies, and the long, detailed ones issued by other venture capital companies.

A short letter may contain a paragraph that sets out in simple terms everything the bank is willing to put in writing. Here is a typical short commitment letter:

J. W. Entrepreneur, President
The Entrepreneur Company
123 Main Street
McLean, Virginia 22102

Dear J. W.:

The First National Bank does hereby commit to lend your company $5 million for five years at 2 percent over prime on our standard terms and conditions. Our loan will be secured by a first deed of trust and a first secured interest in all the assets of your company and will be personally guaranteed by you and your spouse.

Sincere best wishes,

B. J. Banker
Assistant Vice President

You might wonder why some venture capital companies will not issue commitment letters or why commitment letters from banks lack detail. Primarily, it is because banks operate in a competitive community. If they give you a commitment letter and you take it to another financial institution, there is a high probability that after seeing a competitor"s commitment letter, the other bank will be more interested in your company. The competitor might offer you better terms and conditions. Needless to say, entrepreneurs who use commitment letters as a bargaining tool are frowned upon in both the banking and the venture capital communities. Any potential lender hearing of such behavior may rescind the commitment letter as soon as possible. The preferred method of operating is to stay with one venture capital company until you agree or disagree. If you cannot agree, then you should move to the next venture capital company. If the agreement is in the form of a commitment letter, you should stay with the agreement.

COMMITMENT LETTERS

The normal method for preventing an entrepreneur from using a commitment letter to bargain with other financial institutions is to require the borrower to make a commitment deposit in order to hold the commitment outstanding. This procedure seems only fair, since the venture capital company at this point will have reserved some of its funds for your company. Also, the venture capitalist will have to make a commitment of time and expenses to analyze you, your company, and your industry. There should be some commitment on the part of the entrepreneur. Be advised that the points or percentages of the investment are normally required as commitment deposits, especially by those venture capital companies that are leveraged. For example, if 1 percent is required as a deposit on a $5 million commitment, then you will have to put up $50,000 to hold the commitment. The current norm is 1 to 2 percent as a commitment deposit.

Usually the fee is paid before the venture capitalist visits your company. If for some reason the venture capital company does not go through with the commitment, the fee is refunded. If you do not go forward, normally you lose the fee. You are legally free to shop for the best deal you can find from the venture community. You should remember that the venture community is relatively small and somewhat friendly. You may damage your relationship if a venture capitalist hears that you are using his commitment as a bargaining tool. Even worse, the venture capitalist may cancel the commitment on the basis that your company and the VC fund have an agreement.

Some venture firms do not issue commitment letters, because they believe such letters would bind them to make the investment. They do not want a suit if they back out. Even the firms that do issue commitment letters make certain the letters contain loopholes that let the firms off if they do not wish to go forward. Some venture capitalists do not like commitment letters because they reveal their full intentions to tie the entrepreneur in knots with conditions the entrepreneur must meet. Nonetheless you should insist on a commitment letter, or at least a letter outlining the basic terms of the agreement. This last one is called a "term sheet."

A detailed commitment letter is the subject of this chapter. It is the first step toward obtaining your funds. In the example below, the structure is preferred stock with options to own stock.

WHAT IS IN THE COMMITMENT LETTER?

Commitment letters vary greatly from one venture firm to another. They also vary greatly depending on whether they are preferred stock or a mezzanine loan. And of course, a well-done commitment letter is much more preferable to its shorter brother, the term sheet that gives you only a small part of the deal. Since most of the deals done today have a venture investor and at some point a mezzanine investor, we will mix a discussion of both as we go through the commitment letter.

The standard commitment letter contains five basic segments. The first segment states the terms on which the investment is being made to your company and the terms of any equity option. The second section states the collateral for the investment and this section usually exist only for mezzanine loans. The third part talks about the conditions of the investment, both negative and positive. The fourth outlines the representations you have made that have induced the venture capital fund to make a commitment. The fifth part deals with the conditions on which the commitment was made. Each part is discussed in the following pages.

SECTION 1: TERMS OF THE INVESTMENT

In this section the venture capital fund will try to state in clear terms precisely what it intends to do.

"The venture capital fund will purchase preferred stock in the amount of $3 million with a preferred coupon of 8 percent per annum paid in additional shares of preferred stock (PIK), paid quarterly on the first of each quarter." Or if this were a mezzanine loan the terms would be something like "12 percent interest paid monthly in arrears on the first of each month."

In this sentence, which is self-explanatory, the venture fund agrees to purchase $3 million of preferred stock at 8 percent preferred rate. This means the VC fund will get its money plus an 8 percent rate, paid before the common stock investors, like you, get anything.

"The preferred stock will be redeemed by the company at the end of five years from closing."

This means you have to give back the money in five years plus the 8% preferred return. If this were a mezzanine loan, this next sentence might say, "The loan shall be interest only for the first 36 months, and beginning with the 37th month you will pay principal and interest sufficient to fully amortize the loan over the remaining 60 months. All principal and interest outstanding at the end of 8 years shall be due and payable in full."

"The preferred stock may be redeemed at any time. Or for a loan, the loan may be prepaid in whole or in part, at any time with no prepayment penalty."

This part indicates that you may buy back the preferred stock or prepay the loan in whole or in part at any time. Thus, if you had a large public offering and had surplus cash, you might want to pay off the note in order to free any collateral that the loan had encumbered. Of course, it is difficult to obtain preferred stock or a mezzanine loan, so you may not want to eliminate it. At any rate, this gives you the flexibility to eliminate the investment. Always avoid prepayment penalties in this section. Sometimes the VC will require you to prepay if the company has a public offering.

"Disbursement and takedown of the investment shall be 100 percent at closing."

This is a very important section. Sometimes the venture capital firm will agree to invest in your company but will not let you draw it down unless certain conditions are met. Here, no conditions are stated. Disbursement by the venture capital firm and the takedown of all the funds by you will be 100 percent at closing. This means you will get all the money on the day of the legal closing. If possible, you should attempt to have all the money disbursed at closing with no conditions. This gives you control over the funds.

"In connection with this financing, the venture capital firm shall receive at the closing separate stock options to purchase stock in the company. The cost of the options to the venture capital firm will be $100. These options, when exercised, will provide stock ownership in the company of 20 percent at the time of exercise. The exercise price will be $20,000. The options will expire ten years from closing. The venture capital firm will share pro rata in any redemption of stock by the company in order to expand its pro rata ownership."

This paragraph explains the equity option granted to the venture capital firm. A piece of paper signed by you will give the venture capitalist the right to own stock in your company. This piece of paper will cost the venture capital firm $100. However, when the firm exercises the option described on the piece of paper and receives the stock, it will have to pay $20,000 for it. It will have this option for up to ten years. That is, the option will hang over the company for the next ten years unless a different agreement is negotiated in that period of time. The venture capital firm will also share in any redemptions of stock. If there are various stockholders and the company agrees to buy out one who owns 10 percent of the stock, the venture capital company would receive the same offer—in this case an offer to acquire 2 percent more of the company and thus have an option to buy 22 percent of the company for $20,000. Sometimes the actual number of shares and price per share are stated in this section. If so, there will also be an antidilution clause stating that if you sell stock below the price to be paid per share by the venture capitalist, then you will issue additional shares to the VC fund.

"There shall be an "unlocking" provision whereby if there is a bona fide offer to purchase the company and the venture capital fund wishes to accept the offer but the company does not, then the company is required to acquire the venture capitalist's interest on the same terms and conditions as the bona fide offer. If you do not buy out the venture capital fund, then you must sell the company according to the terms of the bona fide offer."

This "unlocking" provision gives the venture capitalist an opportunity to exit from your company if there is a bona fide offer to purchase the company. In essence, it says that if someone offers to buy your company and the venture capitalist thinks you should sell the company but you do not agree, then your company must buy back the venture capitalist fund's equity ownership on the same terms and conditions as those made by the bona fide offer.

"There shall be a "put" provision whereby anytime after five years the venture capital fund may require the company to purchase its stock options or the resulting stock from the options at the higher of the following:

1. $5 million cash.
2. 120 percent of book value times 20 percent ownership.
3. Five times net pretax earning for the year just ended times 20 percent ownership.
4. Two times sales for the year just ended times 20 percent ownership.
5. Ten times cash flow times 20 percent ownership.
6. Appraised value times 20 percent ownership."

The preceding list names just a few of the ways the VC fund finds a way out of your company if there is no public offering or no one to buy your company. A very important provision in the option agreement will be the "put" provision. Here it is agreed that the venture capitalist can require the company to buy the VC fund's option according to six possible formulas. The minimum amount is, obviously, the cash price of $5 million. This means that any time after five years the venture capital fund can require your company to purchase the VC fund's stock option for $5 million. The amount is the amount you negotiate with the VC firm.

The other formulas are related to the equity ownership of the venture capital firm. For example, the third formula uses the company's pretax earnings for the year just ended times five, and then multiplies that number by 20 percent which is the equity ownership it has an option to buy. If pretax earnings had been $1 million, then the venture capitalist could require you to buy the VC fund's equity position for $1 million cash ($1 million earnings times five, times 20 percent, equals $1 million).

"There shall be a "call" provision for a period of three years after five years from closing; after the venture capitalist's investment has been paid in full, then the company can purchase the stock options or resulting stock from the options on the same terms and conditions as specified in put provisions."

This section enables you to buy back the stock option held by the venture capital company after five years at a price based on the higher of the formulas set out in put provisions. In this situation you have a limited time to buy back the option. It is three years, and the clock begins running five years after closing. Most venture capital companies will not give you a call because it puts a cap on the amount of profit they can make. So don't be disappointed if you can't obtain a call. The call does not obligate you; it is a benefit. It is the put option that puts you under the gun.

"Anytime after five years from closing the venture capitalist may require a registration and public offering of the shares owned by the venture capital fund at the company's expense."

This section gives the venture capitalist the right to make you register and publicly offer the shares owned by the VC fund. This could be quite expensive in that you would have to go to the Securities and Exchange Commission, register the shares, and give the venture capitalist the right to sell the shares in the public market. In theory, this seems to be an onerous task. In practice it is not. Most venture capitalists would not dream of requesting a public offering of the company's shares without having a stockbrokerage firm as an underwriter. An underwriter will not register and sell the shares of a floundering company or one that cannot meet strong projections.

Therefore, if your company is not doing well, an underwriter/stockbroker will not be willing to take your company public. If it is doing well, the venture capitalist does have a means of pushing you into a public offering. It might be at a time when you do not want to have it, but nonetheless, the VC would have the right to push you in that direction. If you can avoid this paragraph in your commitment, do it.

"The venture capitalist shall have full "piggyback" rights to register the shares owned by the VC fund whenever the company or its management is registering shares for sale, and such registration of the venture capitalist's shares shall be paid for by the company."

This paragraph enables the venture capitalist to ride your coattails if you register shares for public offering. This means that if you have lined up a stockbrokerage firm and it is willing to sell shares in a public offering, then the venture capitalist will have the right to ride piggyback on that registration and sell its shares also. Generally, a brokerage house will not permit the venture capitalist to sell more than 10 to 20 percent of its holdings in the initial public offering. The fact that the venture capitalist has the right to sell all of the shares of the VC fund shares in the public offering could provide for an impasse between the brokerage house and the venture firm. This is seldom more than a momentary impasse, because most venture firms recognize that having 20 percent sold is better than none and they will probably go along with the offer to sell some shares. The "piggyback" paragraph is a standard one.

SECTION 2: COLLATERAL AND SECURITY

Most of the parts of this section usually apply only to a mezzanine loan, and as you read it you will see which ones fit the preferred stock investor. This section of the commitment letter sets out the collateralization of the investment with certain assets of your company and, in some cases, your own personal assets.

"A second deed of trust on land and building of the business subordinated as to collateral to a first mortgage of $2 million from a bank on terms acceptable to the venture capitalist."

According to this paragraph, the venture capitalist will have a second deed of trust mortgage on the land and building owned by the company, subordinated only to a $2 million first mortgage by a bank. There may be no equity in the land and building at this time, but the venture capitalist is hoping that if the business gets in trouble after a year or two, perhaps inflation will have increased the value of the land and building and there will be some collateral for him. If you agree to give a mortgage, then this paragraph is standard.

"A second secured interest in all the tangible and intangible assets of the company, including but not limited to inventory, machinery, equipment, furniture, fixtures, and accounts receivable subordinated as to collateral to a first secured bank loan of $1 million on terms acceptable to the venture capitalist."

In this instance the venture capitalist has a second secured interest in all the tangible and intangible assets of the company. They are subordinated to the first secured interest of a $1 million term loan from the bank. Many venture capitalists seek to secure their loans in order to remove themselves as general creditors of the company. This gives them protection in case the company falters or goes into bankruptcy. It's better to be in a second mortgage position and a second secured interest in the company than to be just another general creditor. Sometimes there is something for secured creditors when there is nothing for general creditors.

"Pledge and assignment of all the stock of the company and assignment of any and all leases of the company."

Here, you will pledge the stock that you own in the company as collateral for the loan. If the loan was in default, the venture firm could take the stock and become the owner of your company. That is unlikely. If the company actually was in trouble and the venture capitalist became an owner, the VC fund could be held responsible for some of the liabilities, such as payroll taxes. Often a venture capitalist will take a valuable lease assigned as collateral, especially in a retail situation. Under a default scenario, the venture capital fund can take over the leases and sell them to a third party if permitted by the landlord.

In a preferred stock situation, the investor might ask you to put your common stock in a voting trust with an independent trustee, and if you get in trouble, then the VC will be permitted to vote the shares in the voting trust. This is less a collateral issue than a control issue. In essence it says if you take the company on the road to strong profits, then you get to drive; however, if you slow down or get off the road, then the VC gets to drive.

"Personal signature and guarantees of you and your spouse."

Many venture capitalists will require the individuals involved in the business to guarantee their investment. Frequently, the guarantee is required in order to satisfy the venture capitalist that the entrepreneur will not run away from the business. This requirement is particularly common in cases where the entrepreneur puts in few equity dollars.

Another way to do this is to have the entrepreneur buy stock in the company by signing a note that makes the entrepreneur have to pay back the note. This gives the entrepreneur the incentive to make the company successful, because if the entrepreneur fails, then the entrepreneur has to pay back the loans from personal earnings. This is less about collateral than it is giving the entrepreneur motivation not to be reckless in operating the business.

"Assignment of a life insurance policy on your life for the amount of the loan outstanding with the venture capitalist listed as the loss payee to the extent of the VC funds investment."

Venture capital firms almost always require a life insurance policy on the life of the key entrepreneur. If the key entrepreneur dies, the policy will pay back the venture capital fund the money it has invested. This is not an unreasonable request since the venture capitalist is betting on you to make money.

"Adequate hazard and business insurance, which shall include flood insurance if your business is located in a designated federal flood area. All such insurance shall be assigned to the venture capital firm, which shall be listed as the loss payee to the extent of its interest. In this regard, you will supply the venture capital firm with a list of all business insurance, and such insurance and coverage shall be acceptable to the venture capital firm."

Business insurance is also a requirement before a venture capitalist will invest in a company. Much like any other creditor or investor, the venture capital firm will want the insurance policy assigned to it so that if the business is destroyed, at least it will be repaid for part of the money it invested.

Section 3: Conditions of the Investment

This section enumerates the conditions under which the investment will exist. Wherever possible, you should try to remove many conditions.

"The company will provide the venture capitalist with internally prepared, monthly year-to-date financial statements, in accordance with generally accepted accounting standards (including a profit-and-loss and balance sheet) within 30 days of the end of each month."

As a condition of the investment, you will be required to prepare monthly financial statements and give them to the venture capital firm within thirty days of the end of each month. So, by the end of June each year, you will have supplied the venture capitalist with the May financial statements. This is a standard requirement.

"The company will provide the venture capitalist with a monthly one- or two-page summary of operations with the financial reports furnished in the previous section."

Venture capitalists also like to have in writing a monthly summary of the operations and an indication of important events. If you are in this situation, you must include this summary with the financial statements.

"Within 90 days after the year end, the company will provide the venture capitalist with an annual certified audit from an independent certified public accounting firm acceptable to the venture capital company."

A certified audit from an independent certified public accountant is mandatory in any company financed by a venture capitalist. Some venture firms will permit an accounting firm to review the finances of a small business, but most often they require an audit. Although an audit is expensive, it is useful in the early years because it will permit you to have a public offering at a much earlier date. Normally, you need to have the last three years audited in order to have a public offering.

"Within 30 days of the year end, provide the venture capitalist with projections for the next fiscal year in the same format as the financial statements."

Venture capitalists want to have updated financial projections. In this instance, you will have to provide the venture capitalist with projections for the next fiscal year within thirty days of the year end. You can expect the venture capitalist to discuss these new projections with you in detail.

In an early stage deal, the projections of cash flow may be done weekly to determine when you need to raise capital and how fast you are "burning" capital. The well worn term "burn rate" refers to how fast a company is spending cash after adjusting the burn rate for how much cash it is collecting.

A weekly burn rate of $100,000 when you have $1 million in the bank, means you can last another 10 weeks before you "hit the wall." This is just another cute term for running out of cash so you cannot pay your bills.

"Within thirty days after they are filed, provide the venture capitalist with a copy of all material documents filed with government agencies such as the Internal Revenue Service, Environmental Protection Agency, and Securities and Exchange Commission."

In an effort to obtain additional information on the company, the venture capital firm will want a copy of filings before government agencies. These documents will enable the venture capital firm to continue to monitor your company.

"The president of the company will provide the venture capital company with a certificate each quarter stating that no default has occurred in the terms and conditions of this investment."

In this instance, you will certify that to the best of your knowledge nothing has come to your attention that would indicate that the company is in default on any of the default provisions in the loan agreements to your banks or mezzanine lenders and any of the representations you have made. Falsifying this kind of statement could lead to charges of fraud. You should take every precaution to make sure that what you are signing is correct.

"On a quarterly basis and within 30 days of the end of the quarter, provide the venture capital firm with a list of inventory, accounts receivable, and other collateral to be compared with certain ratios."

This is more the domain of banks and mezzanine lenders. But here the venture capital firm often follows certain ratios and levels of assets and sales. You may be required to provide the venture capitalist with this information, including the calculation of certain ratios.

"In accordance with generally accepted accounting principles, the company will maintain:

1. A current ratio of one to one.
2. Accounts receivable to loan balance of one to one.
3. Inventory to loan balance of percent.
4. Sales of $1 million per year.
5. Net worth of $3 million."

This, too, is more for banks and mezzanine lenders. In your quarterly statement set out in the previous section, you will have to mention the ratios that you agreed to in this one. When you agree to one of these ratios or absolute numbers, you should look at your projections to make sure the ratios will be maintained throughout your projected future. Ratios are less popular among venture capitalists, and you will be able to remove all or most of them, especially if this is a preferred stock deal.

"There will be no change in control or ownership of the company without the venture capital firm's expressed written approval."

Under the terms of this section, the venture capitalist does not permit a change in control of the company. If you or the others who own the company were to sell it to somebody else, the venture capitalist would then be in bed with a different partner. No venture capitalist wants to wake up the next morning to find a different management team and different owners. Expect the VC to insist on this one.

"Management will not sell, assign, or transfer any shares it owns in the company without written approval of the venture capital firm."

Here the venture capitalist makes sure you will not sell, assign, or transfer your shares in the company without his approval. After all, if you sold all of your shares, even though they did not amount to control of the company, the venture capitalist, again, would not have the same manager the VC had before. Your incentive would no longer be to make the stock of the company worth a great deal since you no longer would be an owner of the stock. When venture capitalists bet on a racehorse, they want to make sure the same jockey stays on the racehorse that finishes the race; they don't want to change jockeys in the middle of the race.

"The company will have board meetings at least once each quarter at the company's business offices. Although the venture capital firm's representative will not serve on the board, its representative will have the right to attend each meeting at the company's expense, and the venture capital firm shall be notified of each meeting at least two weeks before it is to occur."

By agreeing to this paragraph, you and the VC agreed to have a meeting at least once each quarter, and the venture capitalist will come to the meeting. Venture capitalists will often become board members and, therefore, they will not attend the meeting as a representative, but as a member of the board of directors. The usual discussion here is how many board seats the VC gets as opposed to the right to attend.

"The company will pay no cash dividends, and the company will not sell any assets of the business that are not part of the regular course of business without the venture capital firm's approval."

The company will be prohibited from dividend payments. In all likelihood, the company is in its strong growth mode and does not intend to pay any dividends. Nor will the company sell any assets of the business that are not in the regular course of the business. This clause will prohibit the company from selling its machinery or equipment if it wants to shut down a certain part of the business. The only assets that could be sold are assets that are regularly sold. For example, if you are a manufacturing company and trucks and cars are used in the business, then it is ok to sell a truck and replace it with a new truck. This is a standard paragraph.

"The company will not expend funds in excess of $300,000 per year for capital improvements without written approval of the venture capital firm."

In this instance, the company is prohibited from making capital improvements. In total, this will cost more than $300,000. Obviously, the venture capitalist does not wish to have the company buying a great deal of capital equipment without permission of the VC fund. If your company needs additional machinery, equipment, or other assets, you will need to negotiate the $300,000 figure up.

"The management team, including you, will live in the metropolitan area where the business is located. The business will not be relocated without the express written permission of the venture capital firm."

Many venture capitalists require entrepreneurs to live in the city in which the business is located. It is a universal rule among venture capital firms that a business cannot be run on an absentee basis. This is possible in a few situations, but most often you will be required to live where your business is located. If you intended to move away and retire after the financing, you would not be allowed to do so.

"The company will not pay any employee nor will it loan nor advance to any employee money that, in total, exceeds $150,000 per year without the written approval of the venture capital firm. "

Here the VC fund is keeping you and your management team from paying out all the capital you are raising as salaries to yourselves. This is standard, and you need to agree to some figure. The venture capitalist will want a ceiling on the salary the entrepreneur can take from the company. The reason for this is simple. If the entrepreneur is taking out hundreds of thousands of dollars in salary, then there will be no incentive for the entrepreneur to take the company public or to go forward with any action that will give the venture capitalist an opportunity to cash in on the investment. It is my experience that most venture capital firms do not mind entrepreneurs making a large salary but they would prefer this to come in the form of bonuses at year end rather than as a monthly payment. The board can agree to the bonus subject to approval of the venture capitalist. Then permission can be obtained from the venture capitalist if the entrepreneur has done a great job during the past year.

A second part of this paragraph may be: "If the company is in default for nonpayment on its loans, or if the company is not profitable for any calendar quarter, then the company will not pay any employee nor will it loan nor advance to any employee money that in total exceeds $100,000 without written permission of the venture capital firm."

This is a penalty clause that says that you need to run the business correctly, or it will hurt your salary—just another of the little incentives built in to keep you going in the right direction.

"The company will not pay any brokerage fees, legal fees, or consulting fees in excess of $50,000 per year without written approval of the venture capitalist."

Venture capitalists do not like to have a consultant or broker on the payroll unless it is one of their own. For this reason, they limit the amount of money that can be paid out in legal fees, consulting fees, and brokerage fees.

"You will pay all closing costs and recording fees, which include all attorney fees, even those of the venture capitalist's attorney. You may use any attorney you want, but the venture fund's lawyer will control the documents and draw them up."

Invariably, you will pay all closing costs, recording fees, and attorney fees, including the fees of the attorney for the venture capital firm. These all come out of the proceeds of the financing.

SECTION 4: REPRESENTATIONS

The approval of the investment in your company was based on the following representations, which were made by you and were inducements to the venture capital firm making this commitment. If any of these representations is not true, this commitment letter may be declared void by the venture capital firm. Do not sign a representation you cannot fulfill.

"The company is a corporation in good standing in (your state). You will provide the venture capital firm with a certificate of good standing and a copy of the charter, the bylaws, and the organizing minutes of the company."

This is a standard certification that your company is in good standing and incorporated in a certain state. Your attorney can make sure that these representations are correct.

"The company is primarily engaged in the business of (type of business)."

The venture capitalist seeks to define in legal terms what business you are in. It is a representation to him that you are not in some other business.

"There are no lawsuits against the company, its directors, or its officers, nor do you know of any that may be contemplated. If there are any suits outstanding or contemplated, your attorney will provide the venture capital firm with a letter stating the nature of such suits and a copy of such suits at least 30 days prior to closing. You will provide the venture capital firm with a copy of all lawsuits you have filed against others."

You will have to certify to the venture capitalist that there are no lawsuits against your company. This is a moment of truth. If you do not inform the venture firm of any lawsuits that are outstanding, you are in effect certifying that there are none.

"The company is current on all taxes owed; in this regard you will provide the venture capital firm with a copy of the last three years' tax returns plus a copy of the receipts for payment of the last four quarters for payroll taxes."

Here you are certifying that you have paid all payroll taxes or other taxes owed, including real estate taxes. If you owe any taxes, again, this is the time to let the venture capital firm know. Indicate in the commitment letter whether you owe taxes. In the instance above, you are certifying that there are no taxes outstanding.

"You have presented financial information, business information, and a business proposal that you represent to be true and correct."

In this paragraph the venture firm is seeking to incorporate all the information that you have supplied to it under a representation that you believe this information to be correct. If you state in your resume that you received an M.B.A. from a renowned business school and you did not, then the commitment letter could be automatically voided by this misrepresentation. Is everything you stated to the venture capitalist true? Be sure it is before you sign this statement.

"Your personal financial statement showed that you have a net worth of $1 million."

According to this paragraph, you presented information to the venture firm that your net worth was $1 million. If this representation is incorrect, then the commitment letter will be voided.

"You will invest an additional $500,000 of cash in the company as equity on or before the closing on this loan on terms acceptable to the venture capital firm. You will provide the venture capital firm with written information on the terms of this investment."

Somewhere along the way, you indicated to the venture capital firm that you intended to invest additional equity in the business, in this case, $500,000. The venture capital firm is documenting your representation.

"A group of investors will invest $1.5 million in the business as equity on terms acceptable to the venture capital firm. You will provide the venture capital firm with written information on these investments."

You have also represented to the venture capital firm that a group of investors would invest another $1.5 million in equity in the business and the venture capital firm is documenting this representation.

"The money borrowed will be used as follows:

    1. Pay accounts payable, $500,000;

2. Pay bank debt, $300,000; and

3. Provide working capital, $3 million."

You have represented to the venture capital firm how you intend to use the money. Later, if you do not pay $300,000 on the bank debt but pay off only $100,000, you will be in violation of a material representation. Be sure the representations you make with regard to use of proceeds are correct. Then, follow through when you receive the money.

"Upon closing of the investor's loan, you will have approximately the following assets:

1. Cash, $3 million;

2. Inventory, $700,000;

3. Accounts receivable, $1 million;

4. Machinery and equipment, $500,000;

5. Land and building, $0; and

6. Other assets, $20,000."

Here, the venture capital firm is representing part of the after-financing balance sheet, that is, the assets your company will have after the financing occurs. Look at this representation to make sure it is accurate, because if it is not, your representations may be in default.

"With regard to all material leases, you will provide the venture capital firm with a copy of each lease."

In this section, you are agreeing to provide the venture firm with a copy of all material leases pertaining to the company. If you have forgotten to tell the venture firm that you are leasing a large warehouse and you do not provide it with a copy of this material lease, the loan agreement could be in default.

"You will pay no brokerage fees, legal fees, or other fees in connection with this loan without the venture capital firm's written approval; and, in addition, you will indemnify the venture capital firm against all such fees."

Many financial brokers, who have not been involved in financing a venture, later claim that they were the brokers in the financial transaction. In this paragraph, you are representing to the venture firm that there are no brokers and you are indemnifying the venture capital firm against such fees.

"During the past ten years none of the directors, officers, or management has been arrested or convicted of a material crime or a material matter."

You are representing to the venture firm that none of your officers are criminals.

"The company has a commitment from a bank or other financial institution to borrow $2 million on terms acceptable to the venture capital firm. With regard to this commitment, you will provide the venture capital firm with a copy of your commitment and closing documents."

You are representing that a bank is willing to lend the company $2 million. If the bank has said only that it was interested in making the loan, you may have difficulty living up to this representation, as you do not have a commitment letter. You should obtain a commitment letter from the bank for $2 million before you sign this representation.

SECTION 5: CONDITIONS OF COMMITMENT

If the following conditions are not obtained, the venture capital firm's commitment will be void:

"In connection with this financing, the venture capital firm will receive a 2 percent fee. Upon acceptance of this commitment letter, you will pay the venture capital firm $15,000 of the fee and the remainder at closing. Should closing not take place through the fault of the venture capital firm, then the fee in total would be returned. Otherwise, the paid portion of the fee would be forfeited, and the unpaid portion of the fee would be due and payable immediately. Acceptance by you of this commitment letter and the return of one copy of this letter to the venture capital firm fully executed by you with the fee must be received before (date)."

It is customary in the venture business for the venture firm to receive a commitment fee. After all, the venture firm is committing to invest the money in your company. In the instance above, it is to receive a 2 percent fee. You may be able to negotiate a smaller fee. Note that the commitment above is open until a certain date. If you miss that date, then the commitment letter is void. Once you pay the fee and sign the letter, then the commitment is open until the date set out in the following section.

"Closing on the investment before (date)."

Closing on the investment means the day the legal papers are signed and the money is transferred from the venture capitalist to you. If you do not close by the date listed in this section, then the venture capital firm can keep your commitment fee and they do not have to go through with the deal.

"All legal documents must be acceptable to the venture capital firm."

The venture firm does not have to close unless all the legal documents are acceptable. Obviously, if your lawyer tries to insert provisions in the legal documents, whether or not they seem reasonable to you and your lawyer, they must be acceptable to the venture capital firm. If they are not, the venture capital firm will not have to go to closing.

"A favorable credit check of you and your business and a favorable "due diligence" review of you, your business, and your industry must take place with no adverse occurrences before closing."

Venture firms will run a credit check on you and the business. If they do not like something in your credit file, such as an unpaid bill, they can renege on their commitment. Also, an adverse occurrence before the closing, such as a 15 percent drop in sales, would allow the venture firm not to close on this loan. The due diligence report is prepared by the venture capitalist. Almost anything could make it unfavorable. All venture firms include these types of loopholes in their commitment letters.

"A favorable visit to your business operation by the venture capitalist must take place."

This short sentence is probably the open-ended item in this section in that no one knows what a favorable visit to your business really is. If the venture capitalist wanted to get out of the commitment, the VC could make a visit and say that it was unfavorable for almost any reason. This would void this commitment to you. It will be hard to remove this due diligence visit clause. Every venture capitalist wants to see where the VC fund is investing.

"The entire funds set forth in this commitment letter must be raised."

This section merely states that unless all the funds that are sought have been raised, then this commitment is void. If you are not willing to put in the $500,000 in equity, if the investors are unwilling to put in their $1 million, and if the bank is unwilling to lend you the $2 million, then any of these occurrences can void the commitment letter.

COMMENTS ON THE COMMITMENT LETTER

The reason behind each of the foregoing items seems self-evident. To the extent that you can remove some of these items from the commitment letter or keep them from being added to the legal documents, you will simplify the relationship between you and the venture capitalist. However, the venture capitalist's lawyer will make sure that whatever is in the commitment letter is in the legal documents, so remove troublesome items before you sign the letter. The example letter contains most of the reasonable items a venture firm should ask for.

Most letters will contain only some part of the items listed. You should negotiate every point in the letter, but do not quibble over details.

WHAT IS AN INVESTMENT MEMORANDUM OR TERM SHEET?

Over the years the commitment letter has given way to the "Term Sheet or Investment Memorandum." These are much shorter versions of the commitment letter. They have far less information in them, and you are left to sign a term sheet and fight over the details later. The firm calls this letter an investment memorandum or a term sheet, even though it is in the form of a letter. An investment memorandum usually states all the terms and conditions of the stock purchase. Set out below are the five categories as they appear in a term sheet or investment memorandum, for the purchase of stock.

SECTION 1: TERM OF THE INVESTMENT

In this section the venture capital company will state exactly what it intends to do in purchasing the shares.

"The venture capital firm will purchase 1 million shares of preferred stock in the company at $3 per share."

"All shares will be purchased at closing."

"If any stock of the company is sold by the company for less than $3 per share at any time within five years from this sale, there shall be antidilution for the ownership of these 3 million shares."

"If the company has not had a public offering of its stock within five years from the closing date, then the venture capital firm will have a "put" provision whereby the venture capital firm can require the company to redeem the shares resulting from this purchase at the higher of the following:

1. Book value per share.
2. Earnings per share times 10.
3. $6 per share, fixed price."

"Anytime after five years from closing the venture capital firm may require a registration and public offering of the shares owned by the venture capital firm at the company's expense."

The venture capital firm will have full "piggyback" rights to register shares any time the company or its management is registering shares for sale, and such registration of the venture capital firm's shares shall be paid for by your company.

SECTION 2: COLLATERAL AND SECURITY

In this section of the investment memorandum, or term sheet, the venture capital firm will set out what security or what preferences are given to its shares.

"Should the company be liquidated, it is agreed that the shares being issued to the venture capital firm shall have priority in liquidation to the shares owned by anyone else. This means that any funds remaining after all creditors have been paid will be first paid to the venture capital firm to the extent of its investment of $3 million and the remainder shall go to other stockholders who are assumed to be management until the cost of the shares is repaid. If any funds remain, they shall be divided pro rata."

"You will have a life insurance policy on your life for the amount of $3 million with the venture capital firm listed as the loss payee."

"The company will have adequate hazard and business insurance. In this regard, you will supply the venture capital firm with a list of all business insurance, and such insurance and coverage shall be acceptable to the venture capital firm."

SECTION 3: CONDITIONS OF THE INVESTMENT

In this section, the venture capital firm will set out the conditions under which it has made the investment and you must live up to these conditions even after the closing date.

As long as the venture capital firm owns any of the shares resulting from the purchase of shares at the closing, and as long as those shares are equal to 5 percent of the equity capital of the company, then your company will comply with the following items:

"Provide the venture capital firm with monthly, year-to-date, financial statements, in accordance with generally accepted accounting standards, within 30 days of the end of each calendar month."

"Within 90 days after the year end, the company will provide the venture capital company with an annual certified audit from an independent certified public accounting firm acceptable to the venture capital firm."

"Within 90 days of the year end, provide the venture capital firm with projections for the next fiscal year in the same format as the financial statements."

"Within 30 days after they have been filed, provide the venture capital firm with a copy of all documents filed with government agencies, such as the Internal Revenue Service, the Environmental Protection Agency, and the Securities and Exchange Commission."

"There will be no change in control of the company, nor will there be any change in ownership of the company without the venture capital company's express written approval; further, management will not sell, assign, or transfer any shares it owns in the company without the written approval of the venture capital firm."

"The company will have a board of directors that does not exceed five persons. The venture capital firm will have the right to elect two members to the board of directors, and you and your associates will vote all your shares to effect such election of two members to the board of directors."

"The board of directors will meet at least once each month at the firm's business office. The venture capital firm's board members will be notified at least two weeks before each meeting, and your company will pay the transportation expenses of the venture capital board members as well as customary fees."

"The company will pay no cash dividends, and the company will not sell or assign any assets of the business that are not part of the regular course of business without the venture capital firm's approval."

"The management team, including you, will live in the metropolitan area in which the business is located. The business will not be relocated without the express written permission of the venture capital firm."

"The company will not pay any employee, nor will it loan or advance to any employee money that in total exceeds $150,000 per year without the written approval of the venture capital company."

"You will pay all closing costs and recording fees related to this financing, which include attorney fees of the venture capital firm."

Section 4: Representations

The approval and commitment made by the venture capital firm was based on representations that were made by your company as follows:

"The company is a corporation in good standing in the State of (state). You will provide the venture capital firm with a certificate of good standing and a copy of the charter and bylaws and organizational minutes of the company."

"The company is primarily engaged in the business of (type of business)."

"There are no lawsuits against the company, its directors, or its officers, nor do you know of any that may be contemplated."

"The company is current on all taxes owed and in this regard you will provide the venture capital firm with a copy of the last three years' tax returns and the past four quarterly tax receipts for payroll taxes."

"You have presented financial information, business information, and a business proposal, all of which you believe to be correct and true."

"The money will be used as follows:

1. Research and development, $1 million.

2. Accounts payable, $100,000.

3. Remainder for working capital."

"You will pay no brokerage fees, legal fees, or other fees in connection with this investment without the venture capital firm's prior written approval; in addition, you will indemnify the venture capital firm against all such fees."

"During the past ten years none of the directors, officers, or managers has been arrested or convicted of material crimes of any manner whatsoever."

"You have a commitment from a bank to borrow $1 million on terms as presented in the bank commitment letter."

"There are 3 million shares of stock outstanding and no stock options."

Section 5: Conditions of the Commitment

This investment commitment is conditioned on the following, which, if not obtained by you, will make the venture capital firm's commitment void.

"In connection with this venture capital investment, the venture capital firm will receive a 1 percent fee. Upon acceptance of this investment memorandum, you will pay the venture capital company the $20,000 fee. Should closing not take place through the fault of the venture capital firm, then the fee in total will be returned. Otherwise, the fee will be forfeited. Acceptance by you of this investment memorandum and return of one copy of this investment memorandum fully executed by you with the fee must be received before (date)."

"Closing on this investment must take place by (date)."

"All legal documents must be acceptable to the VC fund."

"There will be a favorable credit check of you and your business and your management team with no material adverse occurrences before the closing date."

"There will be a favorable visit by the venture capital company to your business operation."

Consulting Agreement

As you can see, the investment memorandum is similar to the commitment letter, but it is less detailed. The investment memorandum may contain one other condition that is previously not listed; that is, a consulting arrangement with the venture capitalist. The consulting arrangement usually reads something like this:

The company will enter into a consulting arrangement with the venture capital firm whereby the venture capital firm will provide consulting services to the business for $10,000 per month. This consulting agreement will be in effect for the first 12 months subsequent to closing on the investment.

Sometimes the venture capital company uses the consulting contract as a mechanism for becoming part of the management team and for improving its understanding of the business. Sometimes it wants to make sure that the invested funds will not be squandered by the management team. Often it is just another method for the venture capital company to take money out of the small business. It has been my own practice to avoid such consulting arrangements unless the venture capital firm has someone to provide actual services to the company.

VOTING TRUST

Another item that often appears in the commitment letter is the voting trust arrangement. That is, all the shares owned by the entrepreneurs (which, in essence, represent control of the company) are placed in a voting trust. The voting trust is controlled by the venture capital firm. Should things get out of hand, the venture capital firm can exercise its rights under the voting trust, vote the shares of the company, and elect a new board of directors favorably disposed to the venture capital firm. Then they can make any needed changes, including firing the management team. Many of the conditions set forth in a voting trust could trigger the venture capital company into wanting to operate your business. Some of the basic causes for concern are (a) failure to meet all projections agreed upon; (b) losses greater than anticipated; and (c) key employees leaving the company. A typical voting trust clause is set out below:

All shares of the company will be placed in a voting trust. The trustee shall be an officer of a bank acceptable to both you and the venture capital firm. If the company's sales are less than $1 million in any month, then the venture capital firm may name two additional trustees to the trust. A majority vote of the three trustees may vote the shares placed in the voting trust.

Voting trusts used to be common in the venture capital business but are now less common. Nonetheless, as an entrepreneur trying to raise venture capital, you should be prepared to deal with the voting trust arrangement should it arise.

NONLEGAL COMMITMENT LETTER

You should remember that the commitment letter, the investment memorandum, and the term sheet are not intended to be legal documents. Their main purpose is to convey in writing the business understanding between the venture capital firm and your company. If you ask a lawyer to go through the commitment letter and bring it up to snuff as a legal document, you will probably pay a great deal and not achieve the objective you are seeking. Good business judgment on your part is probably worth more than a lawyer's review of the commitment letter.

Remember, you still have one more pass at this with your lawyer when the legal documents are drawn up. If one of the legal documents contains a paragraph that is supposed to expand and clarify a portion of the commitment letter, and you do not understand the clarification, you have the opportunity to walk away from the deal.

It is important that the commitment letter spell out the business deal, not the legal deal, between the two of you. If it does not clearly state the business deal, you should revise it and make sure it states the business deal. Once a commitment letter is signed, it is usually given to the lawyers to use in writing the legal documents. The legal documents will be 25 times the length of the commitment letter.

ARGUING OVER MINOR POINTS

The commitment letter contains some definitive statements. It states some factual information, and it has all the elements of the venture capitalist's deal with your company. If any of these major items are not what you have agreed to, you should not sign the commitment letter. You need to renegotiate the business deal.

You should not spend a great deal of time arguing over minor points, word changes that are insignificant, commas, misspellings, and so on. The letter is not a legally binding letter that you will be able to use in court, because it has too many loopholes for the venture capitalist to jump out of. The commitment letter is nothing more than a letter of understanding. It represents two businesspeople trying to put on paper what they believe they have agreed to in a meeting. Commitment letters can go through several iterations but only on major points. You should not revise the commitment letter for any minor points. Don't waste your time and your venture capital partner's time. Minor points can be ironed out in the legal documents.

ITEMS YOU SHOULD NOT SIGN IN THE COMMITMENT LETTER

If the commitment letter contains any items that you believe are not true or you do not wish to enter into with the venture capital firm, then don't sign the letter. The commitment letter is not written in a foreign language. It is written in English, and if it does not say what you expected it to say, then you should not sign it.

You should also review the commitment letter for what it doesn't say. If you and the venture capitalist reached an agreement on certain points and they are not covered in the commitment letter, then you should ask to have them inserted. Once you sign the commitment letter, that letter is the business deal. If you receive legal documents that don't contain items that you thought should be in it, and that weren't in the commitment letter, you shouldn't be surprised. I remember signing a commitment letter with an entrepreneur who was part of a large syndication. The letter specifically said in one of its paragraphs that we would invest a certain amount of money. The company actually needed three times as much as we were willing to invest. The commitment letter nowhere specified who would raise the additional funds. It did indicate that all the funds had to be raised before our commitment would be valid. For some strange reason, the entrepreneur assumed that we would be raising the money for him, even though there was no agreement on the part of our company to do so. Make sure you understand the words in the letter so the basic deal is clear.

OBJECTIVE

As can be seen from the term sheet and the commitment letter, the venture capital fund can void its commitment to you in a number of ways. Some of the basic items listed are due diligence, credit check, and favorable visit. This means that the venture firm has not completed all of its investigations of you, your business, and your industry. Five items could cost you your commitment: (1) a visit to your business to meet the people and to understand the business; (2) detailed checks of the backgrounds of you and your management team; (3) a credit analysis of the business; (4) a study of the industry; and (5) a change of heart by the venture capital firm.

Needless to say, the commitment is not a commitment at all. The venture capitalist can simply say that the management of the venture fund does not believe the business will make it, renege on the commitment, and return your commitment fee. This option is always open, and you should be aware that you do not have a commitment until you have the money in hand. Most venture capital firms are reputable and will honor their commitments. If they want to get out of a commitment, it is very easy for them to do it. Your objective is to get the commitment letter. Afterward, you should continue to push for closing. When you have the money in your hand, you know the venture capitalist has made a real commitment.

7

DUE DILIGENCE

WHAT DO THE VENTURE CAPITALISTS
WANT WHEN THEY VISIT?

WHAT TO EXPECT FROM
INVESTIGATIONS OF YOUR PROPOSAL.

When you and the venture capitalist have reached an understanding on the terms and conditions of the investment, the venture capitalist must begin what is known in the VC world as "due diligence." To be sure, before the VC made a commitment some due diligence was completed. Some venture capitalists will not issue a commitment letter or term sheet until all of their due diligence has been completed.

Due diligence simply means that the investor must conduct background checks on the management team, complete an industry study, and verify the representations in your business proposal. In essence, the VC is reviewing you, your management, your company, and the industry in a detailed study. The venture capitalist will try to find misrepresentations in your proposal or other reasons not to invest in your business. The VC is trying to determine the potential of your company to make money. Even though some venture capitalists will conduct their due diligence before they sign a commitment letter or term sheet, you should know the kind of deal to expect from them before they perform their investigations and analysis of your business.

WHAT TO EXPECT FROM A VISIT TO YOUR BUSINESS

One important step in the due diligence process is a visit to your business. If you are a start-up, there is less to this part than if you are an existing business. Most venture capitalists will fly into your city and will need transportation from the airport to your plant or business.

Although not necessary, it is a friendly gesture to pick up the venture capitalists at the airport or to have someone from your company pick them up. Furthermore, the drive to your office will give you some extra time to become familiar with each other on a personal basis. During the drive you will have an opportunity to exchange some pleasantries and take the edge off a new relationship. It is a good time for the venture capitalist to ask some personal questions like: "How many children do you have? What do you do for relaxation? What recreational activities do you like?" The VC may ask some political questions. These give him a better understanding of the person the VC fund might invest in. The trip will also give you a little time to better understand the venture capitalist and make the VC feel at home. Remember, you are still trying to sell the idea that this is a great deal for the venture capital fund.

HOW TO GIVE A GOOD COOK'S TOUR

The starting point in a visit is normally a "cook's tour." This means a tour of the entire operation with introductions along the way to key people in the company. During such a tour, the venture capitalist tries to see as much of the business and as many people as possible. The VC may stop along the way and ask questions of people who are working.

Once in a while walking through a plant with several venture capitalists, a friend of mine tarried behind the group. He asked a woman who was running a drill press what she was making. Her answer was, "Oh, I'm not making anything. They just hired me for the day and told me to look busy." It seems the entrepreneur wanted the plant to look busy so he hired a few extra people for one day and told them to pretend they were busy employees. Needless to say, the venture capitalist did not make that investment. Such deception is unacceptable.

A tour of the business will usually take 20 minutes for a small operation and hours for a larger company, such as a large LBO. During the walk-through the venture capitalist will try to understand the daily operations of the business. The VC will try to understand the type of people needed to make the business successful. The VC will absorb as much visual information about the business as possible. During the tour, the venture capitalist may ask some seemingly stupid questions that have nothing to do with the real world of your business. They will reflect ignorance of your business. Please forgive the poor VCs; it is the only way they can learn. They have a formable task—learn enough about your business in 30 to 60 days to invest in it. Not an easy assignment.

During the tour, you should be the tour leader and explain the various aspects of the operation as you walk through the plant and offices. Introduce the people along the way and describe the role they play in the organization. Leave time for the venture capitalist to ask questions of each person. As you both walk through, explain the layout of the business. Help the venture capitalist visualize sections such as accounting, purchasing, and manufacturing of the first and second product. Show the venture capitalist the manufacturing process or the process that you go through to deliver your product or service to the customer.

If your business is manufacturing, then begin the tour with the raw materials entering the factory; follow them as they progress through the manufacturing process and end up in shipping. If this is a service operation, then walk the VC through the process of delivering the service that you deliver. If you are writing a software program, then start with the creation of the software and show what inputs from inside your company and from the outside world go into creating the software. Then describe how the software is sold to the customer and how it is performing. It is your responsibility as the tour director to make sure the venture capitalist understands how your business operates. You may want to practice the tour once before the venture capitalist arrives.

You might think a venture capitalist, who has seen many operations or plants would not need a tour of another facility. As it turns out, every operation is different. Often a tour will reveal some interesting details about the entrepreneur. Venture capitalists have one generalization about operations and plants. A clean operation indicates the desire to have a well-run company. The way the physical operation is run, the way the facilities are laid out, and the cleanliness of the place are a direct reflection of how the entrepreneur operates the business.

Another reason for the visit is to see the entrepreneur in the entrepreneur's environment. It is interesting to observe how the entrepreneur works with the employees and to see the surroundings the entrepreneur feels comfortable in. Most venture capitalists become disturbed if they discover plush surroundings and a go-go environment. After all, why is the company using so much capital for the physical comforts of the entrepreneur? Why does the business need more money? Perhaps to complete an indoor swimming pool and sauna for the management? The judicious use of capital is the mark of a great manager.

If your proposal is for a start-up venture, obviously the plant or service operation does not exist. There is no opportunity for a tour. Usually the entrepreneur has rented office space where some of the team operate. Some venture capitalists will nonetheless make a trip to see this initial operation in order to observe the management team on its own turf. Such a visit helps the venture capitalist understand the team members and how they interact.

In the high-tech world some VC's look for what they consider the right work environment. They may poke around to see if there are any sleeping bags for the team that is pulling "all-nighters." To them this indicates that people are working every waking hour and using cots or sleeping bags to get a few hours sleep each night. And more than one VC has gone to the lunch room to see if there is plenty of coffee and other caffeine drinks available for employees. These are signs that the staff is working as hard as possible to write code, design Web pages, create a new product, etc. The VC is looking for clues of a "we will win or die trying" atmosphere.

If the proposed plant site or retail location is nearby, the venture capitalist will want to drive by the site. Pictures of the site can sometimes substitute for a visit, especially in start-up situations for a retail location.

ADDITIONAL QUESTIONS ABOUT THE PROPOSAL

After the tour of the operations, usually two to four hours of discussion takes place. This may include lunch or it may be one long session. Typically, the venture capitalist will have already begun the due diligence process and as a result will have further questions about the industry, about the product, or about other critical areas of the business. The venture capitalist may delve into every aspect of your business in order to test you. Again, you must know your industry and your product or service in detail and be able to answer questions without hesitation. If you do not know the answer, write down the question and deliver an answer to the venture capitalist as soon as possible. Also, your financial projections will raise numerous questions; be prepared to answer them during the visit.

For readers who are gluttons for punishment, there is a book that covers the process of due diligence from the perspective of the VC. It is called *Venture Capital Investing* and is published by Prentice Hall. It has been written for venture capitalists to use in their investigation of businesses.

Sometimes a venture capitalist will be confused about one item in the business proposal. It may take the VC an inordinate amount of time to understand the concept. Be patient. The VC is trying to understand something taken for granted by people in the industry. The venture capitalist is also likely to ask the same question twice. This may be due to ignorance, or it may be that the VC did not like the way you answered the question the first time and the VC wants to hear how you answer it the second time.

Then, again, the venture capitalist may ask the same questions twice as a test of consistency. That is, the VC may want to see if the entrepreneur will answer the question about the business the same way twice. If the entrepreneur fails, the venture capitalist may think the entrepreneur does not know the subject, or worse, that the entrepreneur is lying and cannot remember the lies. For sure the VC will try to ask the same question to several members of the management team at different times to see what comes out.

ADDITIONAL QUESTIONS ABOUT THE BUSINESS

The venture capitalist will ask you all the questions you have not answered in your business proposal. You should expect questions like those that were set out in Chapter 4. After the operations tour some venture capitalists sit down with the entrepreneur and methodically run through a list of questions that they use in every investigation. These may be questions that were not asked during the meeting in the venture capitalist's office. During the visit to the entrepreneur, the venture capitalist will want to spend time with the person in charge of marketing and ask the marketing person about the industry, the competition, and the marketplace. The venture capitalist will also want to meet the person who is in charge of production to ask the production expert questions about production, inventory control, labor, and management.

The venture capitalist will spend even more time with the person who is in charge of finance to ask about the banks and other places financing was obtained. The venture capitalist will ask about financial ratios for the business and compare them with others in the industry. The cash flow of the business will be of keen interest.

Finally, if the deal has not been completely negotiated, the venture capitalist will set aside some time to discuss the final aspects of the deal. The VC may take out the commitment letter and go through it point by point to make sure all parties have the same understanding. If the venture capitalist thinks the risks are higher than he perceived before the VC conducted due diligence, or if the potential return is viewed as lower, the venture capitalist will open the negotiations by saying that the VC fund needs additional equity, a higher interest rate, additional collateral, or some portion of the three. You should listen to the venture capitalist's concerns and attempt to reduce the perceived risk. If you cannot reduce the risk, you will have to negotiate your deal again. Negotiations may take a short time, or they may be left unresolved. If possible, it is better to settle the negotiations at this sitting; this will make it more difficult for the venture capitalist to open the negotiations again.

ADDITIONAL QUESTIONS ABOUT MANAGEMENT

During your first meeting with the venture capitalist in the VC's office and later during this visit to your business, the venture capitalist will be trying to answer the question, "What makes you tick?" The VC wants to know what motivates you—in other words, what is the driving force in your life. The VC wants to know why you, of all people, think you can make a venture successful. You should remember that during any meetings between you and the venture capitalist, the venture capitalist will be looking for the seven items discussed in Chapter 5. They are honesty, achievement, energy, intelligence, knowledge, leadership, and creativity. Before every meeting with the venture capitalist, you should review these seven items again so that you can present yourself in the best light.

The venture capitalist will ask you some personal questions. They will usually not be as direct as the business questions. They will usually come during a more relaxed part of the meeting. The VC may ask you where you grew up, what your background is, what sports activities you have been involved in, what hobbies you like, when you were married, how many children you have, and the ages of your children. Basically, the venture capitalist is trying to understand your personal environment. The VC wants to determine if your private life is strong enough to withstand the time and energy you will have to put into this new business. Being an entrepreneur will put a great deal of pressure on you at work and at home. If you have a spouse and family, your business will take up much of your time and leave only a little for your family. The venture capitalist will want to know if your personal life can withstand the pressures of your entrepreneurial activities.

Also, when the VC looks at your personal life, the venture capitalist will be looking for stability and maturity. The VC will be trying to determine if you are a person who has reached the point in your life that allows you to cope with the difficulties of running a growing small business. An unsettled personal life will detract from your ability to operate the small business that is being financed by the venture capitalist. Personal problems will not allow you to give the business all your time and attention. Your energies and emotions will be reduced by your personal situation.

One situation I am familiar with concerned an entrepreneur with tremendous personal problems. For five years the entrepreneur had diligently worked to build his company and neglected his home life. One cold January day the entrepreneur's spouse left and took their two small children. The spouse boarded an airplane and left the entrepreneur forever. The separation destroyed the entrepreneur. Suddenly the entrepreneur was faced with the loss of spouse and children. The entrepreneur went mad trying to find them. After six months, a crisis developed in the business. The number two person in the business was not strong enough to step into the number one position. The business was on a disaster course. The venture capitalist moved in and tried to save the business. The only alternative was to sell the company. So the entrepreneur lost both the business and his family. It was terrible for all concerned. Now you can understand why the venture capitalist is concerned about the personal life of the entrepreneur. A stable personal life is a crucial element in the equation.

INVESTIGATING THE INDIVIDUALS

Before or after the visit, the venture capitalist will investigate the backgrounds of the individuals. This will be a never-ending process for the venture capitalist. The VC will continue to follow leads that might produce additional information about your entrepreneurial team. The venture capitalist often feels like a private detective when looking into people's backgrounds. In checking out the background of an entrepreneur, the VC first requests a personal credit check on the entrepreneur and on each member of the management team. Credit checks often give the potential investor leads to follow. The venture capitalist looks for unpaid bills, which can indicate that the entrepreneur has credit problems. Also, unpaid debts indicate how the entrepreneur is likely to treat the venture capitalist after the investment in the business takes effect. The logic is that if the entrepreneur does not pay personal bills, why should one believe the entrepreneur will pay the venture capitalist?

The second method of checking the background of an individual is to call business and personal references. Of course, entrepreneurs always give references that will say favorable things about them. The venture capitalist usually asks business references if they know someone else who knows the entrepreneur. This question enables the venture capitalist to develop secondary references. Then the VC can call the secondary references and ask additional questions and request other references.

In addition to doing their own work, VCs may hire a firm to help. There has developed a large cadre of investigators that perform what is called "background checks" on individuals. These used to be pretty sleazy private investigators, but the profession has evolved into some very reputable organizations. Some of the large accounting firms have very high-quality groups that do this for a fee. You should expect the VC to have one of these groups complete a background check on you. You will be asked to fill out a set of forms that suggest you are applying for a top secret clearance at the CIA. That document is the beginning point for the background check.

VENTURE CAPITALISTS ARE PARANOID

While the venture capitalist looks for achievements and a record of hard work in the entrepreneur's background, the VC is developing a picture of the entrepreneur's reputation. Venture capitalists are suspicious by nature. They start each relationship believing the entrepreneur is trying to cheat them. As a result, their constant concern is to determine whether the entrepreneur is honest. You should appreciate the predicament of a venture capitalist. Anyone who has money to invest is bombarded with proposals from crooks. Normally it is difficult to fool the venture capitalists and swindle them, but it happens from time to time.

There is the story of a group of venture capitalists that invested millions of dollars in a new business started by an entrepreneur with impeccable credentials. In their background check the venture capitalists found that the entrepreneur was born and raised in a small Midwestern town, had attended a distinguished Midwestern university, and had worked for several conglomerates on the West Coast. In both his university and business environment he had served with distinction. But, no sooner had the venture capitalists invested their money than the entrepreneur disappeared, leaving a trail indicating he was in a South American country. After contacting the FBI about the possible fraud, the venture capitalists found that the entrepreneur was a crook. He had previously testified for the U.S. government in the criminal prosecution of underworld figures. He had been given a new identity under the witness protection program. He had used that clean background to swindle the venture funds. Needless to say, the venture capitalists were extremely upset with the U.S. government.

In revealing information to a venture capitalist, you must tell the VC of any problems in your background. If you do not, and the problems are uncovered during the background check, your deal will most likely be killed. The venture capitalist will perceive your omission as an attempt at deception. Your reputation will be shattered. Venture capitalists do not like to run into surprises when they check your background.

Another story tells of the venture capitalist who was investigating a promising entrepreneur. The venture capitalist was sure she wanted to invest in the business. The venture capitalist could not find anything derogatory in the entrepreneur's credit record, and many of his references praised his business acumen. A secondary source happened to mention that he thought the entrepreneur had encountered severe difficulties 10 or 15 years ago and had actually served time in prison. When the venture capitalist asked the background checking service to go back further in time and search specific criminal records, the agency found that the entrepreneur had spent three years in prison. The fact that this important item in his past was never revealed to the venture capitalist killed the deal, even though the entrepreneur may have been a good investment risk since he had paid his debt to society.

The venture capitalist's analysis usually starts with an individual's early life and follows in detail, both where the entrepreneur has lived and where the individual has worked since college, or at least for the past ten years. Most investigations follow a chronological order. This kind of continuity check gives the venture capitalist an idea of the kind of people you and your team members are. The VC can determine whether the entrepreneur hops around from job to job, moving frequently, or is a solid citizen with an outstanding record in business.

The venture capitalist usually takes the entrepreneur's resume and verifies where the entrepreneur was and what that person was doing each year. The venture capitalist will often check on a military record. Was the individual honorably discharged? Did the individual achieve the rank of second lieutenant, or a corporal? Invariably, the venture capitalist will call the school mentioned in a resume to verify that the entrepreneur received the degrees that is set out in the resume. More than one venture capitalist has found an entrepreneur lying about this detail. All of these checks are necessary in order to confirm that what was presented as a talented entrepreneur is what the VC will get running the company.

OTHER ASPECTS OF THE BACKGROUND CHECK

There is a saying in the venture capital business: "You can predict an individual's future by what they have done in the past." This is particularly true of successful entrepreneurs. Success seems to breed success, and conversely, difficulties may be an indication of a problem personality. It is hard to separate these two entrepreneurial talents. On the one hand the VC wants a hard-charging entrepreneur driven to win at almost any cost. On the other hand, the VC wants an entrepreneur that is not determined to kill to win. There is a balance, but it is hard to draw a line where one ends and the other begins. Most VCs pride themselves on being able to make this distinction.

What the venture capitalist is looking for in an individual's past is the level of achievement. What has the entrepreneur achieved in the past? Most venture capitalists believe there is a high correlation between achieving personalities and success in entrepreneurial endeavors. So if the venture capitalist finds many achievements in your background, then the VC will be happy.

Of course, every venture capitalist is looking for an honest individual. The VC does not want to be in a deal with a cheater. The VC will ask references point blank if you are honest, if you are trustworthy, if you are hard working, if you have bad habits, would cheat under pressure, and in a general way, are a person somebody should trust. Although many people will not answer these questions, most will give some indication of how they feel about you and members of your team. After a venture capitalist has talked to half a dozen people about an entrepreneur, the VC will begin to get an idea of the entrepreneur's honesty and the personality traits that make up the basic character.

DO THEY HAVE A TEST FOR ENTREPRENEURS?

Most venture capitalists do not use personality tests on entrepreneurs. Most believe they can learn as much as they need to about the entrepreneur's personality by using conventional question-and-answer methods. Psychological testing for entrepreneurs has not been used much in the United States but it has been used in Europe. Most U. S. venture capitalists do not believe that any reliable tests for entrepreneurship exist today and the reason is simple. Entrepreneurship spans all industries.

At the same time, various industries may require different personality types. For example, in a white-collar, highly technical environment, management by objective (MBO) may work best. MBO works well among highly motivated people who need to achieve goals. In an industry where the entrepreneur must deal with some rough-and-tumble employees, management by intimidation (MBI) might work best. Unless the entrepreneur has an aggressive personality and is willing to scream and yell, the entrepreneur may not get the point across. Giving a businessperson a test to determine whether the businessperson is an entrepreneur would not indicate whether a certain businessperson could succeed in both businesses. The management style required is different, and no one test on entrepreneurship would be applicable to these two different businesses.

I am told in Europe that use of a personality test and a job qualification test is standard. However, I have not heard of them being successful when given to entrepreneurs. It would be wonderful if the Europeans could lead the way in this endeavor. We need a large body of data to see which test can give VCs help in determining entrepreneurship.

A few large credit companies use handwriting analysis (graphology) to determine whether an individual is creditworthy. Perhaps a graphology test could be used by venture capitalists to determine whether an individual is a good credit risk has an achieving personality. Most venture capitalists don't believe that graphology can predict anything about an individual. There is a rumor among venture capitalists that one firm has used a graphology test. It seems hard to believe, but given the difficulty of the problem it is not surprising to see any technique tried at least once.

A battery of tests on the market today are used to determine an individual's honesty. Many employers give these tests to employment applicants, and these tests are prevalent in the retail business. Venture capitalists do not use these tests yet. It is doubtful that they would work on intelligent entrepreneurs, because such tests are easy to foil. Perhaps the test would help the venture capitalist weed out some of the stupid individuals seeking money.

EXPERIENCE IS THE WATCHWORD

When a venture capitalist looks at an individual's background, the VC tries to determine how much experience the entrepreneur has had in the chosen industry. People who profess a general management ability in operating any business have yet to prove themselves to the venture capitalist as operators of small business. Being a general manager in the small business environment seems to be a contradiction in terms. It may be true that the president of one large company can be just as effective as the new president of another large company. Managing a bureaucracy in one large company is probably similar to managing a bureaucracy in another company. However, the rubber meets the road in small business entrepreneurship, where it is difficult for a general manager to survive at all.

An entrepreneur must have in-depth knowledge of the business in order to play the game according to the rules of each industry. An entrepreneur entering the construction business, for example, would probably be eaten alive by subcontractors unless that same entrepreneur had experience with them. Similarly, an entrepreneur with experience in the construction business who entered a manufacturing environment would probably be slain by the white-collar workers and the inability to collect the accounts receivable.

It is true that a smart individual can become adept at handling practically any industry, but it will usually take a year or two. It takes time to become proficient in operating a small business because there is no layer of middle managers between the president and daily problems. The president is on the firing line every day. If a business can survive during the time it takes the new entrepreneur to learn the business, the business may become a profitable enterprise for the entrepreneur. However, the venture capital investor must realize that the VC will have to wait an additional year or two for the investment to gain momentum. The venture capitalist must wait while the entrepreneur learns the ins and outs of the industry and the business itself. Not many VC's are interested in "on the job training" for the entrepreneurs they back. They want an experienced person at the helm.

When it comes to due diligence by the venture capital fund, the entrepreneur should know that most venture capitalists will be quite thorough in investigating their background. To lie about one's experience or to distort it in a manner that would fool the venture capitalist on paper will only be the entrepreneur's undoing when the venture capitalist begins this background check. The venture capitalist will use a lot of energy to determine how strong your credentials are for operating the intended small business. So if you worked in the marketing department of a company but did not run the place, do not say in your resume that you ran the company's marketing department. Tell it like it is.

INVESTIGATING THE ENTREPRENEUR AND THE TEAM

When investigating the experience of the entrepreneur and the management team, the venture capitalist generally starts with the business references on the individuals. The questions most venture capitalists ask references are the standard ones about achievements, competence, character, commitment, honesty, and so on. You may be surprised to hear that some other questions are asked of your references. One will be, "Does he have a problem with drugs?" This has become an important question for new entrepreneurs as drugs can diminish one's ability.

A long-standing question asked by venture capitalists continues to remain on the list: "Does the entrepreneur have a drinking problem?" Many venture capitalists reviewing the poor performance of a small business have looked behind those problems and found an alcoholic. A company that has gone up and down over the years will often place so much strain on an individual that the entrepreneur will resort to drugs or alcohol as a temporary treatment for the problem. People with an alcohol problem are not successful entrepreneurs.

Other questions asked by venture capitalists are: "Does the entrepreneur like a high style of living? Does the entrepreneur have a bar-hopping life style?" This is often a problem in sales-oriented companies where the entrepreneur salesperson is on the road a great deal. If you act like a "big shot," you may impress your friends but not the venture capitalist. In order to determine whether the entrepreneur is living "high on the hog," the venture capitalist will have the background agency drive by the prospect's house, note what kind of car the entrepreneur is driving, and ask neighbors about the individual.

Don't be surprised if the VC asks for a copy of your personal tax return. Some entrepreneurs think this kind of investigation is an invasion of privacy, but if the venture capitalist intends to risk a lot of money on an individual, the VC wants to know exactly who the individual is, what his or her life style is, and what problems the individual has.

QUESTIONS FOR OTHER PEOPLE IN THE ORGANIZATION

The venture capitalist may go one step below the management team and talk with other people in the organization. A specific individual the venture capitalist wants to talk to is the marketing manager. The VC needs to know how the head of marketing perceives the marketplace for this product or service. The venture capitalist also wants to find out how the production person views producing the product and what problems there may be in production.

Of course, the venture capitalist always spends a great deal of time with the finance person in order to understand the numbers that have been presented. As part of this procedure, one venture capitalist spends at least several days with the management team and lower people in the organization. After hearing the bright picture painted by the management team, this VC is often quite surprised to hear the controller's remarks about the financial status of the company. The VC may be rudely awakened when the production boss says the item in question cannot be produced easily. More than once marketing people have told the VC the products in question are difficult to sell. Lower-echelon people should be as convinced as the entrepreneur that the company is a great opportunity. If they have not been convinced, it probably will be difficult to convince an investor like the venture capitalist, because in the interview process the VC will get a different story from the people at a lower level.

In addition to these inside people, the venture capitalist tries to talk to all the directors of the company to find out what their involvement may be in the company. The VC will want to know how they came to be on the board of directors. Also, the venture capitalist wants their views of the company. The venture capitalist will talk to principal stockholders. Now and then a stockholder of 10 or 20 percent of the company is not a director or part of management. The venture capitalist will want to know why the investor owns such a large percentage of the company and what the price was for the stock. Further, the VC will ask the big stockholder why this is such a good investment.

Every venture capital firm is hungry for information about the people who will make the company grow. The more information you can give the venture capitalist about your team, the happier the VC will be.

INVESTIGATING THE BUSINESS, THE PRODUCT, AND THE INDUSTRY

While the venture capitalist is investigating the entrepreneur and the team, the VC will also be investigating the product/service, the business, and the industry. To do so, the VC will call many users or potential users of the product or service. The VC will ask them many of the questions that a marketing survey would include: "Why do you like the product? Is it too expensive? Is it a major purchase for you? How could the product be improved? Are you satisfied with it?" One other question the VC will usually ask a user is, "Do you intend to purchase additional products or services from the business?" If the answer is yes, the VC tries to determine the dollar volume of their purchase. This helps the VC understand the backlog. The VC will normally call many of the people listed on the backlog in order to verify that they do have an order for the amount specified in the backlog report. The VC will usually ask those people on the backlog list why they ordered a product from the company and what they like about it.

Many venture capitalists will engage a marketing research firm to get a better handle on the business. The market research firm will do a complete study of the industry and the product or services of the business as perceived by the customer. Some VCs hire production experts to come in and verify the production of the product. And the VC will almost always hire a very knowledgeable consultant in the industry to give them a perspective of the situation. These are usually hired by calling the local trade association and getting an expert. In addition, many of the VCs have invested in a certain business area time and time again. They know as much as almost anyone in the segment and can call dozens of experts and people working in that segment to get a read on your particular situation. If you get this expert VC on your team as an investor, that individual can add a lot of value.

On the other end of the scale, the venture capitalist almost always calls suppliers in order to determine how promptly they have been paid, what they like about the company, and how they are treated as suppliers. Suppliers can be a tremendous source of capital for a small business since they can extend credit. For this reason alone, you should have good relations with suppliers. The venture capitalist will conduct discussions with suppliers in order to determine what kind of business you operate. If you do not pay the supplier on time, the venture capitalist will assume you will not pay the interest on the subordinated debt or the dividends on the preferred stock that the VC fund is going to invest.

INDUSTRY STUDY

A study of the industry is often difficult to undertake, especially if it is a new and dynamic industry. Research reports of public companies and credit reports of private companies in the industry may not give a clear picture of what to expect. Industry studies by "think tanks" or large sophisticated research firms may not yield a great deal of information, either. If the industry is new, the estimates may be based on hunches or on inadequate data. If the industry is further along in its development, some companies in the industry will be public, and the reported information on public companies will help the venture capitalist understand the industry.

Sometimes a private competitor's financial statements can be obtained through normal credit reference services. They can give an added dimension to the industry. All of these sources give the venture capitalist insight into the potential for your business. You should have covered some of this same ground when you studied the industry. How well you know your competition is one of the things the VC will investigate about you. You can help the venture capitalist in this survey by providing details you have already uncovered.

After becoming acquainted with the industry, the venture capitalist usually tries to relate the industry study to the projections made by the entrepreneur. How do the projections compare with the growth of other public companies in the industry? How do the ratios in the projections compare with published ratios for companies in the same industry or those in similar industries? These are important questions. The entrepreneur should not merely pick some ratios out of the air that seem to be attainable. A common mistake of entrepreneurs is to assume that gross profit ratios or other ratios will hold up, when, in fact, the industry does not function in that manner at all.

UNIQUENESS OF THE PRODUCT

The venture capitalist will investigate the uniqueness you describe in your business proposal, attacking the problem from various perspectives. Often an idea may seem unique to the venture capitalist, but it will be old hat to people in the industry. It does not take long, however, for a venture capitalist to determine whether the entrepreneur has a unique approach to a problem or if it is just a variation on a theme. When the venture capitalist talks to people in trade associations and experts in the field, the VC will soon uncover the uniqueness of a product or service. The Standard Industrial Classification of investments made by a venture capitalist is recorded by the trade association of VCs and can be consulted by VCs for the names of venture capital firms that have direct experience in the industry. These firms can give your venture capitalist a sophisticated appraisal of the projections presented in your business proposal. If necessary, the venture firm will hire an expert to review your assumptions about the industry. For sure, the VC will hire an expert to review your patents or other out-of-the-ordinary ideas for conquering the industry you are in. Many VC firms have an advisory council to which they refer all unusual technological ideas.

Trying to give the venture firm a "snow job" on your product will waste everyone's time, especially yours. It will also tarnish your image in the close-knit venture capital community. I remember an entrepreneur who made his product sound unique. After a few hours of investigation, we determined that most of the components, and indeed the product itself, could be purchased from a local retail electronics store. The store had been selling the product for the last three years. Needless to say, I no longer trusted this entrepreneur. He had spent no time researching the product. He thought he had "invented" it and so concluded that it was unique. What a nut case.

Another entrepreneur had a product that seemed unusual by every measure that one might use. However, when the venture capitalist began to talk to users of the product, they did not mention specifically the product's special traits touted by the entrepreneur. When the venture capitalist asked about the extraordinary aspects of the product, customers informed her that those particular aspects had no bearing on their choice. They liked the product simply because "it worked" and because "it was delivered on time." The unique aspect did not influence their purchase of the product. The users informed the venture capitalist that many products on the market could do the job without the special feature of this product. In essence, the entrepreneur was touting a uniqueness that did not make any difference to the customers. Venture capitalists find it disconcerting to uncover this type of information on their own, especially when the entrepreneur has told them how important the unusual feature of the product is to each sale.

Many entrepreneurs think that a patent on a product "proves" its uniqueness. A patent may prove uniqueness, but the worth of the product and the extraordinary features must be demonstrated conclusively. Having a patent does not make a product worth something. There are millions of worthless patents.

In addition, a patent is not conclusive evidence of uniqueness. Patents have been overturned and patents can be granted on grounds that can be disproved in later years. A patent may preclude a competitor from manufacturing an identical product, but a competitor can change minor details and bypass the patent protection. If a patent exists, the venture capitalist will usually talk to the patent counsel to determine how strong the patent is and how wide it reaches and to hear the patent attorney's justification of the uniqueness of the product and how it would be defended against an encroachment by a large firm. There are endless stories of small companies with patents being kept in the courts for years trying to win money from large companies that used their patents.

QUESTIONS FOR BUSINESS REFERENCES

The venture capitalist will want to speak with many business references, not only users and suppliers, but banks, accountants, lawyers, and various other people who know the business and the reputation of the management team. The venture capitalist will call a number of the outsiders that you have mentioned during your discussions and those on the list you have provided. The VC will ask each of these outsiders a number of questions, and you should be aware of what the VC is seeking from these various sources. You may wish to forewarn some of them that the following questions will be asked.

Suppliers. You will probably have given the venture capitalist a list of suppliers. The VC will call many of these suppliers, especially the largest and most critical ones, to ask them some simple questions such as, "Does the company pay on time? Have you had any problems with payments? Will you continue to supply the company? What credit limit do you have for the company? Have you ever shipped supplies COD?" Any company that is being shipped supplies COD is a company that the supplier does not trust. If the supplier is short of goods, he will cut off the COD orders and ship only to his best customers. If the supplier's product is a critical item, the venture capitalist will want to know that the supplier has financial strength and a capacity large enough to provide the items needed. At one time the toy business did not have enough computer chips to satisfy the demand for electronic games. Therefore, slow-paying manufacturers of electronic games usually had to wait an inordinate amount of time to receive the chips they needed for their games.

Customers. If you have industrial customers or are selling to retail outlets, the venture capitalist will call the largest of these, and perhaps a number of the smaller customers, to determine your reputation. The VC will want to know if the customers have been shipped poor products and what happened when the customer received faulty items. The VC will want to know if the customers will continue to buy the product. Is the customer satisfied with the price? How many units can the customer use or sell? What is the current outstanding order that the customer has with the business? This last question will be used to check on the backlog that you have reported to the venture capital firm.

The venture capital company may call many of the customers listed on the backlog to verify that the backlog is correct. The venture capitalist will also ask the customer who else he or she buys from—that is, who the competition is. The venture capitalist will try to understand who these competitors are and how they are regarded by the customer.

Every VC knows that the customer is one of the three foundations on which a business is built (the other two are employees and suppliers). So expect the VC to get to know your customer. It is a critical area.

Competition. Many venture capitalists investigate the competition's product and even talk to salespersons representing the competition. They may pretend to be a customer looking at various products. The venture capitalist might indicate that she is buying your company's product as opposed to the competition's product in order to hear how the salesperson sells the product against yours. Sometimes the venture capitalist may know someone who works for the competition. She will be able to obtain additional information about the competition and how they view your product by talking to that person too.

Stock Market Analysts. Stock market analysts often follow a particular industry. Many of the companies they follow will be the competition for your business. The venture capitalist will contact several of these analysts to discuss the industry and the competition in order to determine what the market is like. The stock market analyst may also be the person who will help the venture capitalist and you with a public offering of shares somewhere down the road.

Associations. Every industry has an association, and lists of these associations are compiled by several publishers. Every public library has a business section containing an updated publication on associations. The internet is full of association Web sites with information. The venture capitalist will locate your association and discuss the industry, the competition, and the market with the association executives. The association may not be knowledgeable about the market and may suggest another individual that it uses for market analysis; the venture firm will probably contact that expert too. Most associations will have data on the market, its size, and its growth rate. The venture capitalist will obtain this information in order to back up statements you have made in your business proposal.

Government Sources. The U.S. government publishes billions of words about business. It has conducted study after study of various segments of our society. Some of these studies are filled with useful information. Venture capitalists generally know where to uncover such sources of industry information in the government. You should be aware that they will contact the Commerce Department and the Bureau of Business and Labor Statistics seeking information on your industry. Most of these sources have Web sites that contain a good deal of information.

Accountants. Many venture capital companies will not contact your accountant. Those who do contact your accountant will ask only minor questions about accounting principles. Other venture capitalists have learned the importance of verifying the accuracy of the audit they received. I was once involved in a case in which the entrepreneur had used the letterhead of an accounting firm to construct his own audit, complete with the accountant's unqualified opinion. The original audit had shown him losing $450,000, but after the entrepreneur redid the audit, it showed him making $250,000 in profit. Only a telephone call to the accountant to verify the numbers unraveled the scheme. The entrepreneur was sent to jail for this fraud.

Accounting firms often issue management letters, which the venture capital firm will want to read because they are critical to your operation. Some venture capital firms will hire an accounting firm to complete a "businessperson's audit" of your company. This means the accountants will come into your operation and go through the books and records in order to determine whether they are being accurately kept. Some venture firms ask accountants to review projections in order to determine whether they are reasonable.

Lawyers. The venture firm will contact your lawyer, primarily to find out whether any lawsuits are outstanding and to ask if any suits are pending. The venture firm will ask if the entrepreneur has discussed any suits with the lawyer. All venture capitalists are lawsuit shy and will not invest in any company that has a long history of litigation or that shows signs of many possible suits in the future.

A venture capitalist will contact your patent counsel if you represent that your unique product has a patent. The basic questions for the patent attorney are, "On what basis was the patent applied for or granted? What makes this product so unusual?"

Bankers. The venture capitalist will discuss your general business with your banker. The VC will verify that you have a credit line, and will want to know if you have made payments on your prior bank loans on time. If you have switched banks in recent years, the VC may call your prior banker to ask if any problems arose in the prior relationship.

Consultants. Some venture firms will hire experts or consultants to review specific parts of your business. You should welcome these free experts since they will be studying a situation that you intend to build a business upon. Sometimes you may hire a consultant to do a study, in order to prove or disprove that a product will work, or that a market exists. You should expect the venture capitalist to contact your consultant and discuss the report.

Insurance Agents. If your company deals with a hazardous product, your venture partner will want to know if the product liability insurance covers all the aspects of the business. The venture capitalist will also want to know if the company carries liability insurance for directors. This will be important to the VC as a member of the board of directors.

Unions. If the work force is unionized, the venture capitalist will want to see a copy of the union contract and may wish to contact the union leader. The VC will question the union leader as to the relationship between the union and the company, and more particularly, the relationship between you and the union leadership. If the venture capitalist finds an intransigent union that will surely make enormous demands the next time the contract comes up, the VC may not invest.

There are some VCs that have accepted money from pension funds that are controlled by unions. Many times the VCs have entered into side agreements that say that any investment made by the VC fund (with the union-controlled pension fund's money) will not be hostile to unions. Some VCs have entered into far more significant agreements. For example, they may have promised that any firm they invest in will be open to collective bargaining by the union. The VC may have promised that any company they invest in will be pro-union or at least neutral to union organization. Be sure you cover this point with any prospective VC.

Appraiser of the Property and Equipment. If you give the venture capitalist an appraisal of property and equipment, he will talk with the appraiser to determine how competent the appraiser is and to ask questions about the appraisal. Sometimes the venture capitalist will hire an appraiser for property and equipment, especially where the VC is providing subordinated debt to be collateralized by these assets.

Manufacturers of Machinery. Is the machinery you use in your business built specially for you? Sometimes the machinery is used for a special purpose and is built to the customer's design. The venture capitalist will want to know if the machinery will work, and the VC will try to determine this by speaking directly to the manufacturers of the machinery. There have been many new companies that have ordered new equipment with many special features critical to the business, only to find out later that the equipment did not work as expected—a very rude shock for both VC and entrepreneur!

Other References on the Business. Any references you give the venture capitalist probably will be contacted. Any other names that the VC may come up with that relate to a special part of your business will be approached to determine how critical they are to the success of the business. The more critical to your success, the more time the VC is likely to spend with that person. You should identify these for the VC and arrange for the VC to meet with critical persons. It will show the VC you know what you are doing and save a lot of time.

WHEN THE VENTURE FIRM FINDS SOMETHING WRONG

You can be sure that the venture capital firm will find something wrong with your proposal or will uncover something during its due diligence work that will be worrisome. There is no such thing as a perfect proposal. You should not be overly alarmed by this prospect. In the venture capital business it is an accepted axiom that no deal is perfect, and that every deal has something wrong with it. You should try to minimize the effect of this negative item. Make sure the venture capital firm understands that the problem is not critical and that the business can go forward and make money. Some negative features are the result of a lack of knowledge about a certain subject. To satisfy the venture firm, you may conduct an intensive research effort in order to obtain additional information that will remove the item from the critical list for the venture firm. You can be sure that the venture firm will find something wrong. Do your best to minimize it for them as well as for yourself. After all, if the venture capitalist is concerned, you should be concerned, too.

You may have already listed the primary risk in your business proposal. The venture capitalist will be concerned about the risk. The VC will ask you to explain why you are willing to take such a risk. If the risks listed in your business plan are the only concerns of the venture capitalist, you are 90 percent of the way to a deal with the venture capitalist.

QUESTIONS FOR THE VENTURE CAPITALIST

While the venture capital company is conducting its due diligence on you and your industry, you must conduct your own due diligence on the venture capital company. Chapter 1 covered the first five questions you should ask a venture capital firm, but it is worth mentioning them again at this point.

QUESTION ONE—MONEY TO INVEST

The first question, "Do you have money to invest?" Obviously, this question must be answered in the affirmative, or you should not be spending any time with this venture firm. If the venture capital company does not have funds, you should ask for the name of a venture capital company that does have money.

QUESTION TWO—REVIEW OF PROPOSAL

Do you have time to complete a review of my proposal? If the venture capitalist is so busy that the VC does not have time to complete a review of your proposal for two months, then you may wish to work with another venture capital firm. If the venture capitalist gives you a date in the future, you will have to gauge in your own mind the likelihood that the VC will keep this promise.

QUESTION THREE—AVAILABLE TIME

If the venture firm is interested in investing, how long does it take to get to a commitment and disburse the funds to your company? Again, if it takes the venture firm a long time to go through the process, you may wish to seek money from another firm. Investing in a company in two weeks is very quick. The average time from inception to investment is approximately six to eight weeks. A waiting period of over eight weeks is considered long. Keep in mind that complex companies and syndications of venture investors will take longer than a simple investment.

QUESTION FOUR—INTEREST IN THE INDUSTRY

"Are you interested in investing in my industry?" A no here means you are bucking a mental block or a policy at the VC firm. You should go elsewhere. If the venture capitalist does not like your industry, do not try to persuade the VC that this is a great opportunity. You are wasting your time.

Another way of approaching the situation is to ask, "Have you ever invested in this industry or do you have specific knowledge of this industry?" If the venture capitalist is interested in your industry or is already investing in the industry, you will find it easier to convince the VC that your deal is a good one, since the VC already understands the economics of the industry. It is helpful if you can find a venture capital firm that has experience in your industry, but it is not essential.

QUESTION FIVE—OTHER VENTURE FIRMS TO CONTACT

"Do you mind if I contact other venture capital firms at the same time I am working with you?" Obviously, this is a touchy question. Venture capitalists do not want to openly encourage competition. They would like to have you all to themselves. Another way of approaching the issue is to ask: "Would any other venture firms that you have worked with before be interested in reviewing my proposal at the same time you work on it?" Most venture capital firms work with other venture firms that have a similar approach to investing. They probably welcome having you send your proposal to their friends, and since most venture firms syndicate their investments, you will be one jump ahead of the syndication process.

BACKGROUND INFORMATION ON THE VENTURE CAPITAL COMPANY

In order to verify that you have contacted a reputable venture capital firm, you will want to obtain the names of some references. A good start is the banker for the VC. You will want to ask the banker a number of questions; your main purpose, of course, is to verify that the venture capital firm has money to invest. After you have determined that the banker believes that the firm has money to invest, you will want to ask about the reputation of the venture capital firm. In a similar vein, you may ask your own banker to ask the venture capitalist's banker about the venture firm.

Some bankers will talk more openly with other bankers. You may want to ask your accountant about the venture firm's accountant, and you may want to ask your lawyer to ask about the firm's lawyers. If your banker, accountant, and lawyer tell you that the venture capital company's bank, accountant, and lawyers, are all of poor quality and have a poor business history, then you may not want to deal with the venture capital firms. Guilt by association is not necessarily true, but birds of a feather do fly together.

In talking with the venture capital firm, you want to obtain a list of companies they have invested in. You want to call the entrepreneurs of these portfolio companies because soon you will be stepping in their shoes. You will want to ask some questions along the following lines:

- How long did it take to get your money from the venture firm?
- Is the venture firm reasonable?
- Are the managers of the venture firm honest?
- Can you trust them?
- What types of negotiators were involved?
- Were they difficult to deal with?
- What is the management of the venture firm like to "live with"?
- What have they done for you besides invest the money?
- Have they given you any assistance that you didn't have to pay for?
- Do they act like they are your partner or do they act like they own you?
- What is their attitude toward you, and how do they treat you?
- How active are they in your business?
- Do they try to tell you how to run your company?
- Are they helpful?
- Do they hinder the operations?
- What is the relationship between you and the venture capitalist?
- If your company has had some operating problems, how did the management of the venture firm act during the period of difficulties?
- Would you say their contributions were helpful or did they create greater problems?
- If you could sell your company and go out and start over again, would you do it with the same venture capital company?

All of these questions are oriented toward the relationship between the venture capitalist and the management of the portfolio company. If you decide during your discussions with portfolio companies that the venture capitalist is unethical and overbearing and tries to take over portfolio companies, you may wish to switch to another venture capital firm.

TIMING QUESTIONS FOR THE VENTURE CAPITALIST

You should question the venture capitalist about the status of the legal papers necessary for closing. Ask the VC, "What is the procedure for closing so the legal documents can be signed?" This question should be asked without trying to push the venture capitalist over the brink. Usually venture capitalists are already pressed for time, so that adding one more deadline that needs to close "tomorrow" might create difficulties for the venture capitalist. However, it does not hurt to ask about the procedures and the timetable before closing.

OBJECTIVE

Your objective during the visit by the venture capitalist is to give the VC an extensive tour of the plant or service operation and to answer the thousand questions the VC will ask you about your business proposal and about the business in general. You should finalize any negotiations left undone. You should also try to make the VC feel at home, and try to become friends on a first-name basis. The more you can become friends and partners and the more the VC will feel at home with your business, the more successful the visit will be. The more successful the visit, the quicker the venture capitalist will want to have a legal closing, as covered in Chapter 8.

You also need to complete your homework on the venture firm. You must determine whether the firm will be a good business partner. If you do not take the time to do this, you may end up in business with a gorilla.

8

THE CLOSING

Sometime after the due diligence is completed and the visit to the business is past, the venture capitalist's lawyer will contact you about "the closing." This term means completing the legal documents for the investment and dispersing the money to your company. You may even hear from the lawyer before the due diligence is completed. This will be your first exposure to the lawyer who is looking out for the interest of the venture capitalist. It is important that you have a lawyer of your own to look after your interests. Never sign legal documents without having an independent lawyer who represents you read them with your interest in mind.

The venture capitalist's lawyer will draw up the legal documents that are necessary for closing. The legal documents should follow the commitment letter or term sheet that you signed with the venture capitalist. The lawyer for the VC will forward a copy to you and your attorney. Sometimes there will be oral changes to the commitment letter that will be incorporated in the closing documents. You should read the legal documents to determine whether the documents are in agreement with the business deal. The legal documents will contain standard paragraphs known as "boilerplate" paragraphs. Your lawyer can explain these to you. There are many boilerplate paragraphs in every set of legal documents.

All during this process you need to manage the legal process just as you would any service you buy. Lawyers get paid by the hour. While many are judicious in billing their hours, there are plenty that will bill you for more hours than you ever dreamed could have been billed. All the service professions (accountants, lawyers, and architects) are chided for billing hours. There are few VCs that don't manage the billable hours of their lawyers.

In this chapter we discuss two types of closings: first, a loan with options to own stock, and later on, an agreement to purchase preferred stock.

FIRST CLOSING: LEGAL DOCUMENTS FOR LOANS WITH OPTIONS

It would be wonderful if you could sign an IOU and receive your money. You cannot. There must be adequate legal documentation before the loan can be closed and the proceeds of the loan disbursed. Three fundamental legal documents are involved in a loan with an option to buy stock: a loan agreement, a note, and a stock purchase option. Each document has specific objectives, and each covers separate ground. It is important for you to realize that these documents will govern the legal relationship between you and the venture capitalist. Please read all legal documents carefully. There is nothing frightening about legal documents. They are written in English, not a foreign language. Sometimes lawyers use stilted language that can be confusing. If that happens, just tell them to rewrite it in common English. As you read the documents, make sure they say precisely what you and the venture capitalist have agreed upon. There can only be two reasons why they may not. Either the venture capitalist has changed his mind and instructed his lawyer to change the documents, or there has been a mistake. In either event, you should discuss the changes with the venture capitalist not the VC's lawyer. This will head off any expensive arguments between you and your lawyer with the venture capitalist's lawyer. Now, let's examine each of the three basic legal documents in the first closing.

DOCUMENT ONE: THE LOAN AGREEMENT

By far the largest document will be the loan agreement. It will contain 25 to 100 pages, and possibly more if the investment is a complicated one. To some extent, the loan agreement will include the items in the commitment letter plus items standard for loan agreements. (Remember the boilerplate?) There are ten sections to the loan agreement and each is discussed in turn.

1. Purchase and Sale. In this section the lawyer will use specific language to describe the loan with all its terms and conditions. The lawyer will describe the equity option with all its terms and conditions. This section will describe in detail the securities to be purchased and will specify the following:

- The interest rate per annum.
- When repayment of principal will begin and over what period it will be repaid.
- Dates payments are to be made, such as the first day of each month.
- Delivery date of the funds by the venture capitalist to you.
- Description of the venture capitalist's stock option.
- Ownership in the company by the venture capitalist.
- Cost of the ownership by the VC.

In addition, this section will establish that the company has authorized and empowered its management to enter into the sale of the note and the option to the VC fund. It will discuss any other venture capital participants and the amount that they will be purchasing in your company.

2. Collateral Security and Subordination. This section will describe the collateral for the loan in great detail, and it will refer to a collateral security agreement that will be an exhibit to this agreement. Normally, the lawyer will describe each piece of collateral as set forth in the summary terms below:

- A mortgage on specific land and building.
- A secured interest in machinery and equipment of the company.
- Personal guarantees of certain individuals.
- Assignment of certain leases.
- Assignment of life and casualty insurance.

3. Affirmative Covenants. This section covers all the actions you agreed you would take as long as this loan or option to own stock is outstanding. Your company will do the following:

- Provide the investor with detailed financial and operating information on a monthly basis.
- Provide the investor with any documents filed with the Securities and Exchange Commission or other government agencies.
- Provide an annual budget by a specific date each year.
- Advise the investors of any adverse changes in the company's status.
- Maintain certain current ratios, working capital amounts, or net worth amounts.
- Maintain life insurance on certain executives of the company.
- Maintain property and liability insurance in sufficient amounts.
- Elect a representative of the VC fund to the board of directors, or, if the VC is not on the board, notify the representative of the venture capital company when board meetings will occur so that the venture capital representative may attend the meetings as an observer.

- Provide access for the venture capitalist to the premises and to the books and records of the company.
- Keep all equipment and property in good repair and in working order.
- Comply with all applicable laws and regulations.
- Pay all taxes and other levies of taxes against the company.
- Maintain its corporate existence and other business existences.
- Give the venture capital firm the right of first refusal on new financings in the future.
- Maintain a standard system of accounting in accordance with generally accepted accounting standards.
- Notify the venture capitalist if you are in default on any loans or leases.

The items above will be spelled out in their own separate small paragraph in the Affirmative Covenants section of the Loan Agreement. Be sure you agree with each covenant, because once you sign the agreement you must perform or the loan will be in default. If a new covenant is brought up as a "standard" or "boilerplate" covenant, discuss it with the venture capitalist, not the venture capitalist's lawyer.

4. Negative Covenants. As you can imagine, this is the section where you agree not to do certain things. Typical negative covenants include the following:

- There will be no change in control of the company.
- Management will not sell, assign, or transfer its shares.
- The company will not change the basic business it is in.
- The company will not change its current business format—that is, change from being a corporation to a partnership.
- The company will not invest in other companies or unrelated activities.
- The company will pay no cash or stock dividends.
- The company will not expend funds for capital improvements in excess of certain amounts.
- The company will not pay nor loan to any employee money in excess of a certain amount per year.

- The company will pay no brokerage fees and the like in excess of a certain amount.
- The company will not transact any business with members of the board of directors or management or its officers or affiliated individuals.
- The company will not dissolve, merge, or dispose of its assets.
- The company will not change its place of business.
- The company will sell no additional common stock, convertible debt, or preferred stock.

Each of these will be covered by a short paragraph in the legal documents. Violation of any of them will be considered a default, as set out subsequently. Each item should have been discussed with the venture capitalist. If a new item appears, you need to discuss it with the venture capitalist, because it will have an impact on the way you conduct business. If material new covenants appear in this section, you may need a meeting with the venture capitalist to negotiate the terms in the legal documents.

5. Events of Default. This section describes items that will cause a default of the loan. A default means you have violated one of the items previously listed. A default may require you to repay the loan in full on the day of default. A default is usually called on any of the following items:

- If you do not carry out all of the Affirmative Covenants.
- If you violate any of the Negative Covenants.
- If the representations and warranties you made in the legal documents are not true.
- If you do not make timely payments on the loan.
- If you do not pay other debts as they come due.
- If you have any other loan called in default.
- If you have any lease called in default.
- If a final judgment is rendered against the company by the creditor.
- If bankruptcy or reorganization of the company should occur.

In this section the lawyer will also specify what remedies are necessary to remove the default. As an example, suppose a default is called because you have not made a payment; making the payment within ten days of written notice of the default may be the solution to remove the default. Some defaults can happen easily, as with the case of a payment that is not made on the due date. If you miss the payment date by only one day, the venture capital firm can call the loan in default. A grace period should be provided in the legal documents. This refers to the amount of time you have to correct a default once notified. In negotiating grace periods from the venture capitalist, remember that the longer they are, the better for you. Do not be unreasonable, because you will lower the venture capitalist's opinion of you and may make him think twice about closing the deal.

6. Equity Rights. Here the agreement may cover a wide range of items relating to the equity of the company, the equity of the venture capitalist, or option to own equity held by the venture capitalist. These items include:

- The right of the venture capitalist to force the company to register the venture capitalist's shares in a public offering, free of charge.
- The right of the venture capitalist to include the VC funds shares in any registration of the company's shares, free of charge.
- Any restriction on the transfer of the shares being received by the venture capitalist.
- A section referring to certain Securities and Exchange Commission regulations to which everyone must conform.
- An indemnification of the venture capital company against any violations on your issuing the stock.
- Representations on your part about the number of shares and options outstanding.
- Any rights the venture capitalist may have to require you to repurchase the shares held by him. This is the put.
- Any rights you have to repurchase the shares at a later date. This is the call.

This section covers all the equity rights that the venture capitalist will have. This part of the document should cover all matters that you and the venture capitalist have agreed upon with regard to the equity rights the VC will have in your company. These equity rights are the mechanism whereby the venture capitalist will someday realize a profit on its equity ownership. It is the VC fund's exit. Be sure you understand how the venture capitalist will realize a profit on the equity. Be sure it is in concert with your agreement with the fund. This section is particularly critical to the venture capitalist, and you should exercise caution about trying to remove provisions from this section. As you can understand, the venture capitalist wants to exit from your deal some day, and these equity rights will be the mechanism for doing so.

7. Representations and Warranties. In this section you are representing and warranting to the venture capitalist that certain things are true:

- Your corporation is in good standing.
- You are in compliance with all laws.
- There is certain capitalization of your company.
- There are no subsidiaries.
- The financial statements are correct.
- There have been no material adverse changes since the last financial statements.
- There is no litigation going on, or if there is, a description of it is attached as an exhibit.
- The company is in compliance with all government regulations.
- There are no defaults on current borrowings.
- The company is current on all taxes.
- The company has rights to any patents that it owns.

Paragraph after paragraph of such representations and warranties can be expected in the legal documents. Each one has a specific focus and meaning. Your lawyer should be able to substantiate most of the claims. Read each one and be sure that on the closing date all representations made by you are true. A false representation can mean a legal problem for the company and for you personally.

8. Fees and Expenses. This section will explain who pays the fee to the lawyers for drawing up the documents, who pays the fees for filing any legal documents at local courthouses, who gets notices, and so on. Normally, your company, the borrower, will pay all the lawyers and closing costs. Most lenders stick you with all the closing cost.

9. Definitions. In this section the lawyers will define every technical or legal term appearing in the document. You should understand the definitions, because they are an integral part of the entire document.

10. Conditions of Closing and Miscellaneous. This last section includes items such as indemnification, waivers, notices, and addresses. In this section, too, the lawyer will list all the conditions for closing. Condition-of-closing items are things such as:

- Certificate of incorporation.
- Copy of bylaws.
- Certificate of incumbency.
- Opinion of entrepreneur's lawyers.
- Certified audit.
- Certificates from the secretary of state.
- Copies of all corporate action taken by the company to authorize its execution of these documents.
- Copy of letter from senior lender consenting to this transaction.

There will also be a final page for your signature, the venture capitalist's signature, and the signatures of any guarantors.

This is a general overview of the loan agreement. You should find that the loan agreement follows closely the terms and conditions set forth in the commitment letter. If it does not, something is wrong.

DOCUMENT TWO IN THE FIRST CLOSING: THE NOTE

Usually the note will be written on one to five pages. The note will be an in-depth, detailed statement of the terms of the loan. It will specify:

- How much money is being loaned.
- When it is to be repaid.
- The interest rate.
- What day of the month it is to be paid.
- Guarantors.
- Conditions of prepayment of the loan.
- Collateral for the loan.
- Subordination of the loan to other loans.
- References to covenants in the loan agreement.
- A complete list of defaults.
- Waivers and amendments.

It will be signed by the president and usually the secretary of the corporation, along with any guarantors of the note. The corporate seal will usually be affixed to the last page.

DOCUMENT THREE IN THE FIRST CLOSING: THE STOCK PURCHASE OPTION

Finally, you can expect a four- to ten-page document describing the stock options to purchase stock in your company. It will provide details such as the following:

- Duration of the stock option.
- Any covenants of the company during ownership of the stock option.
- The mechanism for securing the option in exchange for stock.
- The exact price that must be paid when the option is exercised.

- Adjustments to the exercise price; that is, the formula that will be used in case shares are sold at a low price or additional shares are issued by the company.
- The availability of shares owned by the company to be issued if the option is exercised.
- Any written notices that must be given.
- A definition of common stock.
- Expiration date of the stock option.
- Transferability of the option.

Normally this option will be signed by the president and the secretary of your company on the final page of the stock purchase option.

OTHER DOCUMENTS: EXHIBITS

As few as five but usually about ten exhibits will be attached to every financial agreement. Most of these were listed when we discussed the sections of the loan agreement. Be sure you understand what each exhibit states because you will be agreeing that it is true and correct. Typical exhibits listed for a closing include the following:

1. Security agreement describing the collateral security for the loan. Be sure you have given the venture capitalist only the collateral agreed upon.
2. Financing statement that includes UCC-1 forms that will be filed in the records of the courthouse. This statement will let all creditors know who has a claim on your assets.
3. Opinion of your counsel as to the validity of the transaction.
4. Copy of all corporate actions taken by stockholders to effect the transaction.
5. Copy of certificate of incorporation.
6. Copy of the bylaws of the company.
7. Certificate from the secretary of state evidencing good standing.
8. Copy of a certified audit from your accounting firm.
9. Any forms necessary for government-related financing.

The description above is a simple overview of the documents and exhibits. When you receive the real documents, you should read each one in detail to make sure you understand what you are signing. Some presidents of companies rarely read the legal documents. Some entrepreneurs ask their lawyers if everything is all right, and if the lawyer nods a yes, the entrepreneur signs it without reading the legal documents. The lawyer's nod only means that the legal documents are in legal order. The lawyer's nod does not indicate that the business deal is correctly presented in documents. Only you can determine that. Some venture capitalists do not read legal documents, but most take the time to read the documents before they sign them. Be smart; read your legal documents. Ask questions if you do not understand the legal descriptions.

SIMPLE IS GOOD

The complexity of legal documentation has baffled American entrepreneurs for decades. The simpler the legal documents are, the better it is for all parties. If there is a simple way to say something in a legal document so that everyone will understand it, that should be the order of the day. Some lawyers are carried away with a great deal of verbiage. You should ask them to refrain from following this practice. In legal documents, simple equals good.

The best legal documents are those that you never refer to after the closing. If, during your relationship with the venture capitalist, you never have to look at the legal documents, then the deal has worked well. If you or the venture capitalist are constantly referring to the legal documents and questioning the meaning of every word, then something is wrong. You and the venture capitalist have a problem.

UNETHICAL VENTURE CAPITALIST

When the legal documents arrive, you may find them quite different from the commitment letter or the understanding you have with the venture capitalist. Rather than wasting legal time, you should immediately take the documents to the venture capitalist. Determine whether the VC is trying to renegotiate a better deal. If you find that the venture capitalist is fairly rigid and will not come around to the original understanding, then you should have your commitment deposit refunded so that each of you can go your separate ways. You should not deal with a venture capitalist who pulls a surprise punch by writing the legal documents to suit a new position.

One venture capitalist is known to obtain excruciatingly binding conditions from many of his entrepreneurs. When asked how he was able to obtain such onerous conditions from his entrepreneurs, he explained the technique. At the last minute at closing, he merely walks into the closing room with a set of preprinted forms and says to the entrepreneur, "Of course, you will want to sign our Form 406." Most entrepreneurs seeing this preprinted form assume it is a standard document that the venture capitalist uses on every deal and merely sign the several copies presented before going on to the other legal documents. The entrepreneurs do not realize that the provisions they have signed virtually tie them in knots. Only the smartest entrepreneurs have read and questioned each item on this preprinted form. Do not get caught signing "Form 406!" Read everything before you sign it!

SECOND CLOSING: LEGAL DOCUMENTS FOR THE PURCHASE OF PREFERRED STOCK

You would think that the purchase of stock would be a simple transaction—that the venture capitalist would write you a check and you would issue the VC fund some stock certificates. As it turns out, that is far from the truth. There will not be a note as there was in the first closing described above, and there will not be a stock option (unless options are an additional part of the stock purchase), but there will be a fairly lengthy stock purchase agreement and the stock certificate itself. The stock purchase agreement will be similar to the loan agreement described previously, but let us discuss the points again from the perspective of a stock purchase.

STOCK PURCHASE AGREEMENT

The stock purchase agreement has 10 to 12 sections. Many of the sections will be similar to the ones covered below.

1. Purchase and Sale. In this initial section the lawyer will describe the sale of stock and the price being paid, as in the corresponding section of the loan agreement.

2. Affirmative Covenants. Many of the affirmative covenants that were covered in the Loan Agreement will be set forward in this section.

3. Negative Covenants. Again, many of the same negative covenants will appear in this section for the sale of stock.

4. Equity Rights. In this section the lawyer will carve out the liquidation rights of the stock: Are the shares sold to the venture firm on the same basis or do the shares get preference in liquidation? What dividends do they receive? What rights do they have to elect directors? It is typical for venture capitalists to have the right to elect one to three directors, as long as they do not elect a majority. Although they may have the right to elect as many as three directors, they often elect only one. This single director will follow your company, attend the board meetings, and if things become critical, the VC will ask you to elect two additional directors who will then have more to say about the operation of your business.

Covered in this section are the many equity rights of the venture capitalist, including the right to register the shares they own in any public offerings, and the right to require you to register the VC owned shares free of charge. Be sensitive to the fact that these equity rights are the primary exit for the venture capitalist. The VC will be reluctant to change any of these equity rights.

5. Representations and Warranties. A full set of representations and warranties similar to the ones in the Loan Agreement will appear here.

6. Fees and Expenses. Again, this section explains who will pay all the legal fees; usually it is the seller of the stock.

7. Definitions. There may be a short definition section, but usually there is none.

8. Restrictions. Some restrictions may be placed on your operation of the company. You may have to operate under certain guidelines as long as the venture capitalist owns shares. This section will describe any operating restrictions.

9. Voting Trust. A voting trust may be involved in a sale of stock. If so, this section will discuss the voting trust in detail. Here is how a voting trust works. Usually a trust is set up at a bank trust department with a bank trust officer as trustee. Your shares and the shares of other managers are put in the trust. The venture capital firm controls the voting trust, but only under certain conditions can the venture capital firm vote the shares in the trust. In all other circumstances you vote the shares that are in the trust, even though you do not hold them. This section will give you the precise details on what the venture capitalist has in mind when setting up a voting trust.

10. Employment Agreement. Many times the venture capital firm will want to ensure that key employees continue to work for the company, at least for a specific period of time. The venture capitalist may therefore ask key employees to sign one-way employment contracts ensuring that the key people will be with the company as long as the venture capital is an investor. As part of the agreement, the employee may be asked not to reveal confidential company information if he or she is permitted to leave the company.

The employment agreement can be turned around, of course, to the advantage of the entrepreneur. It can ensure that the entrepreneur's job is secure during a period in which the venture capitalist firm may have an opportunity to take over the company. Usually this security for the entrepreneur is overshadowed by the one-sided nature of the contract. A venture capitalist told me of three young M.B.A.s who signed employment contracts. The contracts provided that these gentle souls are paid a reasonable sum despite their brief experience in the business world. However, the contracts were for five years. As fate would have it, the business failed. Among the "assets" of the business were the three employment contracts. The institutional investor who had invested the funds foreclosed on all the assets of the business and picked up the employment contracts of the three M.B.A.s. For the remaining four years of their contracts, these men were virtually the slaves of this corporate giant. You may wish to avoid having an employment agreement, and if there is one, make sure there is a way to break the agreement if you are not running the company.

11. Consulting Contract. Many venture capital firms play an active role in the management of the company in which they invest. They may help the company establish marketing or financial controls or to address any number of problems that may arise in a new or small, growing company. They will want compensation for the time and attention their consultants take to help the new business get off the ground.

Compensation is usually arranged through a contract with the venture capital firm for management consulting services. This agreement will recite the description of the services to be rendered and the terms and the amount of payment that will be made to the venture capital firm for these services.

12. Conditions to Closing. As in the first closing above, there will be a section on indemnification, waivers, and notices. There will be a list of items that must be completed before closing can occur. At the end there will be a page for you, the venture capitalist, and other parties to the agreement, to sign.

STOCK CERTIFICATE

The second item is the stock certificate itself. Usually it is taken directly out of the corporate binder, and the stock certificate has the VC fund's name imprinted on it and a legend placed on the back that says the stock has not been registered.

LAWYERS AS BUSINESSPEOPLE

Many lawyers will take it upon themselves to tell a client not to enter into a business arrangement because it is a bad business deal. All venture capitalists want to know if something is wrong from a legal perspective, but they become upset by lawyers who jump into the business fray in order to "save" their client from signing a bad business deal. Some good lawyers are certainly good businesspersons. However, very few practicing lawyers are good entrepreneurs or venture capitalists. (And the opposite is true too; there are few good businesspersons that are good lawyers.) It's difficult for anyone to carry on two professions successfully. Every venture capitalist can tell you about a lawyer who killed a business deal because the lawyer felt the client was not getting a good deal. If lawyers would stay in the legal profession and leave the businesspeople to the business profession, the world would be a better place. And the legal profession would be a lot better place if businesspeople stopped trying to write legal agreements. I am personally guilty of this one.

In one instance my lawyer told me not to invest in a company because the lawsuits against the company were material. I could not see it but listened to the lawyer. Within a year of turning down the deal, the company took off. It was worth over a billion dollars and my VC fund would have owned more than 80 percent of the business for about $10 million. I still cry about that one and I don't use that lawyer anymore.

You should encourage your lawyer to refrain from trying to renegotiate the deal for you. Your venture capital partner will appreciate it. If your lawyer tries to renegotiate the deal, the venture capitalist will assume that you have directed your lawyer to do so. The VC will believe you are trying to change the deal, or find a way to get out of it. Needless to say, this will take the VC's attention away from closing the deal and move the VC away from investing in your company. Be very careful before you instruct your lawyer to openly negotiate with the venture capitalist. If there is something you do not like about the legal documents, go to the venture capitalist and negotiate for yourself. Do not use a surrogate who is not familiar with the business relationship.

EXPERIENCED LAWYERS ARE BEST

A lawyer experienced in reviewing legal documents for venture capital investments is worth a pot of gold. A lawyer trying to bluff his way through this type of investment agreement will destroy your chances of a quick and successful closing. So hire a lawyer with experience. Remember, you will pay all legal costs unless you do not go through with the agreement. Be economical in your use of lawyers; they are expensive.

One of the main factors to slow down the legal process is the lack of time that lawyers have to work on legal closings. Legal documents sent by a venture capitalist's attorney to the entrepreneur's attorney could sit on the desk of the entrepreneur's lawyer for weeks before the entrepreneur's lawyer gets around to reviewing them. It is incumbent upon you to find out when the legal documents have been sent by the venture capitalist's lawyer, and to remind your lawyer daily, if necessary, that you cannot close until the lawyer reviews the documents. Do not expect anyone else to ride herd over your lawyer.

You may not realize it, but your lawyer may have incurred a liability if the lawyer doesn't perform quickly and reasonably. Any lawyer who does not close a deal that should have closed could be held liable for whatever damages are caused to your company. Certainly a lawyer who does not act on legal documents sent for review within five days is courting disaster, especially in a deal that must close quickly because the company needs the funds. So make sure you hire a lawyer who has time to work on the deal.

LEGAL FEES KEEP GOING UP

Legal fees are rarely low. In fact, of all the fees that businesspeople complain about, legal fees probably top the list. The question is not whether legal fees are too high. The question is whether a specific legal fee is fair, in view of the work that has been performed by the lawyer. Some attorneys are unethical in their billing practices. They think nothing of padding a legal bill with 10 or 20 hours of work, and mail the bill to the client without a great deal of explanation. Some legal bills consist of a single line, "for services rendered," followed by a dollar amount. Never pay these. Insist that the time be accounted for. Even then it is difficult to determine whether it is a fair bill. Most detailed bills have the hours worked each day and the subject of the work. The subject rarely is very descriptive, and even if it was, who is to say that a lawyer should have spent only five hours on a subject not six. It is a maddening problem.

Because legal bills have become such a large part of business life, most businesspeople are attempting to manage the fees. The most common method of managing legal fees was introduced by large corporations, many of which now require very detailed legal bills. The bill must include hours worked, the specific project on which the time was carried out, the billing rate of the individual working on it, and the name of the individual authorizing work on the project. Besides these detailed bills, many smaller businesses are requiring the law firms to give them advance estimates of the time it will take to complete a project. They ask the lawyer to call them once the lawyer reaches a certain amount of time or money expended. By doing this, the small business keeps track of the law firm's hours and does not let it run up a big bill. Even with all this, it is difficult to keep legal bills in check.

If you have agreed to pay the legal fees for both your lawyer and for the venture capitalist's lawyer, it is incumbent upon you to manage the legal fees. This means contacting the venture capitalist's lawyer and discussing fees. You must discuss the procedure for working on your deal and how the bill will be rendered. Do not be surprised when you arrive at the closing table and see the legal bill. If you are surprised by the amount of the legal bill, then you have not been managing your lawyers very well. All too often, entrepreneurs receive a shock at the closing table. The venture capitalist may be in a poor position to help you negotiate these fees. If the lawyer for the venture capitalist has a close relationship with the venture firm, the venture capitalist will have a hard time questioning his friend about legal fees, even if they seem too high. The venture capitalist cannot be expected to manage your legal fees. It is important that you manage all your legal fees so that you are satisfied with the amount that you are charged at the closing table.

HOW LAWYERS RUN UP YOUR LEGAL BILL

Besides the unethical padding mentioned above, watch for the many methods employed to run up your legal fee. Listed below are five of them.

DISAGREE ON LEGAL POINTS

Your lawyer or perhaps even the venture capitalist's lawyer will often disagree on many points. This means that they will have to spend innumerable hours discussing these points and working each one out to their satisfaction. If you have agreed to pay legal bills, remember that when these two lawyers disagree, you are paying the bill on both sides of the table, even as they argue about miniscule points. There is a fairly simple way to cure this problem. When your lawyer has reviewed the papers drafted by the venture capitalist's lawyer, tell your lawyer to make a note by each item in the documents where there is a problem. Before your lawyer discusses these points with the venture capitalist's lawyer, ask your lawyer to discuss each one of them with you. Many of them may have no material business significance and therefore you will be willing to let the venture capitalist's lawyer put them into the agreement. Each time you knock out one of these small points for discussion, you save yourself some money.

REWRITE SECTIONS

Some lawyers increase their fees by rewriting sections of the documents over and over again. Suppose the venture capitalist's lawyer presents the VC's written version of the document. Your lawyer may rewrite the documents completely. This means your lawyer will run up secretarial time and drafting time in order to redo entire sections. You should instruct your lawyer, from the beginning, that there is to be one writer of the documents and one commentator on the documents. The venture capitalist's lawyer should be the writer and your lawyer should be the commentator. This arrangement will reduce your legal fees.

RESEARCH POINTS OF LAW

Often lawyers will disagree violently over points of law. The disagreement will send them scurrying to the library, or to other research sources, in order to clarify various points of law. This research can burn up many hours of time. Each lawyer is trying to show which one is the best legal scholar. You should instruct both lawyers that you do not wish them to research various points of the law without your permission and that you will not pay for such research.

LEGAL STYLE

Lawyers will correct each other on usage, style, grammar, and even spelling. They will use up your time for the purpose of "clarifying the language." Tell the lawyers that you are not interested in matters of style. Stress that you want a clear document and that is all.

ARGUMENTS

Most lawyers are by nature argumentative. They spend three years in law school arguing points back and forth. Once they enter the real world, they continue to argue with one another. You should remember that you are paying for all of these arguments. If you have two lawyers arguing with each other, and they are each billing you at the rate of $450 an hour, you are paying $15 per minute to hear them eloquently debate the merits of a legal point. Act as a moderator and get to the heart of the argument. Ask your lawyer what the consequences will be if you agree to the words being proposed by the venture capitalist's lawyer. If these consequences are quite modest, or if the consequences are extremely unlikely, you may wish merely to sign the document rather than fight to remove the words. On the other hand, if the consequences appear to be drastic, you must adjourn the legal meeting and call a business meeting with your venture capital investor to iron out the problem.

QUESTIONABLE LEGAL PRACTICES

In some instances, the venture capitalist's lawyer may be too close to the venture firm. The lawyer may be on the board of directors or advisors, or the VC lawyer may be the staff lawyer for the fund. If either is the case, and the venture capitalist's lawyer does the work, you are in a poor negotiating position. If, at the last minute, the venture capitalist's lawyer shows up with a legal fee two or three times larger than you expected, you have little negotiating power. Since the VC lawyer is part of the company, the VC lawyer can keep the deal from closing unless you agree to pay the fee. I remember one syndicated closing where a participant arrived at the closing with his lawyer. The lawyer had performed very little work, except to review the documents, but when closing started he presented a legal bill for an exorbitant amount. Everyone felt embarrassed by the amount; however, since the lawyer was an integral part of the venture capital company, he demanded that his fee be paid. The venture company refused to close on its part of the deal unless the bill was paid, and said the entrepreneur would not receive the entire funding!

There are not many ways to handle this type of problem before closing. You could, at the closing, try to give the lawyer a promissory note and after closing you might be in a better position to negotiate the bill down. However, if the lawyer is an integral part of the venture capital firm, then you are starting your relationship with the venture capital firm on unsure footing.

SYNDICATIONS AND LAWYERS

Sometimes an investment is syndicated—that is, there will be a group of venture capitalists investing at the same time on the same terms. When you are dealing with a syndication of venture capitalists, each venture capitalist's lawyer may want an opportunity to review legal documents. You should agree to pay for the legal fee, but only for the lead venture capitalist lawyer, not for each participant's lawyer who wants to look at the documents. If you agree to pay for all the lawyers, and if four or five venture capitalist's lawyers look at the documents, you are opening up your cash register for the lawyers.

Never just leave the door open to unlimited legal bills; always insist on a cap on the legal fees. If you leave the door open, lawyers tend to review the documents forever. Many lawyers tell an interesting story about the young lawyer who began working in his father's law firm. His father took a much-needed vacation to Europe and left his son behind to continue the legal practice. The first case the young lawyer worked on was a railway right-of-way case. The young lawyer noted that his father had been working on the case for almost 20 years. In several days, the young lawyer assembled the parties in a room and negotiated a settlement. The case was closed. When the young lawyer's father returned from his vacation, the young lawyer explained with glee that he had settled that long outstanding railway right-of-way case. However, the father was extremely upset as he explained to his son that the railway case sent all of the young lawyer's brothers and sisters to college, and the annual fees from the case had even sent the young lawyer to law school. Remember, lawyers receive fees while cases are open. They do not receive fees from cases that are closed.

Another factor to watch for in syndications is the tardiness with which other venture capitalist's lawyers may review the documents. Invariably one of the venture capitalist's lawyers will be slow and not get around to the documents for days. You must obtain the names of all the venture capitalist's lawyers and constantly put pressure on each lawyer to submit comments so that closing can take place. You alone can manage this process. The lead venture capitalist's lawyers cannot do as much as you can.

The Closing: A Moment of Truth

Once the lawyers have drawn up and examined the documents and once the businesspeople have ironed out the business problems, a big pile of legal documents will be ready for signing. Normally, three to ten copies of each document will have to be signed. The closing usually takes place in a conference room.

Every closing seems to have its crisis. Usually the entrepreneur's lawyer will bring documents, such as incorporation papers or life insurance, that are not in the proper form. If all the documents required are not present at closing, the venture capitalist's lawyer will not be able to close the loan. In large deals the lawyers will get together the day before the closing date to see if all the papers are in order and if it is possible to close the loan. This is called a "dry closing" because no money changes hands. An inexperienced lawyer for the entrepreneur or venture capitalist may try to have a closing without reviewing all the documents beforehand. To just pick a date and show up for a closing is almost a sure way to abort the closing.

A closing is an extremely exciting moment, because it is the moment when the venture capitalist parts with the money from the VC fund and the entrepreneur's business gets an injection of capital. The physical process can take hours and be extremely boring. Documents are signed, shuffled around the table, looked at by lawyers, and verified by lawyers. It is, to say it most simply, a lawyers' environment.

Closing Fees That You Pay

Lawyers can spend considerable time on the actual closing itself. Many hold a preclosing the day before the actual closing. This dress rehearsal, as well as the actual event, can be costly.

Envision the entrepreneur who has agreed to pay the lead venture capitalist's lawyer, the lawyer of the bank giving him a loan, as well as his/her own lawyer. These three lawyers may charge as much as $450 per hour each. On top of these fees are those of the junior attorneys, paralegals, and secretaries, which can run from $150 to $190 per hour. All in all, the entrepreneur is probably being billed at the rate of $2,000 to $5,000 per hour. If the deal is extremely large and complicated and involves additional people, that figure can be multiplied by two or three. But for the moment, assume the combined billing rates are $2,500 per hour. Assume the lawyers spend eight hours in preclosing and eight hours in the actual closing, for a total of sixteen hours. Sixteen times $2,500 is $40,000, just for the closing, quite apart from what you will pay for the drafting, research time, and other document gathering.

There is only one way around the expense of closing, and that is to be absolutely ready when a closing date is set. Your lawyer should have reviewed all the documents in detail with the venture capitalist's lawyer to be assured that when closing occurs and everyone is sitting around the table, everything that is needed to close will be at the table. There will be no last-minute scurrying for any documents, and there will be no last-minute changes. If you can impress upon your lawyer that you do not want the closing set until everyone is absolutely ready, then you will be doing yourself a big favor. Do not go to the closing table prematurely. It will cost you a lot of money if you do. What is worse, you will have to do it again if the investment does not close.

What to Remember About Lawyers

You should remember that lawyers are merely specialists in a specific area and have knowledge of an area in which you do not. They are professionals. Just as you are a professional business person, they are professional lawyers. Remember, too, that they are providing a service and that you hire them just as you hire any other employee. Tell them what you want them to do and you will have a satisfactory relationship with your attorneys.

Also remember that lawyers make money by charging for time, and they are disposed to spend a great deal of time working on something. Most of the problems lawyers work on are not legal problems. They are simply problems lawyers have been left to solve by businesspeople. Many business problems turned over to lawyers can easily be solved by two business people in a "head-to-head" discussion. Before you try to solve a problem from a legal standpoint, be sure you have exhausted all other remedies. Legal solutions are expensive. In one case in New York City, a venture capitalist lost $250,000 when the lawyer, who was a member of one of the large prestigious law firms in New York, had been negligent in his closing of the investment and clearly was open to a suit. Once the venture capital firm looked into suing this prestigious lawyer in New York, he soon found that it would probably cost him at least $250,000 to sue. He was told that he would be lucky if he recouped any of the legal fees, much less the $250,000 that the lawyer had lost for the venture capital firm.

Also remember that the number of lawyers in the United States is higher than ever before. By many counts there is a surplus of lawyers. If you do not like the lawyer you are working with, find a new one. There are hundreds of good lawyers seeking work with a growing company.

OBJECTIVE

Your objective through this entire process is to obtain legal documents acceptable to the venture capitalist's lawyer and to the venture capitalist. As soon as that process is complete, you and the venture capitalist can sign the documents. At that point, you will have your money. The quicker you can go through the legal documents and the harder you can push your lawyer to review them and get them back to the venture capitalist's lawyer, the sooner you will have your funds.

Your role or that of some other officer of the company throughout the entire process is to be in touch with the lawyer and the venture capitalist. You should be in charge of getting together as many documents as possible in order to avoid any delays. You should be in touch with all lawyers in order to determine what might be holding up the process. When a problem arises, you must be involved in the solution in order to keep the process moving. You should review the documents and understand them completely, and you should not try to renegotiate the deal. If you can do all of these things, your closing will be an easy one.

9 WORKING
TOGETHER

HOW CAN YOU AND THE VENTURE CAPITALIST MAKE MONEY?
OPERATING YOUR COMPANY TO MAKE THE MOST MONEY.

Raising money from a venture capitalist has been compared to getting married. The closing has been compared to the wedding ceremony. After the wedding, when the honeymoon is over, the two of you must make a life with each other. During the next three to ten years you will be working with the venture capitalist, not so much on a day-to-day basis, but in regular sessions. Your relationship will be one in which the venture capitalist is or has the option to be a major stockholder in your business. The venture capitalist is your business partner.

Most venture capital firms are not passive investors. Most venture capital firms are very active in the management of companies and some have a consulting staff to perform this task. These consultants may supply marketing expertise to help improve your marketing effort. They might also supply production expertise to help you with production or financial expertise to help you with financial matters.

Most venture capital firms are not staffed with consultants. And while they may want you to hire experts, most VCs will not invest in a company unless it has a full management team that can run the company on a day-to-day basis without a lot of consultants. This is not true for early-stage investments. In such situations, the VC may have a retinue of consultants available to provide services. The VC wants to make sure you don't make any obvious mistakes. So the VC has people to help you get the business organized and in full operation with a good staff. If you ask the VC funds that invest in early-stage companies what they spend their time doing, they will answer that they spend about 50 percent of their time recruiting members of the management team. There are many larger VC funds that have general partners that come from recruiting firms and spend all their time finding good people.

By and large, venture capital firms do not have expertise in marketing, nor do they have expertise in production or administrative matters. Most managers of venture capital companies are heavyweights in the area of finance, and, if they have been in the business for an extended period of time, they will have considerable knowledge of small business practices. Many of them have a long list of contacts in the business world. And if they have specialized in a business segment, then they will know a host of experts and operators. You should rely on the VC team extensively when talking about financial matters and should use them as a sounding board for general policy questions. If you need a bank loan, they can help you determine which bank to approach and how to approach it. They may be able to help you with an industrial revenue bond (IRB) to build a building. Sometimes they can suggest the person to talk to about an insurance company loan. These and other financial matters will be part of the venture capitalists general knowledge. The VC is a financial expert and in many cases can save you hundreds of hours of time and effort in seeking additional financing. You should tap this store of knowledge often.

And when it comes to industry knowledge, VCs may have a range of contacts that you do not have. There are some VC firms that specialize in a certain industry and know "everyone" in the business. They can be invaluable in getting you in to see people about marketing or production problems. Use your VC partners as a resource. They may be able to save you a lot of time and money.

MAJOR POLICY DECISIONS SHOULD BE JOINT ONES

All major policy decisions should be discussed with the venture capitalist—first, of course, because they are your business partners, but second, because most venture capitalists have at hand, or have access to, a great deal of business knowledge. An experienced venture capital firm will have seen many small companies go through the development cycle. The VC team will have encountered many problems similar to yours. The venture capitalist's accumulated knowledge can be used to solve some of your problems. Many venture capitalists have been trained in business schools. They have excellent analytical minds. You can use this resource to help analyze your business problems as well as the potential business problems that you contemplate for the future. Keep your partner informed about your business, and use the minds of your VC partners to help solve your problems.

Most venture capital companies are extremely busy places. A telephone call from you every day or so is totally unnecessary, unless you are in a crisis situation. Most venture capitalists would like to hear from you every week, and you should contact the venture capital firm at least twice a month even if everything is great. If you have a loan or convertible debenture, be sure to send the payment that is due. Most venture capital firms think a monthly payment is a useful way to track a company. Send the monthly financial statements as they are due, and always send a written report with the financials. The written report is just a way to keep the busy VC informed. For an early-stage deal, the weekly cash flow statement is a must. Everyone at the firm wants to know how fast you are "burning" through the cash. Most get their e-mail wherever they are in the world, so your messages will catch up with them.

The point to be emphasized is that you are keeping your partner, the venture capital firm, apprised of what is happening in the company. You need not discuss the day-to-day routine. You should discuss items such as the progress being made, the backlogs that exist, projections if they have changed, or the hiring of a key employee. Also discuss problems you foresee in the future, such as market changes and new competition. The venture capitalist, like most investors and lenders, does not like to be surprised. As a minimum, an accurate, written report is necessary to avoid surprises. A quick e-mail will keep the VC from being surprised.

MONTHLY FINANCIALS

Venture capital firms usually require monthly financial statements. Receiving timely monthly financial statements is second only to receiving timely monthly payments on debts owed venture capital firms. You can be sure the venture capital firm will call you if you have not made your monthly payment on the convertible debenture or loan. You can also be sure that if you do not send in your monthly financial statements, the venture firm will think that you are not running a strong operation. No firm can be managed without accurate, timely, monthly financial statements. If you are not receiving monthly financial statements on a timely basis, you cannot possibly make reasonable decisions about your business. Tardy monthly financial statements are a red flag to every venture capitalist. Do not make the mistake of getting off to a bad start with the venture capital firm. Send the payment that is due, and send the monthly financial statements as they come due.

The accuracy of monthly financial statements is also very important. Every venture capitalist has been surprised at year-end when the audited financial statements came in. There are various types of surprises. Usually the surprise is lower earnings—that is, a profit is shown for 11 months and then a whopping loss for the year-end. Typical excuses for the surprise are failure to accrue enough for accounts payable, an inventory write-off, or a difference in standard cost items in the costing system. Neither you nor the venture capitalist should be surprised at year-end by the financial statements. Everyone can accept some accounting adjustments for year-end. It is the magnitude that we are talking about and the reasons for large changes in financial statements at the end of the year. You will destroy your credibility with the venture capital firm as a competent manager if you have a big surprise on the financial statements at year-end.

WEEKLY CASH FLOW USES AND FORECAST OF USES

In early-stage investing it is fairly common to have a weekly cash flow usage and a projected use of cash completed. This weekly forecast shows how much longer the company can continue without new financing. This weekly use of cash is called the "burn rate," a fairly obnoxious term considering it refers to money. But it gives everyone reading it a projection of how fast the money that has been invested will last. Everyone reads the weekly cash flow statements in an early-stage company.

A Monthly Report Is Mandatory

A monthly report can be a letter, a report, or a memo. A typical monthly report is exemplified by the following:

MEMORANDUM

TO: A. V. Capitalist
FROM: J. Entrepreneur
SUBJECT: Monthly Report for October

Attached are the monthly financial statements for the nine-month period ending September 30. The profit-and-loss statement is understated in that our company will probably not pay taxes at the rate of 40 percent this year because of our net operating loss carried forward from last year. This should put approximately 95 percent of the pretax dollars to the bottom line.

As we near year-end, it is evident that next year will be an extremely busy year. Our backlog has increased fivefold over last year. You should also note that inventories have increased approximately 40 percent more than our forecast. This is due to three very large orders that are now working their way through our production line. We have had to add people to the second shift to make sure that the items come through on schedule. None of these three orders will be completed and shipped by our year-end, and therefore we will start out the year with an extraordinary amount of sales in the first several months.

We have talked to four people since we began looking for a controller to relieve some of the duties of our vice-president of finance. However, as of today we have not found a suitable candidate, but expect to find one within the next 10 to 20 days.

Finally, I am happy to say that the second generation of our product has now been completely designed and developed, and should be ready for introduction into the marketplace within six months at the national convention/trade fair. It will be an important milestone for our company; we introduced our first prototype only two years ago, and have since built many of these products. At our next board meeting we may be able to see a second-generation unit.

This sample monthly report mentioned several key items, each of which has a bearing on the future of the company. It also included a brief discussion of the financial statements, which are fairly self-explanatory. The discussion of the financial statements brought out a point that probably was not obvious to the venture capitalist reviewing them for ten minutes. It is incumbent upon you to highlight in the monthly report any negative, or in this case, positive developments.

HOLD BOARD OR INVESTOR MEETINGS AT LEAST MONTHLY

It is important that you have regular board meetings or investor meetings. You can keep your venture capital partner informed with memos and e-mails, but a face-to-face or conference call meeting in which you discuss material items related to the business is an absolute must. Many venture firms meet with their portfolio companies two to four times per month. At a minimum, the venture capital firm should visit your company once per quarter. You should prepare for these meetings. There should be an agenda, and you should go through the agenda as if you were holding a formal meeting of the board or stockholders.

The first thing on the agenda should be the financial statements. A review of the financial statements compared to the statements of prior periods and compared to projections is a must. If you are presenting new projections, then you should explain them in detail. Generally speaking, the beginning of these meetings should have a financial orientation rather than a marketing or production orientation. Numbers speak louder than words to a venture capitalist. As part of the financial discussions, mention the cash you have, plus credit available from your bank line. The amount you have borrowed should be set out. Then turn to the marketing side and the production side of the business. You have already set the stage for this discussion by showing the financials and the projections; now put some "meat on the bones" by explaining the numbers from the perspective of marketing and customers and then in terms of production and suppliers. Keep the venture capitalist up to date on backlogs as part of the discussion too. And don't forget to talk about the employees. You are building a team and a strong employee base. Make sure there is an employee discussion too.

You may want to take the venture capitalist on an abbreviated plant tour to show the VC any new improvements or changes that you have made since the VC made the last plant tour. You may have created a new service that you can demonstrate, or you may have a new piece of software to demonstrate. Keeping your partners up to date is critical.

You will also want to discuss with the VC the next round of financing that you need or a bank line of credit you are trying to negotiate. If you are planning an acquisition or have been discussing an acquisition, now is the time to lay out the figures and let the venture capitalist know what you are trying to accomplish. Other members of the management team should be present at this meeting and should participate in the discussions. Questions asked by the venture capitalist will often make people think about their business differently. It is important that you all get to know each other well.

If this is an initial or second meeting, you should present the venture capitalist with a cash reconciliation statement to show where the VC's cash has been applied and precisely how it was used in the business. If this is an early-stage company, a bank statement will do just fine, since most of the funding will still be in the bank.

OTHER DISCUSSION ITEMS FOR THE VENTURE CAPITALIST

If you have completed some market research or customer surveys, you may want to relate the results to the venture capitalist, especially if they are significant for your company. If you have reviewed the competition and their activities, you may want to pass along this information. Also, if suppliers have changed policies or if you have found new suppliers, discuss this information with the venture capitalist. If there have been any industry studies or articles about your company or the industry in general in trade journals, you may want to make copies of these and give them to the venture capitalist as background information so that the VC can continue to learn and understand all of your business particulars. If you have hired some key people or if you have fired some important people, you should tell the venture capitalist. Hiring a new director of marketing or changing your controller is a material action, and you should keep your venture capital partner informed about your personnel situation.

Any changes in overhead, additions or subtractions, should be explained to the venture capitalist. If you are opening a regional office or just hiring a regional representative, you may want to mention it in one of your monthly reports or in your formal board of directors or investors meeting.

Any large capital expenditure should be brought out in the discussions. Any material changes in the backlog, either up or down, should be highlighted to the venture capitalist. If your audit is going to be late, you should explain why. If your research and development completion dates will not be met, you should also have an explanation. Target dates for introducing a product to the marketplace should be given to the venture capitalist, and if they are not kept, you should explain why.

Your venture capital partner is always seeking material information about your company. The VC will be more receptive to financial information than any other information. You need not inundate the VC with statistics and detailed information, but you should keep the VC up to date and should highlight any material changes in your business or in the industry. You are doing all this so that your venture capital partner can assist in promoting your company's growth. Remember, the venture capital company is a resource for money and it is also a resource for brainpower. The more you keep the venture capitalist involved and interested in your company, the more you will be able to use the brain power to help solve your problems.

YOU ARE BUILDING CONFIDENCE

In the relationship with the venture capital partner, as in any other human relationship, you are trying to build confidence. Being honest and informative with your business partner will build that confidence. Always do what you say you are going to do. If you intend to change something, explain why you will be going in a different direction. Do not make a statement and then fail to live up to it. Call the venture capitalist if there is a major decision to be made. Normally he is only one phone call away. E-mail, voice mail, and beepers keep us all in touch. We are all wireless now, so we can be contacted anywhere day or night.

Do not wait until you have a quarterly or monthly meeting to let the VC know that you have a problem or that you have some good news. If you are behind in developing your product, make sure you let the VC know ahead of time with a phone call or an e-mail note. If there has been a major change in your financial condition, be sure to get the word out. The venture capitalist should receive no surprises.

By being open, straightforward, and informative with your venture capital partner, you will build additional confidence. The benefit of this open-door policy can be stated succinctly: the more confidence you build with your venture capital partner, the less the VC will bother you for information and the more the VC will rely on your judgment. As with any new relationship, the VC will be uneasy in the beginning of the relationship. The more confidence you build in demonstrating your management style and ability, the more the venture capitalist will relax and allow you to run the show completely without undue influence.

WARNING SIGNALS TO THE VENTURE CAPITALIST

Generally speaking, entrepreneurs are unrealistic in evaluating problems. They often fail to recognize the early stages of failure. Entrepreneurs are optimistic. They cling to their dreams until the doors of their business are locked tight and the auctioneer has sold off the last piece of equipment.

In all probability, the venture capitalist will be the first to react to warning signals from your business. These are commonly referred to as "red flags." The venture capitalist will be the first to point out the problems and perhaps burst the dream bubble of the entrepreneur. Many times an entrepreneur will be very antagonistic to the accusations of the venture capitalist. It will be in your interest to be cooperative and to determine whether the venture capitalist has a valid point. If the venture capitalist sees a problem, maybe there is a problem. Listed below are a number of red flags that a venture capitalist will react to.

LATE PAYMENTS

If you have received subordinated debt and are late in making payment, the venture capitalist will see that tardiness as a sign of very tight cash flow. You might think it is acceptable to leave the venture capitalist short and use the money in the business as working capital, but this will only bring suspicion of internal operating problems. You should make the payments to the venture capitalist on time. If you must be late, tell the VC before the payment is due that it will be late and reach an understanding before you stop paying.

LOSSES

If your monthly financial statements show losses, the venture capitalist will be concerned. Losses as such are not bad. They may be the result of a temporary aberration, or you may have presented losses in your projection for a certain period of time until you break even. The venture capitalist will become more upset if you miss the monthly projections that you have presented. This will be a very large red flag indicating that the business is not going well. The same is true for the weekly cash flow statements. If you are missing the projections on a weekly basis, then you may be in trouble.

LATE FINANCIAL REPORTS

Tardiness in sending in the financial reports and other items you are supposed to supply to the venture capitalist will be considered a sure sign that your business is not operating well. It may be thought that you are trying to hide bad news from the venture capitalist, or that you are so disorganized and are running the business so poorly that you cannot get a financial statement out.

POOR FINANCIAL REPORTS

Even if you produce the financial statements but they are poorly prepared or somewhat unreliable, it will be a warning to the venture capitalist that your company is not well managed. Receiving inaccurate financials is worse than receiving no financials. There was an entrepreneur who sent in a financial statement that showed the company was marginally profitable. This was good news to the venture capitalist since the business had been losing money. Then the venture capitalist discovered that several line items had been excluded from the statement—the rent and interest payments. Even worse, when the venture capitalist added up the expense column, he found it was understated by 20 percent! Not a good day in venture capital land.

LARGE CHANGES IN YOUR BALANCE SHEET

If your accounts payable increase drastically, the venture capitalist will suspect that you are not paying your bills. The venture capitalist will soon spot such changes and want to know why they have taken place. On the other side of the balance sheet, if your inventories become very large, the venture capitalist will believe that you are not making the needed sales and you are producing too many items for inventory. In the same vein, ballooning accounts receivable may mean you are unable to collect some of the receivables that you have booked as sales. Any of these developments will be red flags to the venture capitalist.

Unavailable Entrepreneur

Repeated telephone calls and e-mails to the entrepreneur that are not returned are a telltale sign. Why would the entrepreneur not return phone calls or an e-mail message unless the entrepreneur is afraid of being asked questions about the business? Also, an entrepreneur's failure to schedule regular board meetings is perceived as a warning signal by the venture capitalist.

Large Thefts or Unexplainable Disasters

Unexplained large thefts of inventory may be an indication that the entrepreneur is stealing from the company and covering it up by a reported theft. More revealing is a theft that the insurance company does not cover. This normally means the entrepreneur is unwilling to pursue the case with the insurance company because the entrepreneur does not welcome the insurance company's investigation. An unexplained fire falls in the same category. Entrepreneurs in trouble often try to cover up their problems with a large fire. In the south, a large fire that destroys a business is called "selling out to a northern concern." As the story goes, a "good ole boy" will insure all his assets through a northern insurance company; then a mysterious fire will wipe them out, and he will collect from the northern insurance company. Not a good day in insurance land.

Major Adjustments in Figures

A large year-end adjustment in financial numbers is an indication that management is not running the company well. If you have to write off a large part of inventory or if your accounting firm is not willing to capitalize some expenses, the impact on the profit-and-loss statement will be disastrous and a sure indication that management is not running the shop well. This will be a red flag to every venture capitalist.

WHY ENTREPRENEURS HAVE FINANCIAL PROBLEMS

When you ask a venture capitalist, "What makes a good company?" the VC will always say, "Good management." But, in a sense, that goes without saying. If the company shows strong growth and the venture capitalist makes money, then the company has good management. If the company gets in trouble and loses money for the venture capitalist, then the company has poor management. So what did the venture capitalist mean by good management? The VC meant that good management recognizes that the two most critical problems for an entrepreneur running a small company are (1) lack of financial monitoring and control and (2) undercapitalization. The two go hand in hand.

THE FINANCIAL CONTROL PROBLEM

Most entrepreneurs can put together a good business plan and solid projections and can understand the cost of the required capital from banks and venture capitalists. However, only a few will set up a system to monitor progress and analyze the information they are receiving. As an entrepreneur, you should want to know what the sales figures are on a weekly basis. Some retail operations want to know on a daily basis and compare it with the same day last year. Every entrepreneur should be watching the figures closely. When cost figures do not coincide with those projected, find out why. When sales do not match projected figures, find out why. When the projections do not work out precisely, revise the future projections in order to determine how much capital you are going to need to get where you are going.

The most successful entrepreneurs have been "cash flow freaks." These are people who know exactly what is going on in their company from a numerical standpoint. They know when they will run out of cash, the so-called "drop dead date." They know what they have to do in order to increase cash flow. When things get rough, they know how much money they need to carry them through the next stage. They know precisely what they are doing in allocating their scarce resources properly. A monthly profit-and-loss statement is almost an afterthought for them. They ride herd on the company's cash on a weekly and sometimes daily basis. If you are not prepared to do this, you better have a CFO that is. Not knowing the numbers is the first failure point of an entrepreneur.

THE UNDERCAPITALIZATION PROBLEM

Undercapitalization has always been a serious problem for small businesses. Too often the entrepreneur will fail to raise the amount of money needed. The entrepreneur will raise $2 million when the business really needs $3 million. The entrepreneur does this to avoid having to give up more equity to the venture capitalist. This approach is shortsighted. Most businesses need more money than originally projected in order to reach profitability. When the entrepreneur needs the extra money, the venture capitalist may charge a high price, and the entrepreneur ends up with less than if the proper amount had been raised in the beginning. And the VC now does not trust the figures projected by the entrepreneur. The entrepreneur gets two black eyes for the price of one. Always raise enough money.

Smart management recognizes the need to have sufficient capital in the company. It does not tie up excess capital in accounts receivable or inventory. It seeks ways to increase the capital in the company. When the company grows, management knows the company must increase its capitalization. Be a good manager and maintain adequate capital for your company.

WHY ENTREPRENEURS HAVE PEOPLE PROBLEMS

Many an entrepreneur can run a company well when it consists of a small intimate group, but cannot manage the business when it begins growing into a larger company. The failure often relates to the selection and management of people. As can be expected, no business can grow and remain a one-person operation, nor can an entrepreneur remain a chief with many Indians. In order for a company to grow, the business must attract top-notch members of the management team and a strong middle management base on the team. There are five basic reasons that many small businesses fail to build a strong management team.

POOR JOB DEFINITION

Senior management often fails to understand precisely what job needs to be filled. Entrepreneurs are accustomed to dealing with undefined job responsibilities and wearing many hats. They expect the team to join in and work with any defined goal. However, as a company grows, specialization becomes important. Certain jobs must be segregated and defined so that certain individuals can be hired to do those jobs specifically. As manager of the company, you must define jobs.

POOR SELECTION PROCESS

Once the job has been defined, top management may use a poor selection process. It is easy, for example, to let "good ole" Joe continue to be controller of the company, since he has been the bookkeeper from the beginning. Or to hire a relative out of loyalty rather than because of her ability to manage the job that needs to be done. These practices do not ensure strong middle management. They will hurt the team and make it difficult to succeed. Even worse, selecting unqualified people can make those that do perform well angry that they have to carry those who are not performing.

POOR INCENTIVES TO MANAGEMENT

In order to attract a top-notch management team to your company, you need an effective incentive plan. The members of the entrepreneurial team have a high incentive because they own a large share of the company. Their egos are part of the business, and they want to make it a success. New members of the management team won't have the same rewards. In order to motivate them, top management should consider the various traditional methods of compensating top-notch middle management. These include stock options, stock performance rights, good pension and profit-sharing plans, bonuses based on formulas of sales or accomplishments, and the like. If you do not set up a proper reward system for your team members and middle management people, the team will not perform.

POOR REVIEW PROGRAM

Because the management team and the middle managers do not get the same satisfaction out of the growth of the company as entrepreneurs, they need to be rewarded through traditional review programs that let them know when they are succeeding and when they are failing. A good review program will give you an early warning of any problems with middle managers. It will also give you an opportunity to correct the problem. You must have a review system that is in concert with your incentive system. The mark of a good manager is a manager that gives good feedback to the team member and one that knows how each member of the team is performing.

POOR DEVELOPMENT PROGRAM

Sometimes a company outgrows the abilities of the initial middle management team simply because the managers are not given a chance to develop their skills through seminars and other educational methods. This situation can be avoided by having all the middle management team come together to share their ideas and discuss the problems they are having within the company. This interaction permits marketing people to become acquainted with what is happening in production, and allows finance people to better understand the problems of marketing as well as other aspects of your business. This kind of internal professional development program is necessary for any growing company and should supplement a regular development program.

THE PROTEAN ENTREPRENEUR

As the entrepreneur, you will be expected to move from operating a one-man show to managing a team of people. You will be delegating responsibility and holding your managers accountable for their actions. You must be able to use a variety of management styles to keep your team motivated. In some situations you will have to be a tyrant, and in others, democratic. If you are unable to make this transition, it will be difficult for your company to grow. If you cannot manage people, the venture capital company may suggest that a chief executive officer is needed, and that you should play more of a figurehead role. Many entrepreneurial companies outgrow their scientific or technical founder. It is no disgrace for the entrepreneur to become chairperson after hiring a hard-charging manager as president.

Why Do Some Entrepreneurs Succeed? Why do some entrepreneurs succeed while most fail? There are many explanations of success and failure. Venture capitalists spend a great deal of time discussing why one entrepreneur failed and another succeeded, and they think that most successful entrepreneurs have certain things in common. The characteristics most often mentioned by them are as follows:

PROBLEM SOLVERS

Every successful entrepreneur is an excellent problem solver. Venture capitalists agree that this is a predominant trait of the successful entrepreneur. Rarely do entrepreneurs waste any time placing blame on others. They try to determine what the problem is, solve it, and go on to the next situation.

ABLE TO GROW PERSONALLY

Successful entrepreneurs can transcend their accomplishments and move on to the next level of objectives. One accomplishment seems to create a desire to accomplish the next task. Thus, successful entrepreneurs never seem to dwell on past accomplishments; they deal only with the current objectives. Once these entrepreneurs have accomplished their tasks and seem to be living on Easy Street, they move on to the next task. They are unable to rest, and they must constantly be planning and striving for continued growth of their company.

SET INTERNAL GOALS

Successful entrepreneurs seem to be driven by their own internal goals. They love to set goals and then surpass them. The process of achieving goals seems more fun to them than actually surpassing goals. They love to run the race. Hitting the tape and winning is not important. Winning in itself means nothing. It is the art of winning that drives successful entrepreneurs. Money is important, but more as a measure of success than an end in itself.

UNDERSTAND DOWNSIDE RISK

Every successful entrepreneur has sketched out the absolute downside risk of any major decision. What catastrophic occurrence could be brought on by a decision that the entrepreneur has to make? The entrepreneur knows beforehand exactly what the worst case could be and decides whether the company can live with that outcome. If the company can live with it, then the entrepreneur moves forward with confidence. If the business cannot, then the entrepreneur would not take the chance. Betting too much on a single action is a trait of unsuccessful entrepreneurs. Most unsuccessful entrepreneurs fail to adequately determine the downside risk.

REHEARSE COMING ACTIONS

One of the biggest surprises to venture capitalists has been to learn that successful entrepreneurs rehearse coming events. A good entrepreneur imagines almost every aspect of what it would take to achieve something. Entrepreneurs practice in their minds as if daydreaming what they will do. This is a time-honored technique in sports events, particularly in track and field, but it is surprising to find the same trait in successful entrepreneurs. An average entrepreneur might prepare for a presentation by setting out the facts in an agenda. An achieving personality would mentally rehearse a perfect presentation and prepare psychologically for the entire successful presentation.

If you do not exhibit all of the traits set out in the foregoing paragraphs, you may wish to modify your behavior. In the beginning, you will be involved in every aspect of the business, but later you will need to become primarily a people manager. You will need to become a master of delegating authority. You must be able to work through people to accomplish objectives. Rarely will you be bogged down in minor details. Your micro-management days will be over, and you will have to learn to work through people. It is a radical change for most entrepreneurs, and many cannot make the change.

WHEN YOU HAVE PROBLEMS

When you have severe operating problems, the venture capitalist will be trying to make one basic decision: should you be removed as president, and be replaced with a new president? Does the VC still have enough confidence in you to work with you in the hope that you can turn the crisis situation around? Should you find yourself in a crisis situation, the best thing to do is to lay it all out before the venture capitalist. Tell the VC what the problems are, and how you are trying to solve them. If you lie or hide problems, the venture capitalist will have no alternative but to try to remove you. Remember, the venture capitalist's cardinal rule for entrepreneurs is that they must possess integrity.

There is a general rule in the venture capital community that "You only get one chance." This means that if you, the entrepreneur, lead your company into trouble, the venture capitalist will try to exercise control and force you out. Usually the VC will bring in an interim president who may be a turn-around expert. Or the VC may bring in someone to run the place while the VC searches for a new president. In practice, the venture capitalist does not always adhere to the general rule. You will be forced out for sure only if you are dishonest or stupid. If you show that you can bring the company out of the difficult situation, you have a chance of remaining president.

If you find yourself in the terrible situation of running a company in trouble, the best thing you can do is generate a plan to save the company. Present the plan to your directors and your venture capital partner. If the plan is unacceptable to the venture capital company and your directors, you may wish to bow out gracefully rather than embroil the company in a battle. Try to retain as much ownership in the company as possible while bowing out. You will probably make more money by walking away from the company and letting a new president run than you could gain by entering a mudslinging fistfight with the venture capital company.

In most instances where the entrepreneur is an honest, hard-working individual who is willing to make the sacrifices necessary to save the company, the entrepreneur has been retained. Many companies in trouble have been saved because the entrepreneur was an honest individual who had the "will to survive." The entrepreneur did what was prudent to save the company.

ANALYSIS OF THE SITUATION

Another cardinal rule in the venture capital business is not to lose one's principal investment. When the venture capitalist determines that a company is in trouble, the VC will try to minimize the losses. The first analysis will be to determine how the VC fund can get its investment back. Furthermore, the VC will try to determine what actions will return the greatest amount of money to the VC fund. In order to answer that question, the VC will analyze the company from two different perspectives.

First, the VC will analyze the earning capacity of the company. Can the problems at hand be solved? How quickly can they be solved? How much will it cost to carry the company while the problems are being solved? If the problems are solved, can the company be sold? Before the venture capitalist will invest additional funds, the VC will analyze the company in much the same way the VC did when the fund made the initial analysis. Each new dollar invested will be like a new investment to the VC fund. It must have a return. Throwing good money after bad is not a venture capitalist's method of operating. So this first option is to pump in more money and save the business with the thought of selling the business once it turns around.

The second type of analysis will be concerned with apprising the "bricks and mortar" with an eye toward selling off the assets. The venture capitalist will look at all the assets and determine what they are worth in liquidation. Then the VC will reduce any asset's value by the amount of secured liabilities against it. For example, the VC will look at loans to the company and at the probability that suppliers will try to take back inventory. Mechanics' liens, taxes, and other items that have not been paid will be considered. On the positive side, the VC will try to analyze any intangible assets such as a franchise, a license to operate, patents, advantageous leases, and so on. This analysis will conclude with a liquidation value of the business.

Finally, the VC will finish up the assessment by comparing the two alternatives: either fix the problem and later sell the business, or liquidate the assets, perhaps in bankruptcy. It is a hard choice and not a pretty picture.

WHAT THE VENTURE CAPITALIST WILL DO

The analysis made by the venture capitalist may not lead to a satisfactory conclusion. In fact, such analyses usually are inconclusive. Nonetheless, the venture capitalist will have to make a decision when faced with a company in trouble. Let's look at the five basic options open to the VC at this point.

1. FIX THE PROBLEM

The venture capitalist can put additional money into the business and try to keep it going. The VC may hire additional people or do whatever else is necessary to solve the problems of the business and save the investment. This solution may or may not include you as the general manager. Most entrepreneurs plead with the venture capitalist to go forward with the business. It is not always in the best interest of the entrepreneur to continue, because the company may merely slide into deeper trouble and hurt more people.

In one venture capital situation, the company was in the cement business, which is a cyclical business based on the housing industry. In 1980 the housing industry was in shambles, but projections suggested a turnaround was about to take place. The entrepreneur and the venture group bought the company in the fall and used capital during the winter to carry the company. By spring, it needed an additional injection of capital, and the equity partners put in additional capital. By the end of the summer, the housing industry had not picked up and the equity partners were again called upon to place additional equity in the company. Only a few of them put up the additional money. By this point, the equity partners owned approximately 70 percent of the company and the entrepreneur owned 30 percent. The housing market expansion never took place. Finally, the company was sold for a pittance. Venture firms often feed a company month after month in order to keep it alive. Don't expect an experienced VC to do this. Most have already done it once and will not do it again.

2. SELL THE BUSINESS

The venture capitalist may try to sell the company, or merge it with a similar business. Invariably, every business is worth more as an operating entity than one that is shut down. This is especially true of service-oriented companies. Merging the company with a larger entity that can bring money and management to build the new company may be a plus for you and your investment.

In one venture situation involving retail tires the alternatives were to inject additional money in the company or sell the company. Since the venture capitalist had lost faith in the entrepreneurs, their one alternative was to sell the business quickly. As you can imagine, the tire business is made up of leased locations, inventory, and people. Without these three ingredients, you have nothing of value. It was necessary to move quickly to find another tire retailer who wanted to enter the marketplace in which this tire company was located. It was the only way to save the company.

3. FORECLOSURE

If the venture capitalist has invested in subordinated debt rather than stock, there is an option to foreclose on the assets as a bank would. So in this case the VC has the option of acting like a creditor. The VC can seize the assets and try to operate the business, or sell the assets in order to generate enough money to pay back the subordinated debt. This is a very difficult move for venture capitalists. It involves working with the senior lender of a bank to make it work best. And it involves a quick move that rarely happens in the business world.

Sometimes the venture capitalist, if the VC is in a secured debt position with its subordinated debt, has the option of foreclosing. In one business, the venture capitalist foreclosed on a radio station and took over the assets of the company. These assets were primarily a transmitter and studio on a lease site, and a Federal Communications Commission (FCC) license to operate a radio station. The FCC was petitioned to transfer the license to the venture capital firm on an interim

basis, and it did. While operating the station, the venture capitalist always listened to it as he drove over to pay expenses.
One day he heard many classy ads being broadcast. When he
arrived, he asked the radio disc jockey how the DJ had sold
that many ads on the station. The disc jockey replied, "Oh, I
didn't sell anything. I just like to listen to the ads, so I put
them on free!"

The venture capitalist soon shut down the radio station so
he would not have to feed the losses. Then he went looking for
a buyer. The VC was soon able to find a buyer who was willing
to guarantee the repayment of the note in exchange for all the
assets, including the FCC license. Most venture capitalists
realize they cannot operate your business when it is in trouble. In the case of the radio station, the venture capitalist
knew he could not make money with free ads.

4. BANKRUPTCY

Some venture capitalists try to place the company in invol-
untary bankruptcy and have a receiver appointed. They seek
bankruptcy in order to hold off creditors who may have a
senior credit lien to the company's assets. If the senior creditors obtain the assets, there may be little of value in the
remaining assets to pay the venture capitalist anything. Operating in bankruptcy until the business can straighten out its
many problems may be the only way for a stockholder to
receive anything. Often in bankruptcy stockholders are wiped
out completely, and only creditors receive something.

The bankruptcy code is quite lenient to business owners. It
provides for creditors or the entrepreneur-owner to take the
company into bankruptcy to hold off all creditors. Such action
is frowned upon, however, and would probably reduce one's
chances of receiving financing in the future. In one large venture capital situation, bankruptcy was used to hold off a senior
creditor for three years while the company operated as
"debtor in possession," meaning the management team continued to run the company. The senior creditor was unable to
foreclose under its note. Three years later, the company was
able to come out of bankruptcy, settle many of its accounts

payable debts for several cents on the dollar, enter a long-term payout with the senior creditor, and go forward. It happens but it is rare.

5. LIQUIDATE

The venture capitalist can work hard to liquidate the company by selling off the assets, paying off any creditors who are ahead of the venture capitalist, and then receiving the money that is left. Sometimes a business that is asset heavy may be worth more after liquidation than it would be as an operating entity, because as an operating entity, it is projected to lose money indefinitely. If the venture capitalist is placed in this position, the VC will definitely seek to liquidate the company in order to recover as much of the VC fund's money as possible.

None of these choices is easy. You may find yourself at odds with the venture capitalist on which decision to make, because the VC will be influenced by money matters—the VC is usually the one who has to put up additional money. The entrepreneur can easily represent that the business will be fine if the business can just get to cash flow break-even. The venture capitalist must carry the company until it gets there. Once the decision is made, you are probably better off trying to help. Running counter to the adopted plan and the venture capitalist can only destroy the company's chances of recovery.

TEN THINGS NOT TO SAY

In your long-standing relationship with the venture capitalist, there are ten things you probably should not say if you do not want the VC to lose faith in you. Some of these items deal with your manner of speaking rather than with the context. Each item may sound humorous as presented below, but I personally have heard people say these things in one form or another.

1. My wife and I have decided to move to Florida where the weather is warm so that we can both enjoy the outdoors more. Even though the business is located in Massachusetts, I will be able to run it from Florida.

Obviously, the venture capitalist will be upset to see you moving away from the business. Most entrepreneurial businesses cannot be operated by an absentee manager, especially a start-up business or one in a high-growth mode. When you decide to move, like the fellow above, check out the local employment scene, as you will soon be out of work. The legal documents usually will prevent you from moving. That is, a move may be a violation of the negative covenants. Your presence at the company is desirable for all members of the management team. Big failures have occurred when management was not present.

In one venture situation the company was located in Washington, D.C., while its president lived in Westport, Connecticut. He commuted to work. He rationalized his living in Westport by saying there was good transportation and that the company was oriented toward marketing, which kept him on the road a lot anyway. In addition, the company's marketing manager lived in Houston. This meant neither of the top people in this marketing-oriented company lived in Washington, D.C. They were not constantly in touch with the people in the central office. The company failed and was merged with another large company. These two "flying officers" had their wings clipped.

2. Some friends and I got together and we purchased the franchise to a doughnut operation. I am putting $2,000 of my money into the deal through a second mortgage on my house, and my wife and I are going to help operate the doughnut shop.

Taking on a second business when you are supposed to dedicate 100 percent of your time to the business at hand is a stupid move on your part. It will be viewed by the venture capitalist as a sign of poor judgment on your behalf. Getting involved in outside investments when you have to run an entrepreneur business is not acceptable. When you decide to open another business like the fellow above, make plans to proceed full-time, because if the venture capitalist has his way, it will soon be your only occupation.

Most legal documents have a provision saying that you must give your full time and attention to the business, so if you become part owner and operator of another business, you will be in violation of your agreement. There is a second danger in taking on another business. What if the second business were to develop tremendous operating problems? You would then have to spend a greater percentage of your time on the problem company, and of course, leave the first business backed by the venture capital company to run itself. Many venture capitalists know what can happen when one business venture pulls down another venture because management was spread much too thin. Be smart. Stay in only one business.

3. We have been negotiating with another small business and have now entered into a final agreement to acquire it. We're going to give up about 30 percent of the stock in our company in a stock swap for their company. I didn't talk to you about it because it's such a good deal I knew you would like it.

Acquiring a business without consulting your venture capital partner is a mistake. Diluting the VC fund's ownership in your company by 30 percent is a major move. Bringing in a new business, which may or may not have the same profitability chances as your business, will give the venture capitalist reason to think twice about your intelligence. In addition, any merger is usually a violation of your investment agreement.

One of the greatest problems in the game of mergers and acquisitions is the difficulty of merging one company with another. We are so accustomed to reading about acquisitions in the large financial newspapers that we think an acquisition takes only a small amount of time. In actuality, an acquisition can consume years of management's time as they integrate the new company into the old. Much time will be spent on learning about a new business. Most venture capitalists have been involved in a number of mergers and they know the tremendous amount of time small business management can spend on mergers.

4. We came up with a new product. It is unrelated to our business, but it's in the solar energy field. I have been meaning to tell you about it. We have spent about $200,000 developing the product and we are now producing it at the rate of about two hundred a week. We have a warehouse full.

Obviously, taking on a new line of business that is unrelated to your own is a major decision. Spending large sums of money to develop it is another major business decision. All of this should have been discussed with your venture capital partner before you embarked on it. Jumping into a new area without consultation and without the approval of your partner is a bad idea. If you try something like this, watch out! If the product does not move quickly you, personally, will be moved out of your office into the street.

Any new product that you go into will be a violation of your investment agreement. On top of this, a new product will consume an inordinate amount of working capital. The risk of failure by taking on a product that has no close relationship to your own is extremely high. Ask the venture capitalist. The VC is constantly investing in new products and new businesses that may or may not be related to anything the VC has seen before. It will be wise for you to understand that investing in new, high-risk situations should be left to the venture capital professionals, and that you should invest your time and money only in the areas in which you have expertise.

5. We now have seven new regional offices that cost us about $180,000 each to set up. We wanted to set them all up at once in order to penetrate the market quickly. I didn't call you because I knew you would think it was a good idea to make a fast move.

Any fast move of this magnitude that would cost the company over a million dollars should have been cleared with your venture capital partner. Marketing plans seldom require rapid penetration to ward off the competition. A slow rollout can eliminate some costly mistakes. The quick penetration plan is a drastic change in marketing strategy and is a high-risk proposition. If sales do not pick up quickly, the entrepreneur can kiss his leadership position in the company goodbye.

6. I sold 500,000 shares of the company's stock at $1.00 each to some friends of mine. I know this represents 20 percent of the company, but I just couldn't pass up the opportunity for a quick $500,000. After all, you and I only paid $.25 a share and we have been able to sell the stock now for $1.00 per share. That makes the company worth more.

Violating the investment agreement willy-nilly, without even a telephone call to the venture capitalist, is risking sure destruction of your relationship with your venture capital partner. Whenever you plan anything that is in violation of your loan agreement, you should obtain written authority. Giving up equity is always a touchy subject with the venture capitalist because it dilutes his potential ownership and return on investment. Do not treat your partner badly, and the VC will not be a bad partner. One venture capital firm tells the story of an entrepreneur who just could not stop selling shares in his company. All of his marketing talents had been tuned up and turned on for selling stock in his company. Even after receiving venture capital financing, he continued to line up additional investments for private placement and to work with several stockbrokerage firms for a public offering. It seems the public offering never came around, and the entrepreneur spent so much time trying to arrange future financings for his company that he never really got the product off the ground. He was soon relieved of his duties and, what is not surprising, he became a stockbroker.

7. Two of our accounts receivable customers who owed us a total of $2 million declared bankruptcy on the same day, and it would seem that our claim in the bankruptcy court is probably worthless. This will lower our profits by $2 million and, as you know, make the company a break-even operation for the first six months.

Without question, this type of action has great impact on your financial judgment, but it has an even greater impact on the venture capitalist. You never consulted with the VC about a major account, or about the risk you were running by shipping goods to the companies. Now they have gone bankrupt.

Your credibility with the venture capital partner will be very low in these circumstances. You may also wind up bankrupt.

Some entrepreneurs building up a company become so excited about sales, projections and backlog that they forget to analyze fundamental credit risks of the customer. When you have large orders coming from companies that are not too well known, it is better for you to understand their financial strengths early. You should let your venture capital partner know what kind of risks you are taking when you ship a large order to a small client with a poor credit rating. Both of you should make the decision together to expose the company to a potential large loss.

8. I am out of money and can't meet Friday's payroll. I know the cash flow projections showed that we had enough money to last another year, but in checking through my cash flow projections I found a $70,000-per-week mathematical error. I thought we were using cash awfully fast three months ago, but I thought it would turn around soon. I am sorry. What can I do?

For starters, this fellow should look for a new job. Any entrepreneur who makes a $70,000 per week cash flow mathematical error deserves to be kicked out. It may be possible to forgive a mathematical error, but to have known three months ago that cash was being chewed up quickly, not to have looked into it, and not to have brought it to the attention of your business partner—that is a grave error. It will be practically impossible for you to recover from this stupid mistake.

9. We just finished the prototype of our initial product. I immediately turned the engineers loose on four other products we should be developing. It won't take much time or money to sell our prototype and to get the manufacturing process going. Then we'll really be rolling in the money. Meanwhile, I know there are other products that we can develop for the marketplace.

Your first priority, when you are in the development stage, is to develop the product you agreed to develop and develop it on schedule. It has been my experience that development of a product is easy, compared to manufacturing it within the projected cost and marketing it to the new customers. By continuing to emphasize research and development rather than changing your company's focus to manufacturing and marketing, you will demonstrate to the venture capital firm that you are not an entrepreneur. You are, in essence, a research engineer.

If you are to be the guiding light behind your business, you must determine at the outset what business you are in. Most venture capital firms have no interest in backing research and development companies. They are in the business of backing manufacturing and marketing companies. If you are not willing to make the step from research and development to manufacturing and sales, you should realize that the venture capital firm has no alternative but to replace you with a management team that will move the company into the manufacturing and marketing stage.

10. This recession is killing us. Industry sales are off 35 percent. I don't want to cut anymore overhead because I am sure sales will turn around. I put on a television blitz for the last two months. However, it didn't work, and now we are completely out of working capital. Can you invest some additional money?

Embarking on a television blitz in the middle of a recession is playing with fire. When you have a shrinking market, it is very difficult to increase your market share in a shrinking market, but this is not the point of the example. The point is, the entrepreneur's plan did not work. The entrepreneur took precious working capital and spent it on advertising. The entrepreneur did this rather than lay off additional people. Laying people off is difficult. I can remember every time that I have been involved in the process. But if you, as an entrepreneur, are to be a manager, you must manage in good times and in bad. In bad times laying off people is usually required. If you are unwilling to manage the company in bad times, the venture capitalist will have no alternative but to get someone who will.

SECRET OF A SUCCESSFUL RELATIONSHIP

Every relationship is based on trust. If you have entered into a financial deal with a venture capital firm that you do not trust, you have made a grave mistake. You are sure to have some doubts about the venture capital firm in the initial months, but if your checking has been accurate, then the venture capital firm should prove trustworthy. Assuming you both trust each other, there must also be a desire to help each other. The venture capitalist wants to make money, and you want to make money. You both have a common objective. One should not be making money at the other's expense. You should be on the same level, and therefore, should have a desire to help each other. From time to time, you may ask the venture capitalist to help you with various problems encountered in your company. The venture capitalist may ask you to do some things that will enhance the VC's profit position. Remember, you are partners.

More than anything, the secret to a successful relationship is the ability to talk to each other, and to communicate both the good and the bad news to one another. If two individuals can openly discuss the things they like and dislike about a relationship, as well as tell one another what things are good and what things are bad in a constructive critical approach, then the relationship will most likely be a successful one. In turn, the business will probably prosper.

I remember an entrepreneur who was highly motivated, well trained, and an achiever of the first order, but who was unable to admit failure. This flaw dominated his personality to such a degree that not only did he refuse to admit small errors, he would not accept the fact that his company had lost $170,000 at the end of its second year. When he received the audit from a large accounting firm, he would not accept it. He made the accounting firm restate the figures, but give him a qualified opinion. The financials showed the company had made a profit and was in good financial condition. The accountants' opinion had a section which said the financials were not GAAP but were correct, subject to the adjustments made by the entrepreneur. The entrepreneur presented these financial statements to his board of directors, to his bank, and to his investors. He seemed to think that if he could somehow get through the year without anyone except the accountant knowing his true condition, then he would have time to turn the company around and cover up past mistakes. This entrepre-

neur was unsuccessful in his cover-up. The company was liquidated. Many people lost a great deal of money.

There are plenty of entrepreneurs that push their accountants into taking positions that are not sound. For example,
some software companies sell software that is to be deployed
over a multiyear period but book the sale for account at the
time the contract is sold. Accountants will go along with this,
but when the VC finds out, it is a different story. The VC will
adjust the books to be more in line with the actual business.
So while public companies can fool their shareholders with
fuzzy accounting, don't expect the VC to be fooled.

In your relationship with your investors, your board of
directors, and your employees, be open and speak your mind.
Save all of your conniving and devious actions for your competition, as long as your actions are legal and acceptable in the
marketplace where you sell your products.

VENTURE CAPITALIST AS BOARD MEMBER

Most venture capitalists want to be a member of your
board; in fact, they may want several people from the venture
capital group to be on your board. Some venture capitalists
will not sit on your board of directors because of the liability
involved, but they will attend board meetings. Sometimes, you
may find a young venture capitalist monitoring your business
and may feel as though you are training the junior VC in the
ways of business. Many young venture capitalists are oriented
toward "strategic planning" of the type promoted in business
schools. They review your business plan as if it were a strategic plan for the industry, and they look at you as if you were a
large business about to capture a premier position in the marketplace. While it is important to have a long-range and perhaps even a strategic plan for your business, it is more
important to have a growth plan for your company during the
early stages. A strategic plan for the marketplace in the early
years is probably not necessary. However, managing tremendous growth takes a high degree of planning. You should

emphasize your growth plan to your young venture capital board member, rather than your strategic plan.

When you have a syndication of venture capitalists investing in your company, make sure your relationship is a simple one by indicating that you will be responsible primarily to the lead venture capitalist. You should send reports to all the venture capitalists, but you should work with only one of them. Venture capitalists are familiar with the lead investor situation in which they conduct business with the lead investor rather than the entrepreneur. This does not mean you should ignore them. From time to time, you may want to talk to one of them about specific subjects relating to your business and their specific skills. You should have semiannual or quarterly investor meetings in which you bring them all up to date on the company. Your lead investor can help you with these meetings.

DEGREE OF INVOLVEMENT BY THE VENTURE CAPITALIST

The amount of time the venture capitalist will spend with your company will depend on a number of factors.

AMOUNT INVESTED

The amount the venture capitalist has invested in your company, compared with other investments, will determine how much time the VC spends with you. If the VC fund has invested $500,000 in an early stage, the VC may not spend nearly as much time as if the VC fund had invested several million dollars. The larger the amount invested, the more upset the venture capitalist will be if the company goes bust. The more the invested funds mean to the venture capitalist, the more attention you will receive.

NEED FOR ASSISTANCE

If you have a complete management team and do not need assistance, the venture capitalist will usually stay away. If you need a financial adviser or someone to discuss marketing, then the venture capitalist may perform that function. The more help you need, the more the venture capitalist will be concerned and the more time the VC will give your company.

MANAGEMENT'S WILLINGNESS TO ACCEPT ADVICE

If management is willing to accept advice, most venture capitalists are willing to give it. If management resists every suggestion, obviously the venture capitalist will not waste his or her time making suggestions to tell management. There is a fine line for you to walk here. You should be hungry for advice on major decisions, but not on day-to-day operations.

EXPERIENCE IN CERTAIN AREAS

If the venture capitalist is not experienced in a certain area where you have a problem, the VC will not try to advise you on the matter. If the venture capitalist has good financial information and the entrepreneur is not a financial whiz, the venture capitalist will try to help with financial decisions.

LEAD INVESTOR

If the venture capitalist is the lead investor, then the VC will probably spend more time than if he or she was the sole investor. This arises from the VC's feeling of responsibility to the other venture capital investors. While the VC is under no legal obligation to ensure that they make money, the VC's reputation is on the line with his or her friends. The VC wants you to succeed so he or she will probably spend more time with your company.

DISTRESS OF COMPANY

If the company is operating under distressed circumstances, then the venture capitalist will try to play an active role. Every venture capitalist works on whatever problems threaten the VC's investment. Many venture capitalists spend most of their time working out problems, rather than reviewing new deals. In fact, most venture capitalists say they are not in the venture capital business at all, but rather that they are in the business of working out bad deals. They are always trying to avoid losing their money. It seems the good companies take care of themselves. So much of a VC's day is spent working on problems rather than investing in a new company.

Relationship with Entrepreneur

Often a strong bond will unite entrepreneur and venture capitalist. A certain chemistry that exists among people in venture situations draws them together. Great friendships have arisen from these relationships, even in dire circumstances.

Time Availability

As mentioned many times before, venture capitalists are extremely busy. They work on the most pressing problems first. If yours is a small problem or if you are operating well, you can expect the venture capitalist to be "hands off". You should not interpret the venture capitalist's lack of attention to your business as a lack of interest in your company. The amount of time spent on an investment is usually inversely proportionate to the success of the investment. In general, a venture capitalist cannot make a company a success, but the VC can often save the investment when there is trouble.

Venture Capitalist's Objectives

During this period of time, when you are working together, the venture capitalist will have one objective: growth. The VC wants to see your company grow as fast as possible and to see it become as large as possible. The VC wants to see sales go up and profits to follow. Those are the basic objectives for being an investor in your company. The venture capitalist also wants to see you become a leader. The VC wants to see that you build a strong management team and no longer have to be involved in every detail, that you have found good employees, and that you can work through them.

If your company has grown rapidly and is now becoming large, the venture capitalist will be looking toward liquidity. The venture capitalist wants to be able to see part of the investment the VC fund has made turn into cash. The VC receives no bonuses because of your growth and success. The VC receives cash rewards personally when the investment made by the VC fund is returned in cash. You will find that every venture capitalist has a desire to sell part of the VC fund's investment. The only drawback in selling is the matter of price.

OBJECTIVE

Your objective during this period of time will be to build your team and build the company. Make it strong so that you can either (a) buy out the venture capital partner by refinancing the company; (b) go public, so that the venture capitalist and you, the entrepreneur, can cash in some of your ownership; or (c) sell the entire company so that you and the venture capitalist can realize a large capital gain. Your second goal is to use the venture capitalist. You should consult the venture capitalist. They can help you with information that can be of help in making tough decisions. Putting your time and effort into running a good strong business, rather than concentrating on how quickly you can get rid of the venture capitalist, will make life more bearable for you. In the next chapter we discuss how you can move the venture capitalist out of your life.

C H A P T E R

10 THE EXIT

How Can You Remove the Venture Capital Company?

The Way to Own It All.

There has always been a love–hate relationship between the venture capitalist and the entrepreneur. Most venture capitalists are frustrated entrepreneurs. They will watch you make a great deal of money and sometimes they will be envious of your success. Most entrepreneurs, on the other hand, love their venture capitalist the day they receive an infusion of cash from the VC fund, but some years later, when the venture capitalist is able to cash in the equity ownership and make ten times the investment, the entrepreneur is apt to believe the venture capitalist made too much money. After all, the only thing the venture capitalist did was put in money. Another source of friction arises in the company that operates poorly. The venture capitalist may take actions to remedy the situation, and the entrepreneur, thinking the actions are wrong, may try to resist them.

Instead of reacting negatively, both parties should remember that each one took a substantial risk. There may have been many times when both wondered if the company was ever going to make it. Each party had a great deal to lose: the venture capitalist's reputation and money were on the line, and the entrepreneur's reputation and one chance were on the line. Both should respect each other's position and continue to work together as mature adults.

Nevertheless, there comes a time when every entrepreneur wants to be completely free of his venture capital partner. The entrepreneur does not want to be under the influence of the venture capitalist. The entrepreneur wants to have complete operating authority over the business. When this time comes, the venture capitalist will sell the VC's equity ownership in the business.

Every ownership position in every company held by a venture capitalist is for sale. Do not ever think that a venture capitalist wants to own a minority interest or even a majority interest in your firm forever. Venture capitalists are not in the business of owning and operating companies. They are in the business of investing for a period of time, helping build up a business, and then cashing in on those investments by selling their positions. They receive no kudos from the investors in their venture capital fund (the limited partners) when they say to the investors that the VC fund owns 30 percent of a dozen small companies. The only time the venture capitalist is rewarded is the day the VC converts the ownership in your company into cash. Most venture capital managers receive a bonus in proportion to the cash capital gains they generate. This comes in the form of a carried interest they have in the profits of the venture fund. So remember, every venture capitalist wants to sell the ownership position the VC fund has in your company and generate capital gains so the venture capital manager can receive a nice fat cash payment. This can work to your advantage. You know they have to sell, so plan for that day. If you do, you will help the VC and you can own all the business with your management team.

It's All a Matter of Price

Now that you understand what the venture capitalist wants to get out and needs to get out, you have reduced the argument to one of price. As they say in a number of businesses, we know what the VC is, so we are just talking about the price. The price we are talking about is the price at which the venture capitalist will sell the equity the VC fund owns in your business. And that price depends on the value of your company, which in turn depends on the stage of development of the company. If it's early in the game plan for the company, you may have to pay dearly to buy out the venture capitalist. The VC may be prepared to wait for the business to mature and be worth a lot more. The VC will not sell short if the VC sees that the company will be twice as large next year. If your company is mature, the venture capitalist will want out soon and the VC's price can be negotiated more easily.

Don't think all those arguments you made to get the VC to invest will not come back to haunt you when you begin this conversation. All those arguments you used to persuade the VC that your business was worth billions will now be used to push the price up. What goes around comes around. Let's look at the four ways you can take out the VC.

First Method: Going Public

Most venture capitalists will spend a great deal of time talking about the virtues of going public. You and the venture capitalist will like the idea of going public. By establishing a public market, you can cash in some of your chips. The public market gives the venture capitalist an exit for part of the VC fund's holdings and a method of selling additional shares as time goes on. In a publicly owned company in which the venture capitalist merely has an investment, the role of the VC in the policy making is relatively small.

WHEN TO GO PUBLIC

Many brokerage houses will tell you that there is a time to go public and there is a time not to go public. They will discuss the marketplace in terms of being hot or cold for new issues or for the concept behind your company. They may tell you that your company has not achieved an equity value, enough sales, and earnings to permit it to go public. Generally, they will want a growth record of 30 to 60 percent or more. Most brokers are reluctant to take companies public unless they have at least $10 million in net after-tax income unless it is a very hot stock market. From your standpoint, the entire discussion is not material. There is only one time to go public for you and that is when a brokerage house will take the company public at the price you think is reasonable. If one brokerage house says it cannot take you public, go to another one. Make sure you test all the good brokerage houses before you abandon this alternative.

Entrepreneurs usually ask if they should sell any of their shares in the initial underwriting. They ask this question because they believe if management is selling any of their shares, new stockholders who are being asked to purchase shares will be leery. The answer, of course, is that it is a matter of percentages. If you are selling 2, 3, or even 5 percent of your holdings, or perhaps even 10 percent if you hold a large percentage of ownership in the company, then it is perfectly all right for you to sell some of your shares in the initial or secondary underwriting. Every entrepreneur is advised to sell some of his or her shares in the initial public offering if the underwriter will permit it. This makes sense for you as the entrepreneur because it allows you to diversify your own investment.

You should take some of your capital gains as soon as possible and invest them in some other medium, such as tax-free bonds. You want to diversify your own holdings rather than tie them up in one company. Nothing will give you greater happiness and satisfaction than to have half a few million dollars parked in a tax-free money market fund that pays you a handsome income each year, tax-free. This type of money, from the entrepreneur's standpoint, is often called "screw you" money, because if everything were to blow up and the company were to fall on hard times, the entrepreneur would have some money with which to survive and start again. The entrepreneur can say to the cruel business world that killed the company, "Screw you!" When your time comes, do not forget to obtain some "screw you" money.

WHY YOU SHOULD HAVE A PUBLIC OFFERING

There are a great number of reasons to go public.

- Generally speaking, selling shares in the public market will allow you to sell them at a higher price than they can be sold for in a private placement of the shares. The reason is simple. Public shares have liquidity that makes the shares more valuable. The public will pay more for the stock because it is liquid and can be resold at any time. And by selling shares of your company at a higher price, you will have much less dilution in your own ownership in the company. Everyone's ownership will be diluted less by the new shares.

- Once your company is public and the shares are traded, it will be much easier to raise additional equity capital if you do a good job of building your company.

- Having the shares of the company in public hands will establish a market for the company's shares. It will allow you to attract new management talent and to motivate them with stock options. A publicly held company has greater credibility with customers and suppliers as well as lending institutions.

- The most important reason is that a public market creates liquidity through which you as a large stockholder and the venture capitalist as a stockholder can exchange shares in the company for cash. Nothing is sweeter for the entrepreneur or venture capitalist than to take a few shares and exchange them for $5 million or $10 million, or more, in cash.

Why You Should Not Have a Public Offering

Unfortunately, several serious drawbacks have to be considered before one goes public.

- A public company has to disclose a great deal of information about itself. The data can be used by your competition, by customers who deal with you, and by your employees who, when they learn how much money you make, may want pay raises. All your friends and neighbors will be able to buy one share of stock in your company just to keep track of you. Unless you like living in a fish bowl, you should not be a public company.

- All public companies are subject to reporting requirements established by the government, primarily the Securities and Exchange Commission, and in addition must file certain information with their stockholders. This will mean increased time and expenses to your company in the form of reporting, audits, and so on.

- Once you are a public company, your new public shareholders will be desirous of strong performance. They will want the earnings per share to increase each year. If you do not perform, they will sell your shares and drive the price down.

- Particularly troublesome are the cost and management time necessary to accomplish the public offering itself—management will be kept from performing day-to-day duties, and the costs of going public will be very high. The legal fees, the accounting fees, and the underwriter's charges, by any standard, will be exorbitant.

- Finally, in a public company you will be severely constrained by insiders dealing with the company. That is, you will no longer be able to use the company to increase your own personal fortune at the expense of the company's. All transactions must be at "arm's length." If insider transactions are not proper, stockholder suits and an audit by the Securities and

Exchange Commission are sure to follow. There is a whole profession of strike suit lawyers that will be gunning for you if you step over this line.

Underwriter's Fees and the Public Offering

Your stockbroker will charge you a fee for acting as an underwriter of your stock. Part of the fee will go to the stockbrokers who join the syndicate, but most of the fee will go to the firm you choose to be the underwriter, called the lead underwriter. The underwriter's fee can range from 5 to 10 percent. The standard for new, high growth companies seems to be 7 to 8 percent. The fee for high-risk companies, the high fliers, is 10 percent.

Sometimes you can reduce the underwriter's fee substantially by offering the underwriter some stock options in your company. For example, rather than having the underwriter receive 10 percent on all the funds the underwriter raises for you, you might negotiate a fee of 6 percent of all the funds raised, plus an option to own 3 percent of the stock in your company. As icing on the cake, you might offer the underwriter the right of first refusal for the next underwriting of your stock. In a $50 million underwriting, the 4 percent that you have saved is $2 million. Your company will receive the $47 million cash, the underwriter $3 million, and the underwriter will have the option to purchase 3 percent of your company in place of the extra fee of $2 million fee.

The fees you will pay out to other professionals in your underwriting may shock you. Legal fees can range from $275,000 to $2 million. It is not unusual for a complicated underwriting to cost $3 million. Printing the prospectus may cost anywhere from $25,000 to $150,000, depending on the number printed, the color photographs used, the paper quality, and so forth. As time moves on, the Internet distribution of the prospectus may cut down on this one.

Accounting bills seem to be lower. Expect to pay $100,000 to $200,000 to your accountants for their certification of the financial statements and their review of your prospectus. Do not forget your own attorney. The general counsel for your company will want a substantial fee for working with the lawyers of the underwriter and your special SEC lawyers. This fee could range from $50,000 to $100,000. In total, a full-blown public registration and offering may cost you $500,000 to $1.5 million. You should factor this into the amount that you are raising. Thus, if you are raising $50 million and you pay an underwriting fee of 8 percent or $4 million plus $1.5 million in professional fees, then the cost of the money will be 10.5 percent. Your net will be $44.5 million.

You will have to negotiate a letter of intent from your underwriter for this public offering. One of the points of intense negotiation will be the price range being set in the letter of intent. The initial price for the stock is usually related to market valuations of issues similar to yours and to companies that are already public. The initial price will also be related to how hot your new company will be perceived to be by the intuitional buyers such as mutual funds that are expected to buy the stock. Generally, if an underwriter says the range is $13 to $16 per share, the underwriter means $13 per share.

SELECTION OF A BROKERAGE HOUSE
FOR THE PUBLIC OFFERING

As you talk with stockbrokerage firms, friends, accountants, and bankers, the name of a local brokerage house that has participated in underwriting new issues for many smaller companies will be mentioned by more than one person. As you widen your sphere of discussion, you will hear the names of three or four national firms that specialize in new issues. Just as you did when raising venture capital, you should contact a few of these firms and determine whether one is interested in taking your company public. Once you have found a brokerage firm that is interested, you should stay with it until you have reached an agreement. If you cannot reach an agreement, move to the next firm.

In selecting your brokerage house, look for one that has an excellent reputation and a professional status in the underwriting community. You should also look for experience in underwriting new issues, particularly in companies such as yours. You should determine the brokerage's ability to distribute the shares to its clients. If it has a small number of retail customers, the brokerage may not be as effective as one with a large number of customers or one with an institutional client base. Institutional buyers now dominate the stock market for new issues. So the underwriter that has a strong institutional base will be a strong contender for your business.

You should determine the brokerage house's market-making ability. Once the initial offering is over, will it be an active market maker in your shares in order to maintain the price of the stock? You need to pick a firm that can be a strong market maker. Your VC firm can be a great help in selecting a good underwriter. Finally, determine whether the brokerage firm can take the entire issue or if it will have to syndicate the issue through numerous other brokerage houses. In general, having more than one underwriter is strongly preferable to just having one.

As you can see, a public company has its share of problems. Going public will be a method for you to remove the influence of your venture capital partner and perhaps sell all the shares that the VC fund owns. But what you get in place of the VC will be a number of outside stockholders who will be as interested in your company as the venture capitalist was. But since their ownership will be diluted by all the other shareholders, they will not have the same oversight of your business the VC had.

SECOND METHOD: PURCHASE BY THE COMPANY OR ENTREPRENEUR

Obviously the company or you the entrepreneur can negotiate a price for which the venture capitalist will sell the stock owned by the VC fund. If the company does not have the cash, it can borrow the money from the bank and buy the stock owned by the venture capital fund. This sale leaves the entrepreneur and any other stockholders owning 100 percent of a company, but the company now has increased liabilities in the form of the bank loan. The venture capital company might accept part or all of its payment in the form of a long-term note. Whenever possible, you should give the venture capitalist a note for a long-term payout at a medium interest rate in return for the equity position owned by the VC fund. This gives the venture capitalist an exit and solves the liquidity problem in that the VC fund knows that it will be paid out in a specified time.

There is also the remote possibility that you may have some asset such as an investment in another company or stock in some subsidiary that would be more meaningful to the venture capitalist than ownership in your company. You might arrange for a stock swap—the stock you hold in another company for the stock the VC fund holds in your company. Or, you may own the land and building in which the business is housed. You could swap the land and building for the stock in your business. These types of swaps are uncommon, but they have been discussed by venture capitalists and entrepreneurs on numerous occasions. The reason they usually do not work is that they are not cash. The VC wants cash first and publicly traded stock second. Everything else is just junk.

Purchase by Employee's Stock Ownership Trust

A method used by some entrepreneurs to buy out the venture capitalist is to set up an employee's stock ownership trust (ESOT). The ESOT is like a pension and profit sharing plan, except that it buys stock in your company rather than stock of large traded companies. The ESOT obtains money through contributions by the company and therefore builds up cash. The ESOT can also borrow from the bank on the basis of the projected future contributions by the company. The ESOT uses the money to buy the stock that is owned by the venture capital firm. This is a relatively painless way for the company to buy back the equity ownership held by the venture capital firm. Contributions by the company to the ESOT are tax deductible. In essence, the company can use pretax dollars rather than after-tax dollars to purchase the stock. This excellent method of removing the venture capitalist puts the entrepreneur in a complex tax situation. Anyone contemplating this method should contact an expert in the field of employee stock ownership trusts.

Exit by Puts and Calls

When the investment was negotiated, you may have set up a formal arrangement that provides for exit for the venture capitalist. This may be in the form of "puts" and "calls." As we noted earlier, a put is a right given to the venture capitalist to require you or the company to buy the venture capitalist's ownership in the company at a predetermined formula. The call provision gives you, or the company, the right to purchase the venture capitalist's ownership by the same or similar formulas.

There are probably as many put and call formulas as there are minds thinking about how to structure deals. However, there are seven popular ones that you should consider.

1. Price/Earnings Ratio

Probably the most popular is a price/earnings ratio formula that treats your company's stock like the stocks traded on national stock exchanges. The earnings per share are figured for the shares owned by the venture capitalist. A popular price/earnings (PE) ratio is selected from public stocks in the same industry. That PE ratio is multiplied by the earnings per share to come up with a price per share that you or your company will pay to the venture capitalist for the stock the VC owns.

2. BOOK VALUE

A less common formula is based on book value of the company. It's simple to compute the book value per share for stock owned by the venture capitalist. That would be the price you or the company would pay for the shares owned by the venture capital company. Book value per share is seldom used, because in the early years of a company's development the company usually has a small book value. It's only in older companies that have been around long enough to establish a good book value that this becomes the method of valuing the venture capitalist's equity position.

3. PERCENTAGE OF SALES

Sometimes it is inappropriate to use the earnings of the company in a price/earnings formula because in the early years of development, particularly in a start-up company, the earnings may be low owing to heavy depreciation or research and development expenses. It may take several years for the company to become profitable. Using pretax earnings may seem to be more appropriate. However, pretax earnings are held low, often because of heavy salaries or heavy expenditures for promotion. In such a case, it may be easier for you to take the normal profit before tax as a percentage of sales typical for the industry.

You will find statistics on your industry in publications on business statistics. You may find that most companies similar to yours have a pretax earning of 10 percent of sales. It would be simple, then, to take 10 percent of your company's sales and pretend that number is your profit before taxes. Then you would determine earnings per share by using the hypothetical profit before taxes. Using the industry price/earnings ratio, you could easily determine what the value of the stock owned by the venture capital company would be worth if the hypothetical earnings existed. This can be the method used for buying back the shares owned by the venture capital firm.

Using the percentage-of-sales formula to value and buy back the shares owned by the venture capitalist can be very expensive. If, for some reason, sales take off or you invest a great deal in advertising to push sales and market shares up, your formula for repurchasing the venture capitalist's shares will become unbearable. On the other hand, if the formula was based on earnings, you would control the amount of earnings. For example, you might increase advertising in order to reduce earnings and build a name for the company in the future. By using the earnings formula, you will be reducing the value of the venture capitalist's shares. As the venture capitalist sees it, you cannot tamper with sales as easily, and therefore sales becomes a good indicator of the value of the company.

4. MULTIPLE OF CASH FLOW

In some industries cash flow is a more accurate barometer of how the business is doing than are profit-and-loss statements based on generally accepted accounting principles. Using an eight to ten times cash flow formula, we might say a company is worth millions of dollars more than a price/earnings ratio of the profit-and-loss statement would indicate. If we assume a company is worth ten times cash flow, it is simple to compute the value of the percentage of the company owned by the venture capitalist. You can use this as the method for buying back the VC's equity position.

The cash flow formula may work quite well for a stable company, but could be extremely expensive in an asset-heavy, leveraged buyout situation. For example, in a leveraged buyout you may have inflated the value of the assets in order to shelter income. However, when these heavily depreciated assets are removed in the calculation of cash flow, the cash flow number will be much higher than the profit before tax figure. The price you have to pay for the equity of the venture capitalist can be high if it is based on cash flow.

5. MULTIPLE OF SALES

The value of some companies in certain industries is based on a multiple of sales. Radio and TV stations traditionally sell at two to three times gross sales. If you determine the value of a company to be two and a half times gross sales, it would be simple then to compute the value of the venture capitalist's percentage of equity ownership and pay the VC that amount for ownership in the company. As in the percentage of sales calculation above, the multiple of sales valuation also means you will be paying for a company that may or may not have earnings. Many investors in the radio business buy a poorly run station on a multiple of sales calculation, knowing full well that the station's earnings cannot possibly pay back the investment. The investor who is buying the station must put in enough money to carry the station until its sales and earnings can be increased. In fact, the earnings must increase drastically if the investor is to pay back any debt and get an adequate return on the money invested.

6. APPRAISED VALUE

It is often easy to find a valuation firm to appraise the value of the equity ownership held by the venture capital fund. There are a half dozen well-known business appraisal firms that can render a very formal opinion on what the investment held by the VC firm is worth. The appraisal will probably be based on a combination of some of the items mentioned previously. Appraisals are usually computed by three methods. First, the value of the company is determined by its earnings power, both past and future. This formula is similar to the price/earnings ratio, except it uses the stream of future earnings. The appraisal will look at the stream of earnings that the company is likely to produce over the next ten years and discount that cash flow back by an appropriate discount. This is the earnings approach to valuing a company.

The second method is to determine the value of the assets (bricks and mortar) as if they were sold at auction as part of an orderly liquidation. From this liquidation the appraiser subtracts all debts outstanding, and the remaining value is the appraised value of the assets. The bricks and mortar formula is similar to the book value calculations, except there it includes an appraisal of the assets and a restated new book value based on their appraised value. When these two figures do not agree, the appraiser usually selects something close to the higher of the two. For example, if the bricks and mortar formula were higher than the earnings formula, the appraiser would assume that the highest and best use of the company was to sell all of its assets.

The third method is by comparing the business to public companies. In this method, a number of companies that are public are selected because they are similar to your business. Then this "basket of businesses" is used to come up with a multiple of earnings that they are trading at, the price/earnings ratio (the PE). The PE is the ratio one gets by dividing the price the stock is selling at, by the earnings of the company. Then that ratio is multiplied by the earnings of your company to determine the value of your company. So if the basket of businesses is trading at a 12 PE, and your company is earning $8 million, then your business is worth $96 million.

All three of these methods will be used by the professional valuation firms to value your business and determine a price for the shares owned by the VC fund.

7. PREARRANGED CASH AMOUNT

Of course, a simple way to set up the purchase of the VC's ownership is to base it on a put and call option on a single cash amount. That is, at the end of three years the venture capital firm would have the right to require the company to buy its equity ownership position for a certain amount, say, $2 million. Although this method saves a great deal of negotiating and appraising at the end of three years, people find it difficult to agree on a value at the beginning of the investment period. It sort of takes all the fun out of investing if you know what you are going to get at the end. I am convinced that most VCs like their jobs because there is this unknown about what they will get back once they give you their money. It permits them to dream like an entrepreneur about how much they may make. That was kind of mushy, wasn't it?

THIRD METHOD: SALE OF THE COMPANY TO ANOTHER COMPANY

Rather than having the venture capitalist sell the fund's ownership position in your company, you and the venture capitalist may decide to sell the entire company to another individual or a large conglomerate. This will rid you of the venture capitalist as well as rid you of your own company. You may prefer to sell the company, receive a large amount of money, and dissolve your marriage to the venture capitalist. Then you can start a second company with the cash you received from selling the first company, but this time without venture capital financing. Nice thought, huh?

When the entire company is sold to a conglomerate, the venture capitalist and you will be paid in one, two, or three different kinds of payments for the purchase of the stock in your company or the assets of the company. There are six basic ways in which a company may be sold. You should understand each so that you will be ready to negotiate with the buyer of your company.

SELLING STOCK FOR CASH

The simplest of all methods is to sell the stock in your company to someone else for cash. This triggers capital gains and is a straightforward method of selling your company.

SELLING STOCK FOR NOTES

Rather than take cash for your stock, you may wish to take a note from the buyer. That is, the buying company may buy the stock you own in your company by giving you a note that pays off over a certain period of time, say five years. In the venture capital community these notes are called paper, so when you "take back paper," you have taken notes in place of cash. Although cash is made out of paper as well, only these seller notes are called paper. Maybe the word paper is used here because it suggests something that is worthless. Many people have taken notes that later became worthless because the buyer ran the company into the ground.

It is common to give notes in order to establish a deferred purchase and give you, the seller, tax advantage. Most venture capital companies expect to take some deferred payment for their investment. Receiving a note for stock that you are selling can create complications in that you will have a note from an unrelated third party, which may be strong if it's a big conglomerate, or may be weak if it is a group of individuals. A way around the weak note is to have your company buy back all the stock you and the venture capitalist own except for several shares. Your company pays you and the venture capitalist for the stock with a note, and the note is collateralized by the assets of your business. Then it is very simple to sell the remaining several shares of stock for the cash down payment amount to whomever is buying the company. The buying group will be the sole stockholder. You will have collateral for the note that you have received for your stock.

SELLING STOCK FOR STOCK

At times you may wish to take stock in a very large conglomerate or strategic buyer for the stock that you own. This will give you the advantage of not paying taxes until you sell the stock received from the conglomerate. In a tax-free exchange you will not pay the tax until the day you sell the shares of the large conglomerate. Of course, it will be much more dangerous to take stock in a smaller company. It might be ludicrous for you to swap the stock in your company for stocks of another private company, since you still will have neither liquidity nor income from the stock you receive. When dealing with large companies, you should try to obtain registered shares so that you will be free to sell your stock whenever you wish.

In another twist, you may wish to take a dividend paying preferred stock from the large conglomerate that is convertible into the conglomerate's common stock. In this way you can have income until you decide to convert your shares into common stock and sell them in the open market.

SELLING ASSETS FOR CASH

In this situation your company agrees to sell all of its assets for cash. Then all the operating assets and all the operating liabilities are assumed by the buying corporation for a specified cash amount. Your company is left with only cash as its asset. It is quite easy afterwards for you to file a tax plan to liquidate the corporation and distribute the cash to stockholders of the company, including you and the venture capital firm. Unfortunately this method my have some dire tax consequences because the payment may be taxed twice. Please see your tax adviser before you go down this trail.

Under the current tax law the sale of assets is a taxable event, even if you liquidate the company shortly thereafter. Therefore, if you sell the assets for more than book value, the corporation will have to pay a tax on the difference between book value and the price you sold the business for. When you liquidate the company and distribute the cash to the stockholders, the stockholders will have to pay a tax on the difference between their cost of the stock and the amount of cash they received from liquidating the company. This means that there is a double tax on the sale of the company. As you can see, selling the assets for cash and liquidating the company can be a very expensive method of selling the business.

SELLING ASSETS FOR NOTES

Sometimes the acquiring company may not have the cash necessary to pay for the assets it is buying from your company. In that situation, your company may have to take notes, secured by the assets being sold as payment. Once you have sold your assets for notes, these notes will be the only assets of your company. As the payments on the notes are made, your company may distribute them to the stockholders in a liquidation plan. The notes must be for the short term. If there are many stockholders, this is a tricky situation. Someone will have to manage the collection of the notes and the payments to stockholders in order to retire their shares. You may wish to have the buyer issue the notes in small denominations. This will allow you to distribute the notes directly to the stockholders and they can collect principal and interest directly on the notes. Such a multiple note plan may be appropriate for large conglomerates that are acquiring your company, since their credit is good. But it would be inappropriate for a small company that is acquiring your company, because it would be hard for you as a group to get back together and file suit against the small company for nonpayment under the many notes. If there are only a few stockholders—for example, a few key managers and the venture capital company—then the multiple notes can be transferred into proper denominations to the appropriate parties upon sale of the assets without much danger.

Be aware that the sale of the assets of the company for notes can be a taxable event and can require the double tax payment as previously discussed, as if the company had received cash. You need a good tax lawyer or tax accountant to review the transaction before you sign the document to sell the assets.

SELLING ASSETS FOR STOCK

If you are receiving, as payment for the assets, registered shares (or even shares that are restricted), it is quite easy for you to exchange the assets of your company for stock in a large conglomerate. Then you can file a plan of liquidation and distribute these shares to the stockholders of your company. This too can be a taxable event, and you should consult your tax expert.

OTHER FORMS OF PAYMENT

Many other forms of payment can be used in concert with the foregoing structures. For example, you could structure the payment on an "earn-out basis." An earn-out involves paying you cash for the stock and then paying an additional amount for the stock that you own in the company, which is based on the earnings of your company over the next few years. As an example, the company that purchases your company might agree to pay you an additional amount (earn-out) of 25 percent of pretax income in excess of $2 million for each of the five years succeeding its acquisition of your company. This would mean you would get some cash up front, but the bulk of your earnings would come as a percentage of the earnings. Many buyers like to do this because it gives the entrepreneur who is selling the company an incentive to stay at the business and work to build it up so it pays the entrepreneur more money and makes the purchase a success.

Another form of compensation to entrepreneurs who sell out is known as the "W2" method. This method is used when the company is not in good shape, when assets are sold and there is not enough money to pay creditors. In this situation the entrepreneur tells the creditors that as a stockholder he or she is not receiving anything and that, therefore, they should compromise their debt and receive only a partial payment. This arrangement will permit the assets to be transferred to the buyer. What the entrepreneur has failed to tell the creditors is that he is being paid for his stock through his W2—that is, his employment contract with the large acquiring company. They agreed to pay him what they normally pay managers, say $200,000 a year, but at the same time they agreed to pay him an additional $300,000 per year in salary to compensate him for not making anything on the transaction. This type of exercise is called a W2 because an employee's reported salary is part of his W2 government form. What the entrepreneur lost on his stock he made up in his paycheck.

Obviously, the selling entrepreneur can be rewarded with a consulting contract or an employment contract as part of the payment. Of course, this takes something away from the stockholders that they would have received. To use an absurd example, the entrepreneur might agree to sell the assets of the company for one dollar and at the same time sign an employment agreement with the buying company providing that the entrepreneur be paid $1 million per year for the next three years. In this instance the entrepreneur received $3 million and the existing stockholders received virtually nothing. You can be sure the venture capitalist will be upset if you are selling out and part of the overall consideration is your compensation through an employment contract. You will have to reduce the amount that you are being paid for your stock in order to compensate for a large employment contract.

NEGOTIATING THE SALE OF YOUR COMPANY

Negotiating with large companies for the purchase of your company will be an exasperating experience. Big companies rarely move quickly. There are reports, projections, analyses, discussions, and so forth. Negotiating with the acquisition team from a large conglomerate can be a harrowing experience. These people are usually sharp. They frequently play "good guy and bad guy." That is, one or two individuals in their negotiating team will be the good guys and one or more will be the bad guys. The bad guys will tell the good guys and you, what a bad deal this is, what a terrible thing to do, and how overpriced the deal is. At some point the bad guys may scream and walk out of the room. Then the good guys will saddle up to you and tell you they believe they can bring the bad guys into line if you can just agree on some of the remaining minor issues, such as lowering the price by 20 percent. Many individuals on the corporate acquisition team will resort to any method to obtain a good deal. You should be on your toes when negotiating with the team trying to buy your company.

One of the main conditions that you will have to determine at the outset is whether you will stay with the company after the acquisition. The acquisition team will want you to stay. Unless you have an outstanding middle management team, a condition of the purchase will be that you stay long enough for the corporate giant to understand your business. The new owner will need time to prepare somebody to run your company. The transition from running your own company to becoming a wholly owned subsidiary or a division of a large company will be quite a change for you if you are not ready for it. The number of reports, the memorandums, the auditors, the cash disbursements—all these and more will create a great change when you become a subsidiary of a large company. Your entrepreneurial spirit may be broken by the bureaucracy in large companies. In many respects, there is no difference between a large conglomerate's bureaucracy and the bureaucracy of any state or national government. Be sure you reach an understanding about the operation of your business before you sell. If that understanding is not satisfactory to you, make sure the price paid for your company is sufficient so that you can walk away happy when the time comes.

BUY—SELL ARRANGEMENT

The sale of the company may have been triggered by a buy–sell arrangement. That is, you have agreed with the venture capitalist that if a bona fide offer is made to purchase your company and you do not wish to take it, then you must buy out your venture capital partner on the same terms and conditions as the sales offer. If you cannot buy out the venture capitalist, then you have agreed to sell the company on the same terms and conditions as the bona fide offer. A buy–sell arrangement is useful in any agreement. It offers you the same option. If someone offers to buy and your venture capital company does not want to sell, then you have the right to require them to buy you out on the same terms and conditions or they must sell the company. It gives you both the opportunity to look at any bona fide offers that may arise and have either party (you or the venture capitalist) accept the offer.

An example of a more drastic form of a buy–sell arrangement is a deal in which at the end of four years the venture capital company can market all of the stock of the company to the highest bidder. That is, in year four the venture capital firm can approach anyone. It may try to sell all the stock of the company in order to trigger a long-term capital gain for the venture capital firm and for the entrepreneur stockholder. This is a more severe version of the buy–sell arrangement in that the venture capitalist has a built-in exit for all of the shares. You might wonder why the venture capitalist has the right to sell all of the shares rather than just his own. Obviously, a buyer of the stock will pay a premium for owning all the stock, or at least control of the company. It is worth more per share than the same buyer would pay for a minority stock position in a small company. In short, control is worth more than a minority position on a share-by-share basis. This is called the control premium.

FOURTH METHOD: FINDING A NEW INVESTOR

Sometimes you may be able to find an investor who will buy the ownership position of the venture capital firm. Perhaps the new owner can become a working partner with you. You may have a close personal friend who has enough money to purchase the position held by the venture capital firm. On the other hand, you may find a passive investor who wants to be a long-term investor in your company and who is willing to buy the position held by the venture capitalist. Sometimes you can make a better deal with this second investor. You can have the passive investor buy stock in your company, which you in turn use the cash received to retire the stock of the venture capital company. This is becoming more common in the VC world as there is so much money in the industry that deals are "recycled" by selling the business to another VC firm.

CORPORATE PARTNERS

When your company has grown substantially and is moving along at a good pace, you can sometimes find a corporate partner who wants to own part of your company. The corporate partner's objective may be to own all of your company at a future time. It may make good sense for you to have the corporate partner buy out the venture capitalist. The corporate partner may make a better partner than the venture capitalist, because the corporate partner will know more about your marketplace and how to produce your product. The corporate partner will be the logical company to buy your personal stock when the time comes for you to cash in your ownership.

As an example, one venture capital firm was an investor with a large international conglomerate. As the company began to grow, the conglomerate decided it wanted to buy the venture capitalist's position and a bargain was struck. No sooner had that acquisition taken place than the conglomerate decided it had to own the rest of the shares and bought them after strenuous negotiations with the entrepreneur. The entrepreneur made a lot of money. It was a happy ending, even if the entrepreneur did have to learn German.

Having a corporate partner can be dangerous if your company has enough shares scattered around to give the corporate giant the opportunity to buy those shares and squeeze you into a minority stockholder position. You should be careful about taking on a corporate partner for this reason, and everyone's intentions should be on the table before the transaction occurs. There are some very aggressive players in the corporate world.

There once was an entrepreneur who owned part of a small publicly traded company. The company needed additional cash in order to grow. The entrepreneur located a corporation that traditionally had invested in small companies. He raised the necessary cash from them by giving up 20 percent ownership of the company. He then owned 20 percent of the company and the public owned 60 percent.

However, the entrepreneur had not looked into the real motives behind the corporation's investment in his company. After one year, when everything seemed to be going well, he woke up one morning to find that his corporate partner had made a tender offer for all the shares outstanding. The price was approximately 50 percent more than market value. Not only did the corporate partner offer a 50 percent premium over market, but he offered stockbrokers a 25 cent per share for rounding up shares of the company. Needless to say, every broker in the universe was looking for stock. The entrepreneur saw the writing on the wall. He tendered his shares along with everyone else. He made a substantial profit on the investment but within three years the company had grown to three times its original size. He had missed making his fortune. Meanwhile, his corporate "barracuda" partner made millions.

If the company is public but has a thin market and if there is every intention to have an additional public offering so there will be a wider market for the company's shares, then the venture capitalist may be able to sell his or her block of stock to a large institutional investor such as an insurance company or a pension fund. These institutional investors will be interested in buying such a block at a discount from the current market prices. The institution may think long-term growth is available, and it can obtain a higher return on investment with a block of stock in your company than with a small position on a large New York Stock Exchange company. The institutional investor will probably not be interested unless the venture capitalist's position is worth more than $10 million.

NEW VENTURE CAPITAL PARTNER

In certain circumstances it is possible to find another venture capitalist to purchase the position held by your venture capital partner. Your first venture capital partner may be an equity-oriented venture capital fund that invests in early-stage investments. This partner will invest for a medium term, so that once your company reaches a certain stage, the VC fund will be delighted to exit. The new venture capital firm will be oriented to third- or fourth-round financing. This venture capital partner may loan you the money and have an option to buy a small amount of equity in your company. You can then use that money to buy out your first venture capital partner. This happens in the venture capital community quite frequently. It typically happens in the venture capital business when a venture capital group that has backed an individual becomes impatient with the entrepreneurs performance. To put a stop to such harassment, the entrepreneur will try to find a new venture capitalist to take the other one's place.

FIFTH METHOD: LIQUIDATION OF THE COMPANY

More venture capitalists than you would imagine have made their exit by this method. If the business performs poorly, it may be easier to liquidate the company and sell off the valuable assets than to find a buyer for the company. Some companies that grow to a certain stage are worth more dead (liquidated) than alive. That is, the land, building, machinery, equipment, and other assets are worth more in liquidation than they are as a going business. A good example of this situation has been drug wholesalers. For some years these wholesalers were quite profitable and built up a large book value, but, as wholesaling became more competitive, their profits dropped. Several conglomerates began to buy up drug wholesalers; however, they were paying only 50 percent of book value because the earnings were so poor that the book value did not represent true value for the company. As a result, some drug wholesalers sold off the inventories and customer's lists of their businesses to the conglomerate. Then they liquidated the land, building, machinery, equipment, and other assets. All of these in liquidation were worth more than the company by itself as an operating entity.

In the venture capital business, liquidation usually comes about because default provisions in the loan agreement have been violated. This makes all the funds due and payable immediately. Of course, this action puts an intolerable cash demand on the company and usually forces it into liquidation. In a forced liquidation, all assets are worth much less than their value on the balance sheet. Accounts receivable and inventory may be sold in liquidation for 50 percent of their cost. Machinery, equipment, furniture, and fixtures may be sold for 20 to 30 cents on the dollar. Obviously the best way to sell assets is not simply through liquidation but through orderly liquidation.

Liquidation can also be accomplished at a high price when the company requires a large amount of cash in order to generate income from the assets. As an example, think about oil and gas drilling. It takes a large amount of money to purchase mineral rights and to drill several sample wells. The investor hopes one will strike oil or gas. But it takes an inordinately large amount of money to drill many wells over a large acreage of mineral rights. As a result, many independents sell these partly proven mineral rights to large companies in order to avoid having to raise large amounts of cash for drilling.

NEGOTIATING WITH THE VENTURE CAPITALIST

Negotiating to purchase the venture capitalist's shares (option two) or have the VC sell the shares to someone else (option four) will remind the entrepreneur of the day the entrepreneur tried to persuade the venture capitalist to invest money into a new company. Now you are on the other side of the argument. You are trying to tell the venture capitalist that the VC fund's investment in your company has reached a peak. It is time for the VC fund to sell. It would be wise that you not downgrade your own company just to get the VC to sell. The best strategy is to tell the venture capitalist that it is a good time to sell, that it is a reasonable price, but do not downgrade your company. Remember, if you downgrade your company, and the purchase of the VC position does not go through and then your company continues to progress, you will have impaired your credibility with the venture capitalist.

OBJECTIVE

Your objective during this period is to find a way to rid yourself of the venture capital fund. You should be reminded that it is possible to end up with an investor who is worse than a venture capitalist. Helping the venture capital fund find an "exit" may be beneficial to you as a stockholder of the company, because it means you have larger stock ownership.

A secondary objective during this point in your life may be the liquidity of your own investment. Having a marketable security in a public company that has raised a sizable amount of equity can make you rich on paper. Putting a few dollars in your own pocket as a result of selling some of your shares in the public offering (or the sale of your company) can make you sleep well at night. If this is your objective, you will find it totally in concert with the venture capital fund's. The venture capitalist, too, would like liquidity and realization on the investment.

11 USING BROKERS

ARE FINANCIAL BROKERS OR CONSULTANTS WORTH ANYTHING? A BROKER COULD DESTROY YOUR CHANCES.

You may wish to engage a broker to find money from the venture capital community. There are many different classes of brokers in the business of raising money for small businesses. Most venture capital firms do not have a great deal of confidence in financial brokers. Of the thousands of people who call themselves financial brokers, only a few are competent. At the top of the financial brokerage list is the corporate finance department of major banks and stockbrokerage houses. Second are those at smaller stockbrokerage firms. These people call themselves investment bankers. After you go through that list, it's difficult to find more than a few competent financial brokers. The world is filled with people who say they can raise money for you. Be very wary.

There are very few financial brokers in the United States who understand venture capital financing. Of the thousands of people who call themselves financial brokers most are merely packagers of paper, meaning that they will help you assemble some of the information about your business and send it off to a venture capital firm. These packages have no similarity to the business proposal discussed in this book. They usually consist of copies of some of your existing documents put together in a haphazard way. The broker usually looks up the venture capital company in a guidebook on venture capital or on the Internet. Then the broker mails the package. The inexperienced financial broker may call the venture capitalist. The telephone conversation usually proceeds as follows:

Broker: Hello, Mr. A.V. Capitalist. My name is Barney Broker. I am a financial broker and I have a number of clients who are in need of venture capital financing. I would like to send you a package on these good investments, but before I send over these packages, I would like to talk to you to see if you have an interest in them.

Venture capitalist: All right. Why don't you tell me about the business?

Broker: I have a company that's in chemical solvents and it does a great job of making solvents in New Jersey. They have a nice operation and they are growing like topsey.

Venture capitalist: What are the gross sales on the company today?

Broker: Just a minute, let me look that up. [Shuffling of papers heard in the background.] Here it is. Last year they had gross sales of $800,000 and it looks like they had about $700,000 the year before and they are projecting $20.3 million this year.

Venture capitalist: What profits have they had?

Broker: Uh, uh [more shuffling of paper in the background], uh, it looks like they didn't make any money last year, but the year before they had a $25,000 profit. I don't know why they're not profitable this year.

Venture capitalist: About how much money do they need?

Broker: They need $5 million to finish building a new plant and buy some new machinery and equipment, and at least $2 million in working capital. If they get all that money, they can build this into a nice operation.

Venture capitalist: How much money does the owner have in the company?

Broker: I'm not sure that's in the business package, but I can find out for you. But rather than go through this business package with you, I would really like to send it to you.

Venture capitalist: Oh no. [Under his breath]. Well, that will be fine. Send it on down to me, and we will let you know in the next day or two after we receive it whether we have an interest.

As you can see from this exchange, the business broker had no idea of what he was talking about. He had a poor business proposal, in which he could not find basic information. He left a poor impression of the entrepreneur and the business proposal. After receiving one of these phone calls, the venture capitalist knows exactly what kind of business proposal will arrive at the office. It will be worthless. It will not set out any of the key elements covered in our summary in Chapter 2, and it will not come close to providing the detailed information required in a business proposal, as discussed in Chapter 3. The broker in these cases will receive what is known in the venture capital business as a "standard no" letter. Most standard no letters are as follows:

Mr. Barney Broker
Brokers Plus Unlimited Money, Inc.
123 Fifth Avenue
New York, NY 12345

Re: Chemical Solvent Plant

Dear Mr. Broker:

I have discussed your proposal with my associates, and at this time we do not wish to make an investment in the chemical solvent plant. We appreciate your considering our company for this investment.

Sincerely,

A. Venture Capitalist

If you do not wish to receive a standard no letter, you should complete most of the work yourself or hire a competent professional to help you. Some financial brokers are excellent assistants to entrepreneurs. Some brokers can help you prepare a good business proposal, but you need to know how to use their services in your quest for financing. Let's look at some of the professionals you may wish to engage to help you with financing.

ACCOUNTANTS: HOW TO USE THEM

Most venture capitalists have great faith in the accountants who prepare the financial portion of the business proposal. Accountants spend considerable time on the numbers to make them believable. However, accountants usually lack in-depth knowledge of your business, so they cannot prepare the remainder of the business proposal on marketing, production, and administration, as discussed in Chapter 3. The accountant can help you write those sections but cannot do it without you.

The best way to use an accountant is to have the accountant check the numbers after you have prepared the financial statements on your own. The accountant will make sure that the presentation is correct. The accountant should ask enough questions to test your assumptions. If you do not have the time, you may wish to have the accountant prepare the numbers first. Then you can review the numbers in detail with the accountant. All the assumptions should be yours, and the accountant should merely pull together the numbers or check them.

Many accounting firms do not wish to make projections for new businesses or for entrepreneurs. They believe it may lend their name to an otherwise uncreditworthy financing. The accountants believe that if you obtain financing and fail, you will tarnish their name before the venture capital firm. You may have to employ some strong arguments to convince the accounting firm to prepare your financial projections and put its name on them.

Sometimes the entrepreneur will bring the accountant to the meeting with the venture capitalist. In one such meeting, the entrepreneur was being questioned intensely by the venture capitalist about the projections. After stumbling through some of the projections for several minutes, the entrepreneur turned to the accountant and asked for some assistance. It was obvious to the venture capitalist that the accountant was responsible for completing the projections. What was more obvious was that the entrepreneur had no idea of the meaning of the projections. If you want to display your ignorance about the projections, do it alone with your accountant in the accountant's office. Once you have become fully knowledgeable about the projections, then go to the meeting with the venture capitalist without your accountant.

INVESTMENT BANKERS: WHAT THEY CAN DO

Perhaps the people who can help you with your business proposal best are the investment bankers of stockbrokerage firms and large banks. Most of them have seen many private placements and understand what goes into a business proposal. They usually know many sources of financing and can help you with many of the written items in the business proposal, although they may be weak on the numerical aspects of the proposal. They can give you informed guidance in selecting a financial source. It is appropriate to ask the investment banker to attend the meeting with the venture capitalist. Most brokers, and especially investment bankers, will insist on going with you. They believe they should be in the meeting to help you as much as possible. Sometimes an investment banker can be a bit overbearing. When the venture capitalist asks the entrepreneur a question, the VC expects the entrepreneur to answer. All too often the investment banker will answer. It is all right for the investment banker to contribute to the conversation, but the investment banker should not be the main individual answering the questions. After all, the VC wants to hear you.

As a small businessperson you may receive more service from the small independent brokerage houses than you will from the large brokerage firms. In fact, it is difficult to get the investment bankers of the large brokerage houses to work on a company that is raising less than $25 million. Large brokerage houses are geared to large capital raises, just as the stockbrokers are looking for large underwritings, and your financing will be too small. Small regional brokers are usually more knowledgeable about financing businesses through the financial sources in that region and will take on smaller transactions. So if you have a small amount of money to raise, the local investment banker may be the one you need to see. The fees charged by investment bankers are high.

LAWYERS: ARE THEY O.K. AS FINANCIAL BROKERS?

Generally speaking, lawyers are not good financial brokers. A lawyer should not be consulted when you are writing your financial proposal, except to review it as a friend. If you use a lawyer to help you write your business proposal, it will be filled with legalese. It will be sanitized and devoid of any excitement. It will read like a legal document and will not help you sell your company to the venture capitalist. But it will protect you from making statements that you may later be sued on.

INDEPENDENT FINANCIAL BROKERS: WHAT DO THEY WANT?

Above all, you should be cautious about hiring independent financial brokers as advisers for your company. Some independent financial brokers are outstanding, but many are not well regarded in the venture capital business. By independent, one means not connected with an accounting firm, stockbrokerage firm, bank, or other institution. Every venture capital company and thousands of small businesses can tell you horror stories about independent financial brokers. Usually the small business has paid fees to an independent financial broker and received nothing in return, as illustrated by what seems to be the standard practice of independent financial brokers.

First, the financial broker sets up an office and orders some stationery. The broker contacts people around town, small businesses, accountants, and so on. The financial broker may run ads in the newspapers, usually in the business or financial section of the newspaper. The small business learns of the broker and calls him or her. The financial broker visits the office of the small businessperson. The broker does not want to meet in his or her meager office for fear of giving a poor impression. The broker discusses all the sources of financing that he or she knows. The broker boasts that he or she can obtain financing for the small business. Somewhere along the way the small businessperson asks, "Well, how do we get started?" This will be the invitation for the scam.

The financial broker will indicate that he or she needs to spend time studying your business. The broker needs to pull together a financial plan and must talk to a number of financial sources before he will be able to find financing for your company. In order to complete this process, the broker needs some money. The customary fee will be 2 percent of the amount you are seeking. It may be as low as 1 percent, but the broker will ask for it as an up-front fee. In most cases where an upfront fee is paid to an independent financial broker, the small businessperson receives nothing in return. Once the small businessperson has passed along the money, the businessperson is in a precarious position. The broker now has the money. The broker is a one-person, one-office operation and can disappear overnight. The broker may or may not have financial contacts in the community. Usually the broker will send out a few "packages" and seek "standard no" letters so it can be proven that the broker has worked on behalf of the small business.

Many thousands and perhaps millions of small businesses have lost money in the form of an up-front fee to financial brokers. The U.S. government, through the Small Business Administration, has attempted to curtail the activities of financial brokers. Many local authorities have attempted to shut down these brokerage businesses. In many states, financial and business brokers are licensed by the state. Be sure you understand your financial broker and the broker's motives. Don't become a victim of this scam.

QUALITIES TO LOOK FOR IN A BROKER

As in any business arrangement, you should look into the background of the person you are hiring. After all, this person will be working for you and representing your company, and this "new" employee will be given some of your money somewhere along the way. The financial broker you hire should have the following qualities.

EXPERIENCE

Extensive experience in helping finance small businesses is a must. Without such a background, the broker will not understand the problems that small businesses have in seeking finances, nor will the broker understand the sources of funds that usually finance small businesses.

PROFESSIONAL

Your business broker should be a true professional—that is, one who is knowledgeable about your company and about his or her own business of financing your company. The broker should be a full-time professional. There are many part-time financial brokers, but it is unlikely that a part-time assistant such as a lawyer or an accountant will be able to systematically help you locate venture capital financing.

CREDENTIALS

The broker should have a strong financial background. A degree from a recognized business school, either graduate or undergraduate, is a plus. Any experience as an investment banker for a brokerage firm is definitely a plus. Experience as a financial officer in a lending institution is also a plus. If the broker has in the past been responsible for buying into small businesses or lending to small businesses, then the broker will understand what the loan officer and venture capitalist are looking for.

OPERATOR OF A SMALL BUSINESS

An individual who has operated a small business successfully can be of help. If, during that period, the broker has raised money for the small business that the broker operated, that is a plus. Generally speaking, however, people who have operated a small business will not understand all the sources for financing a company can tap unless their company was a heavy capital user. As a result, a past history of operating a business may not necessarily be helpful in the venture capital area. A small business owner who has cashed in and whose business was backed by a VC can be very helpful.

SPECIAL KNOWLEDGE

If your company is oriented toward high technology, you may be better off with someone who has a technological background, an engineering degree, or experience in a high-technology company. Capital sources that finance high-tech ventures are a specialty. An individual with a high-tech background may have helped finance other high-tech companies and may be of more help to you. A VC fund that invests only in high technology will have fund managers that have strong knowledge about high technology and will respect the knowledge of someone with a technology background.

The more your broker fits the qualities listed in the preceding sections, the more the broker will be able to help you with your business plan, guide you to the right VC fund, and help you get the funding you need.

AGREEMENT WITH THE BROKER

You should enter into a formal written agreement with the broker. To rely on an oral agreement where services for a fee is involved is to court disaster. Too often an oral arrangement will be contested in court. The arrangement between you and the financial broker should contain all of the elements of a contract. The basic items of that contract are now discussed in turn.

DEFINE THE SERVICE

In this section of the legal agreement you should spell out in detail the service to be performed by the broker. Establish what is expected of you in the way of financial information, data on your business, and so on. You should also clearly state the objective of this arrangement, such as to obtain $5 million of venture capital financing.

TIME FRAME

Every legal document should specify the date on which the relationship terminates. You and your broker should specify the final date for the agreement and, further, you should specify intermediate dates by which certain milestones are to be completed. If you or the broker do not meet these intermediate dates, the contract can be canceled by either party. You will be in a position to call the broker and ask what progress has been made. If none has been made, terminate your agreement with a letter to the broker stating that you are terminating it because specified progress has not been made. Also ask for a refund of any advanced fees. You are free to go to another broker.

TERMINATION CLAUSE

Your agreement should provide for a termination subject to written notices from one party to the other party. This clause will state how, and for what reasons, the agreement can be terminated.

AMOUNT OF THE FEE

State the amount of the fee in detail. It can be a flat fee that covers all out-of-pocket expenses, or it may be a fee plus out-of-pocket expenses. If you are agreeing to the latter, make sure you have in writing an estimate of the out-of-pocket fees.

Be sure to insist that the broker obtains your approval on any out-of-pocket expenses in excess of, say, $150 a week.

REPORTS ON PROGRESS

The agreement should state whether any progress reports are to be produced by the broker. Normally, the broker should report to you orally at least once every week and should give you a written report of the work completed frequently. With e-mail, we are all able to receive progress reports easily.

OWNERSHIP OF WORK COMPLETED

Any work completed by the broker—such as charts or work on the business proposal—should be owned by your company. You have paid for it; therefore, you should own it. If you do not have this clause in your agreement, any work completed by the financial broker may belong to the broker. If you should terminate this agreement for just cause, the broker may keep everything. This will force you to duplicate a great deal of work.

NONDISCLOSURE CLAUSE

There should be another clause in your agreement specifying that the broker will not disclose any of the information in your business proposal, or other information divulged during this process, to any other persons without your prior written consent. This will prevent the broker, under any circumstances, from passing along information to your competitor. For example, if you disagree with the broker over the fee, the broker may try to make some extra money by selling your idea to a competitor. You need to protect your company with this clause.

INDEMNIFICATION

The broker should indemnify you in the agreement against any misrepresentations or wrongful doings that the broker may perform while the broker is in your service. The broker should also indemnify you against violations of federal and state securities laws. If the broker does not indemnify you for actions the broker has taken, the broker could conceivably misrepresent your situation to someone, and that person could sue you because of the misrepresentation. After all, the broker is your paid representative.

COMPLETE AGREEMENT

The agreement should state that this is the only agreement that the parties have entered into, and that any oral understandings are null and void. This written agreement should supersede any previous agreements, and all future modifications should be in writing. Once you have a full, written understanding of the relationship between you and the broker, you will be in a better position to use the broker's services.

SOME TIPS ON DEALING WITH BROKERS

The soundest advice anyone can ever give you is to urge you to check out the broker. Obtain references from the broker and determine whether the broker is legitimate. Call any companies that the broker claims to have helped raise money. Call the presidents of those companies and ask about the broker. Also ask the broker for some names of companies that the broker was unable to help. Contact the presidents of those companies, and ask them why the broker did not succeed. Any information you can develop about this individual will be useful in helping you to decide whether to hire the firm.

Do not believe any broker who tells you he or she can "guarantee" to raise money for you. No agent or intermediary can guarantee funds for your company. Anyone who gives you a guarantee is trying to impress you; that person's influence is being overstated.

AMOUNT AND TYPE OF FEES

If possible, you should not pay any significant cash up front to any financial broker. It may be unrealistic to hold to this idea, however; brokers have to eat, too. The best arrangement is to pay the broker on the basis of performance once you have your money. If you must pay a fee, make a small down payment, and pay the remainder when you are funded.

You can purchase various types of services from a financial broker. First, you may ask the broker to help you with your business proposal. The broker may charge you an hourly rate of $150 to $350 to supervise the assembling of a good business proposal. If the broker writes the business proposal using information presented by you, a one-time fee of $10,000 to $50,000 may be fair. Second, you may hire a financial broker to contact and work with the sources of financing. If the broker merely introduces you to a financial source, the customary fee is 1 to 2 percent of the amount you raise from the source. If the broker actually tries to sell your proposal to the venture capitalist, the fee is higher. If the broker makes the rounds to help you sell it, the formula has to be considerably higher, perhaps 3 to 6 percent. The fee is usually a percentage of the loan, and it can be as high as 10 percent.

The standard percentage of the loan or financing that is paid to the broker usually depends on the amount raised. The standard formula in the financial community for years was "five-four-three-two-one." This means that the broker gets 5 percent of the first million that is raised, 4 percent of the second million, and so on. Smaller financings of $500,000, $800,000 or $1 million, may cost more than 5 percent. However, anything greater than 8 percent is probably too much. As mentioned, some fees are as high as 10 percent of the amount being raised. Fees of this size will make the venture capitalist uneasy, since 10 percent of everything the VC invests will go to a broker.

Sometimes the fee is partly in cash and partly in an option to buy stock. That is, the broker might receive 4 percent of the venture capital investment in a cash fee and an option to buy 2 percent of the stock of your company. This mixed fee is customary for new and untried companies that need every dollar of cash to make their company go. The best advice you can follow in this area is to negotiate no up-front fee, or a very small up-front fee, and then pay the broker a fair and equitable amount when the investment is made in your company. You should not pay the broker when the commitment is made, but only when the loan finally closes. Many deals fall apart between commitment and closing, and you should not pay a fee if that should happen.

Some brokers promise to raise a large amount of money on very attractive terms. For example, one broker might say he or she can raise $1 million in equity for your company for 10 percent ownership. This will sound extremely good to you, but it may be quite unrealistic. What may happen is that you will raise $1 million, but it will be in the form of a high-interest debt that forces you to give up 45 percent equity in your company. You still must pay the broker the percentage fee of the amount raised. Any broker who claims to be able to raise large amounts of money and give up a very small amount of ownership in the company should have the brokerage fee based on delivery of the deal promised. Your agreement should provide that you will pay the broker much less if you have to accept a deal that is not comparable to the one the broker has promised. By defining the terms of your contract in this manner, you can be sure the broker will give you a more realistic appraisal of what is possible.

You do not necessarily have to accept the first financial broker you meet. There are many of them around. You may want to talk to several before you select the one you think is best. After you have selected one and signed your contract, work closely with that broker alone to give the broker a chance to finance your company. Do not expect financing overnight.

WHO SHOULD PRESENT THE PLAN TO THE VENTURE CAPITALIST?

No broker is prepared to sell your deal to the venture capital company the way that you can. Brokers should be used to advise you, but you should do the selling. After all, the venture capital company is not investing in a financial broker; it is investing in you. The most that the financial broker can do for you is to give you an introduction to the venture capitalist. Some skilled brokers can help move the negotiations along during an impasse. The venture capitalist knows that the broker works for you and will treat the broker accordingly.

As mentioned previously, sometimes an entrepreneur will deliver a business proposal containing financial projections that were completed by a broker or an accounting firm. When questioned about the projections, the entrepreneur will behave as though the entrepreneur is not familiar with the numbers. This problem commonly arises when the entrepreneur asks the broker or the accountant to make projections from certain sets of assumptions, but then the entrepreneur doesn't take the time to review the statements to make sure the entrepreneur understands them. You should understand the projections thoroughly—even better than the broker or accountant who put the numbers together for you.

A similar problem can arise when a financial broker, or more likely the investment banking department of a large brokerage house, completes the business proposal for you. Unless you understand every word in the business proposal, you will not be able to answer questions from the venture capitalist. When the venture capitalist begins to ask the really difficult questions, the VC will be impressed only if you know what you are talking about.

OBJECTIVE

Your objective in using financial brokers is to obtain leads to financial sources that you cannot develop yourself. You must check out any financial broker before you pay any amount of money. Be aware that most venture capitalists think that independent financial brokers add no value. Your objective in using accountants is to let them help you complete the numbers in the financial section of the proposal. The investment banking department of a large brokerage house can help you prepare the business proposal and help you find capital sources. Remember, all of the people can only lend a hand in completing the task. They cannot remove the hard work involved in preparing a business proposal and seeking venture capital financing.

12 ADVICE FROM US TO YOU

IS IT WORTH ALL THIS?
HOW TO WIN.

Before you contact a venture capital firm, ask yourself the simple question, "Is it worth going into this business situation?" Many times when the venture capitalist is talking with an entrepreneur who wants business funding, the VC asks a simple question: "Why in the world does a smart person like you want to take the chances that you are about to take?" The VC might add, "Is it worth it?" In your mind, the answer is "Sure!" But think again.

You have probably heard a number of success stories about small business owners. They are very inspiring. They motivate us to want to do the same. Some entrepreneurs have made millions and even billions by starting or growing a small business. But you should remember that thousands of people just like you have failed. The odds are stacked against you. Four out of five small businesses fail in the first five years of their existence. The opportunities for failure in a small business seem to be infinite in number. The basic question for any entrepreneur is, "Are you ready to go through hell; and are you ready to undertake the tremendous amount of stress that will be involved in running a small business?" Every entrepreneur should engage in a moment of soul searching before embarking on the road that is set out in the business proposal. There are very good jobs in larger companies that pay well and have much less stress and demand much less of one's personal time than occurs in building a small business. You need to make sure you are doing what you want to do. Is the risk that you are taking worth the upside return? Once you have completed this soul-searching exercise and determined that this is the right course for you, you can charge ahead.

KEEPING UP WITH VENTURE CAPITALISTS

In order to keep up with the venture capitalists in your area, or anywhere in the United States, you should write to them and ask them to place your name on their mailing lists. Go to their Web sites and sign up for their notification lists. If they are public, ask for an annual report. Other venture capital firms that are in your area will also be delighted to send you their brochures and information about the types of investments they make. Study the venture capital industry so that you will understand it better.

Seeking information about venture capital firms can be compared to studying any new industry. If you were going to invest in the VC industry, you would look at many of the companies and study what they do. You should do the same when searching for a venture capitalist. Study the field as much as possible in order to become knowledgeable about the type of business each venture capitalist firm is interested in and its method of operation. Go to the venture fairs that are held in your area. Go to conferences that are held to join VC firms with small businesses. In every large city there are a wealth of organizations that try to get entrepreneurs together; go to these and discuss venture capital funds with the others at the meeting. This preparation will help you when you begin your effort to raise venture capital.

SELECTING A VENTURE FIRM

In selecting a venture firm, you should investigate its business ethics. If the firm's operations seem to be shady in any way, you should not deal with it. Remember that if you deal with crooks, you will be the victim. Do not think you can outsmart them. Crooks know too many ways to hurt you. Life is too short to deal with crooks.

You should also be careful when you are dealing with rich individuals who have become venture capitalists. A rich venture capitalist is not averse to risk. The rich folks can shoot craps with hundreds of thousands of dollars without missing it. Although this attitude may help you in raising your money, it will not help you get out of trouble, as the rich person can walk away from your situation and not miss the cash. A rich person has no one to report to. The rich do not have partners or stockholders. They get a tax break when they have losses. When possible, take venture capital financing from a professional venture fund. If you have a choice, do not use rich people's money.

This is not to say that there are not a lot of angel investors in the market for investments that do not make good partners. Some angel investors are tops. They have a professional approach to investing and can bring in friends and small institutions all interested in helping you. Going to some of the angel investment groups in your town can be a beneficial experience. It will teach you a lot, and it will put you in touch with some very good people. But at the end of the day, you will be much better off if you raise your money from a VC fund that has as its only motive to grow your business and make money. Too many rich investors have mercurial personalities that get in the way of growing a business.

The best relationship between the venture capitalist and the entrepreneur is one of equals. The entrepreneur should be on equal footing with the venture capital partner. If the venture capitalist is running the small business, it is probably doomed to failure. If in operating the business the entrepreneur is inconsiderate of the investment made by the venture capitalist, a struggle will inevitably arise and hurt the business.

VENTURE CAPITAL PROCESS

Remember that the process of raising venture capital and the relationship with the venture capital company will be a long, drawn-out one. If you expect a quick fix from the venture capitalist, you may be in for a rude surprise. Some venture capitalists work quickly, but they are few and far between. Most are interested in completing a full-blown, due diligence report to make sure they have found the right investment. After all, they invest for the long term. Be aware that the venture capitalist needs a long review period. Understand that few venture firms will be able to react in the time frame you may want. The diagram in Figure 12.1 will help you follow the list of events that must be accomplished. We have discussed them all in this book.

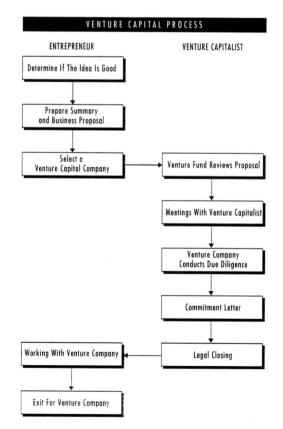

Figure 12.1   Venture Capital Process

VENTURE CAPITALISTS AS HUMAN BEINGS

This book has painted a picture of venture capitalists as wonderful people who can help grow your business with money and advise. Perhaps you have a completely different view. Venture capitalists are not saints. They are probably not as knowledgeable as this book portrays them. They are probably not as reasonable as you have been led to believe. Nor are they as professional as this book would indicate. But, in general, you will find the venture capital community a hard-working group. They will not try to cheat you, but they will try to get the best deal from you. They want to make money for their venture capital fund. Most assuredly, there are some sharpies in the group, but most are good-hearted people. They are not trying to play the game of "I-got-you," whereby they use every opportunity to take your company. They want you to succeed. They want to be your partner, and, if treated correctly, they will make good partners.

Remember that venture capitalists are just human beings. They are trying to do the best that they can. Some venture capitalists like to think of themselves as the highly paid elite, standing at the pinnacle of capitalism, and determining which new companies are created. In reality, most of them are just part of the great middle class of businesspeople who have helped make our country great. They can help make your company great too.

PROBLEM COMPANIES LOOKING FOR FINANCING

Venture capitalists see many companies with problems that are seeking financing. As mentioned before, these are called turnarounds. Venture capitalists also see many turnarounds that are not presented as such by the entrepreneur. A company may have a significant flaw or a problem that the entrepreneur has covered up. The entrepreneur hopes that the venture capitalist will not uncover the flaw and will finance the company. The entrepreneur believes the new money will save the company. If you have a significant problem and do not tell the venture capitalist, and if the venture capitalist uncovers the problem, you have lost all chances of financing. On the other hand, if the problem is revealed, you still stand a chance of being financed, albeit less of a chance.

If you are operating a problem company, you are faced with a critical decision. Should you reveal the business problem to the venture capitalist and risk losing financing, or should you let the venture capitalist conduct his or her own investigation? If the VC does not find the business problem, maybe you will obtain the financing. You should think this one through carefully. If the venture capitalist does not find the problem and invests, the problem will surface sometime after the financing. When the problem does arise, you will lose a tremendous amount of credibility with the venture capitalist. The VC will be outraged. You will probably be sued for fraudulently inducing an investor into your company. Stock fraud carries heavy penalties.

Entrepreneurs are in jail today for stock fraud. I know some VCs who were delighted when an entrepreneur they backed was sent to jail.

Financing for Your Job or Your Ego

Sometimes an entrepreneur will dream up an idea in order to create a job for the entrepreneur. Inventors will push an idea on a venture capitalist in the hopes that the venture capitalist will put enough money into the company to guarantee the inventor a job over the next year or two. The inventor's reasoning is, "At least I will have a paycheck for eighteen months." Such an entrepreneur is unethical. The entrepreneur's motivation for financing an idea is not to build a big company that will go public someday, but merely to use it as a vehicle to receive a paycheck for the next eighteen months. If you are caught trying to sell this type of idea, you deserve no respect whatsoever.

There is another type of entrepreneur who wants the venture capitalist to bankroll an acquisition of a company or a new idea in order to feed the entrepreneur's ego. The entrepreneur wants to be president of a great new company that is doing wonderful things. Acquiring the next company and building a large organization is the goal rather than making money. Profitability is second to rolling up lots of acquisitions or pouring money into a losing situation that will never turn a profit. The entrepreneur in this case may give the venture capitalist erroneous information in order to induce the VC fund to back this "great" new company. The entrepreneur's motivation is one of ego enhancement rather than of making money.

Both of these examples show a divergence of interest between the entrepreneur and the venture capitalist that will create trouble. In one case, the entrepreneur wants a job and is merely looking for a way to finance it. In the other, the entrepreneur has a "big shot" complex and wants somebody to finance his or her ego trip. As you know from reading this book, the venture capitalist is interested in long-term capital appreciation. The VC's interests do not coincide with those of the entrepreneurs described above. You can expect any venture capitalist to turn down your deal the minute the VC determines that his or her goals do not match yours.

TOO MUCH INFORMATION

Some entrepreneurs believe they should avoid giving the venture capital investor too much information. They believe too much information will confuse the venture capitalist and cause the VC to ask too many questions. Such an entrepreneur rationalizes that he or she knows the business will be successful, so the entrepreneur will protect the venture capitalist from wasting time or being concerned with negative information about the company or the industry.

As an example, there was an entrepreneur who had invented a computer product. He had raised venture capital financing to manufacture the product. Soon after he began the manufacturing process, he found a problem that could not be corrected. He decided not to tell the venture capitalist. He delayed meeting with the investors, and when the meeting finally occurred, the entrepreneur indicated that some problems existed with the product but that he believed they would all be worked out. All the while, he worked feverishly to find a substitute product. Finally, after three months, he had a new product and it worked. He told the venture capitalist the entire story. The venture capitalist was furious. Credibility was reduced to zero. The venture capitalist felt he could not trust the entrepreneur. After all, what other information was being withheld? Their relationship was never the same again.

DO YOU UNDERSTAND CREDIBILITY?

If you did not get the message from previous sections of this book, let me repeat it: credibility is the only firm basis on which the entrepreneur and the venture capitalist build a relationship. This relationship will be a close one for many years. If you enter it thinking that you will outsmart the venture capitalist by being dishonest, you are in for a rocky ride. Conversely, if you determine that the venture capitalist is entering the deal with ulterior motives, you should not take the financing. No venture capitalist-entrepreneur relationship can be successful unless there is trust between the two.

TEN COMMANDMENTS FOR AN ENTREPRENEUR

You should follow certain commandments in your quest for venture capital and during your working relationship with the venture capitalist. The Bible, of course, has ten commandments. In order to be successful as an entrepreneur, you need to follow ten also.

THOU SHALT BE TRUTHFUL TO THYSELF

One of the hardest things for entrepreneurs to overcome is their belief in their own promotional material. It is usual for an entrepreneur to promote the ideas or business as strongly as possible. Gasconade is expected by everyone. After all, if the entrepreneur does not promote it, who will? However, after you have stripped away all the promotional items, ask yourself if the basic business is a good opportunity. The ultimate question for the entrepreneur is "Do you really believe in the business you are undertaking?" Some entrepreneurs want to go into business for themselves so badly that they are blind to the bad points of the business. If you are not entirely confident about the situation you are putting together, you should rethink your decision.

To make sure you are not eagerly accepting your own promotional information, you should go through the deal in detail, listing all the good points and all the horrible things you can think of. Now throw out all the promotional points and leave only the solid business reasons. Is it still a good deal? Try the idea out with friends who will tell you the truth. Try to make sure that you are not just doing this to be in business for yourself, and that there is a very strong upside to the business.

In your heart you may think it would be a crime for you to miss such an opportunity. You may rationalize that the venture capitalist has reviewed and approved the investment. If the VC thinks it is a good deal, it must be good. Be realistic. A venture capitalist knows much less about the business than you do. The VC has made many mistakes. You should understand clearly that if you put together a deal that fails, it will be a disastrous experience for you. In being truthful to yourself, you will avoid making a mistake by not going into a poor deal. Even though you might be able to raise the money for the deal, it may not be the right deal. If you have any misgivings about a deal, you should discuss them with your venture capital partner to make sure you are both going forward with your eyes open. The VC may even have a solution for the problems that bother you.

There is the story of an entrepreneur who, during the last recession, had been analyzing and working with a small metal fabricator. By the middle of the recession he had negotiated a purchase price for the business on the basis of the financial statements for the prior year ending December 31. The price seemed fair, according to the company's status as of December 31. When the entrepreneur received the financial statements for the first six months, he saw that the figures had dropped significantly. In discussing this point with the venture capitalist, the entrepreneur made every possible excuse for the reduced earnings, which clearly showed that the company could not carry the amount of debt service needed to purchase it. Unless the earnings picked up quickly, the company would be in trouble shortly after the acquisition. The entrepreneur saw the venture capitalist becoming uneasy. He prepared a long analysis of the situation to convince the venture capitalist to go through with the deal. The venture capitalist did not invest. He was convinced the reduced earnings signaled a drastic slowdown.

Others did invest. The company was a poor performer and did not make any money for years. It was a living hell for the entrepreneur who wasted years of his life trying to make a bad deal come back to life. He could have skipped that deal and found a better one in a year or so and lived a happy life. In this situation, the entrepreneur was willing to overlook the obvious because he was so driven to be in business for himself. He believed his own poor analysis. As a result, he promoted himself into a very poor business situation. You should not make the same mistake.

THOU SHALT RECOGNIZE REALITY

A basic theory about reality is that reality is real! Know reality, or you will lose. Consider the story of the entrepreneur who came upon a business to buy. She began to study the industry. As she studied the industry, she saw that the basic economics of the industry were changing because of increased gasoline prices and increased interest rates. She could find no evidence that interest rates or the price of energy would return to previous levels. High gas prices and interest rates foreshadowed a sure reorganization of the industry in the form of reduced sales. The entrepreneur was unwilling to recognize reality, and instead she stormed ahead.

With venture capital money she purchased the business. Subsequently, industry sales dropped off sharply. The entrepreneur went through hell on earth. She couldn't make enough money to pay off the debt she assumed when she purchased the business. The venture capitalist was unhappy because this was turning out to be a poor investment.

Unless you are willing to recognize the facts as they exist, you are doomed to failure. Do not let emotions interfere with sound business judgments. Seeing reality and disregarding it can only lead to disaster.

THOU SHALT MAINTAIN CREDIBILITY

There is more to credibility than just being honest. Honesty is not telling lies. Credibility also means trying to do what you believe is right. You must maintain credibility with your venture capital partner, with banks, with suppliers, with employees, and with all the other people who depend on you. If they find that you changed the meaning of your statements and you act like a Grade B lawyer trying to win a minor case in a small claims court, you will not fare well as an entrepreneur. When you give someone a set of projections and later are unable to achieve the projections, your credibility will suffer if you merely say, "Well, they were only projections and everybody knows projections are only a guess." When you say you are going to do something, projections or whatever, you must somehow, some way, make it happen. This is the only way to maintain your credibility with the venture capitalist and with all the other people who depend on you.

THOU SHALT BE LOYAL TO THOSE WHO HAVE HELPED YOU

Loyalty is another form of honesty. It means that you stick by your commitments. It means you are fair in your dealings with your venture capital partner, your employees, and all the others along the way who have helped your business. If somebody does you a favor, try to return the favor. This will build your business reputation. If you ask someone to help you, accept that help, and then later turn on that person, you will let the world know that you are disloyal to those who help you.

You may make a few extra dollars in the short run by being disloyal, but in the longer term you must be loyal if you want to achieve greater results. Loyalty will carry you far in the business world. No business is built on one person's ability. It takes many people to build a business. You must be loyal to all the people upon whose shoulders you stand in order to reach the heights that you want to attain in your business.

THOU SHALT BE PREPARED

Knowledge is power. Knowledge of your industry, of your own abilities, of your business, and of your venture capitalist's needs must be assembled in order to make a business venture successful. Always be prepared for any outcome. Think through all decisions so that you know the consequences. Be prepared for any reaction by competition. Be prepared for the transfer of a favorite loan officer at your bank. Be prepared for disasters such as fires or other catastrophes. Think about all the things that could destroy your chances of making this a successful business and be prepared for every one of them. Be prepared for your untimely death. Write a corporate "will" to ensure that everyone knows what you think should be done.

THOU SHALT BE POSITIVE

The general mental attitude of an entrepreneur must be positive. Otherwise, the entrepreneur will not be able to jump all the hurdles that stand in the way of success in the entrepreneurial world. You must always be selling the merits of your company, the merits of your people, and the merits of your products. A positive attitude is one of the outstanding qualities of a good entrepreneur. If you are positive, the people who follow you will be positive in all they do, even in solving problems. Self-confidence and a positive attitude generate respect from others. You must be self-confident but not egocentric. Positive thinking means determining how to get the job done. Do not spend time blaming others. Determine what needs to be accomplished, and adopt a positive mental attitude to achieving goals.

THOU SHALT NEVER GIVE UP

Never giving up is not the same as being stubborn. Never giving up means being an achiever and having a strong desire to win. You must have strong motivation to achieve the goals that you have set out. You need physical and mental energy to accomplish the tasks that have been set out. Without a tremendous amount of physical and mental energy, you simply cannot accomplish all the things in your business plans. Your drive, your ambition, and your desire to succeed are embodied in the phrase, "You shall never give up."

THOU SHALT BE STRAIGHT

This book has been a strong proponent of honesty and it has mentioned some situations in which entrepreneurs have not been honest. But it has not delved into the illegal activities of entrepreneurs. In a few publicized cases entrepreneurs have been involved with organized crime. In some other celebrated cases entrepreneurs have used illegal means to make their company grow faster. A few entrepreneurs have turned to crime in order to save their company. From the standpoint of risk and reward, crime does not pay. The rewards of saving your company or making your company grow faster are not worth the downside risk of a term in prison and a destroyed business life. It is better to be a straight entrepreneur.

THOU SHALT BE LUCKY

When entrepreneurs are asked to account for their success as entrepreneurs, they invariably point to luck. They believe that luck as much as anything else has brought them to where they are. However, when one begins to analyze their careers more closely, the truth of Thomas Edison's statement about creativity comes shining through. Edison believed that creativity was 10 percent inspiration and 90 percent perspiration. It's the same for lucky entrepreneurs. Look at the track record of a successful entrepreneur, and you will certainly find lucky breaks, but they seem to come when the entrepreneur is exerting a tremendous amount of energy in order to succeed. Being successful is 10 percent luck and 90 percent hard work. In other words, the entrepreneur constantly seeks success. The entrepreneur is doing whatever is necessary in order to achieve. Only in those instances where overwhelming odds have destroyed all chances, do you find an entrepreneur who is an achiever, but who is not "lucky."

THOU SHALT PRAY A LOT

We (the authors of this book) have been dealing with entrepreneurs for many years. Some of them are religious and some are not so religious, but all of them have one thing in common; they pray a lot. In their prayers they ask that things turn out all right. They want to get that one critical sale that they need. They pray that the new machine that they purchased will work as it is supposed to. They give thanks that their employees are healthy and happy. While most of their prayers seem to be more material than spiritual, nonetheless they pray a lot. Further, we can tell you from first hand experience that prayer is not limited to entrepreneurs. Venture capitalists pray plenty.

PARTING SHOT

We have never been entrepreneurs in the traditional sense. We have met thousands of entrepreneurs and have backed hundreds of them in many different types of enterprises. This book should give you much of the knowledge you need to deal with the venture capitalist. If you will follow every item covered by this book, we assure you it will bring you good luck.

GLOSSARY

The Words

What Terms Should You Know?

Here Are a Few.

This glossary contains some of the more colorful terms used by venture capitalists. It does not include a large number of standard accounting or business terms that you should know. If you find that you do not recognize some of the terms in this book and they are not covered in the glossary, you should refer to a standard business text or your accounting book in order to find definitions of the words being used.

Arm's length: Refers to business transactions where neither the buyer nor the seller has the ability to dictate the terms and each has every incentive to get the best deal for themselves. In a non–arm's length transaction you might sell a family member some assets of the business at a low price to move assets out of the business.

Board: Meaning board of directors of a corporation. These are the individuals who control a corporation for the benefit of the stockholders. They listen to management's recommendations and set policy for the corporation.

Boilerplate: Boilerplate paragraphs are the standard paragraphs in most venture capital and investment documents.

Bona fide: With good faith; without fraud or deception, genuine.

Bricks and mortar: The assets of your company. The term is derived from a building that is built of bricks and mortar.

Buy-Sell: A buy-sell agreement is one in which, under certain circumstances, the first party in a partnership must agree to buy out the second party, or the second party must agree to buy out the first party. Buy-sell arrangements usually are negotiated between two partners such as an entrepreneur and a venture capitalist.

Buyout: The term refers to the act of selling a business; for example, when the buyer of a business buys it, he or she "buys out" the seller.

Cash flow: The most important aspect of any small business is the cash flow. The money coming in and the money going out is the flow of cash that determines whether a business will survive.

Cash in: When you sell all or part of your stock for cash. Cashing in is an extremely exciting moment because it usually means you are rich.

Closing: The event that occurs when you sign legal documents binding your company and transferring cash from the venture capitalist to your company.

Collateral: The assets you pledge for a loan made to your company. If you do not repay the loan, the collateral can be sold.

Control: Owning 51 percent of the stock of a company or, from another perspective, owning enough stock in the company to control what management will do.

Convertible: Usually refers to debt or preferred stock, each of which is convertible into common stock of the company. Obviously, it is possible to have debt convertible into preferred stock and it is even possible to have preferred stock convertible into debt, although the latter is unusual.

Covenant: Paragraphs in the legal documents stating the things you agree you will do and paragraphs stating what you will not do.

Deal: The bargain struck between the venture capitalist and the entrepreneur. In more general terms, any agreement between two individuals, especially a buyer and a seller.

Debenture: Another word for a debt, notes, or loan.

Debt service: The amount of money (principal repayment and interest) you have to pay on a debt in order to keep it from being in default. If you make the payments that are called for under a note or loan, then you are servicing the debt.

Default: When you do something you told your investor you would not do, as specified in the investment agreement, it is a default.

Downside: The amount of risk an investor takes in any venture is called the downside. If you stand to lose half your money if a business goes under, the downside risk is said to be 50 percent. Not many entrepreneurs know what this term means.

Due diligence: The process of investigating a business venture to determine whether it is worth making an investment in the business.

Earn-out: The contract between the entrepreneur and the buying corporation that provides for the entrepreneur to earn additional money on the sale of the entrepreneur's company, if operating earnings are in excess of a specified amount during the future years.

Equity: Normally it describes the preferred and common stock of a business. Also, it is frequently used to describe the amount of ownership of one person or a venture capitalist in a business.

Exit: The sale of equity or ownership in the business for cash or notes.

Good idea: A good idea is one that makes a large amount of money.

Good people: The supreme compliment to an entrepreneur by a venture capitalist. It means the entrepreneur is honest, loyal, and a straight shooter.

Grace period: The period of time you have to correct a default. See Default.

LBO: A leveraged buyout, see below.

Lead investor: The VC investor who leads a group of investors into an investment. Usually one venture capitalist will be the lead investor when a group of venture capitalists invests in a single business. See Syndication.

Leverage: Another term for debt. Debt is usually referred to as leverage because in using debt, one does not have to give up equity. So for a very small amount of equity and a large amount of debt, one can leverage a business on the basis of its assets.

Leveraged buyout: An acquisition of a business using mostly debt and a small amount of equity. The debt is secured by the assets of the business or the cash flow of the business.

Options: The right given to someone, say the venture capitalist, to buy stock in your company. See also Warrants.

Paper: The notes you receive for the sale of your stock or the assets in your company. These are called paper, because paper is fairly worthless. Many of the notes received by entrepreneurs from the sale of their company to someone else have turned into worthless paper.

PE: See Price/earnings ratio.

Pool: Usually a venture capital limited partnership in which the various investors have "pooled" their investments by purchasing a limited partnership interest in the venture capital partnership. The partnership then invests in small businesses.

Price/earnings ratio: The number you multiply times the earnings per share number in order to determine a fair price for a stock. For example, if a stock is earning $.50 a share and a price/earnings ratio of eight is used, the stock is worth $4 per share.

Pricing: The determination as to the price that an investor will pay to purchase shares of stock in the business. Pricing is determined on the basis of the full value of the company. Every time one share of stock is sold, the sale determines the value of the company and in this way, pricing occurs.

Proposal: The document that must be put together by an entrepreneur in order to propose an investment to a venture capitalist or other investors.

Public offering: The selling of shares to the general public through the registration of shares with the Securities and Exchange Commission.

Raising capital: Raising capital refers to obtaining capital from investors or venture capital sources.

Reality: What every individual should make sure the individual understands before jumping into the small business arena.

Representations: These are the facts about your company that you represent to the investor to be true.

Situation: General term used to refer to any business deal. It is common to refer to a business opportunity as a "situation."

Structure: Term referring to the type of financing that will be used to finance a small business. The structure might be $1 million in common stock and $5 million in debt at 15 percent interest for ten years.

Syndication: The process whereby a group of venture capitalists will each invest a portion of the amount of money needed to finance a small business.

Takeback: Term referring to the situation in which the seller of a business must take back something rather than cash. The takeback usually refers to a note with reasonable terms and conditions.

Turnaround: This word is used to describe a business that is in trouble and whose management will cause the business to become profitable so that it is no longer in trouble.

Underwriter: The stockbrokerage house used to raise funds for a small business in a public offering. In a public offering the stockbrokerage house that underwrites the small business is the one that buys the shares from the small business and sells them to the general public.

Unlocking agreement: A legal agreement between two parties meaning that one party may require the other to buy it out under certain circumstances—thus, the so-called unlocking of the partnership.

Upside: The amount of money that one can make by investing in a certain deal is called the upside potential. See also Downside.

Warrant: A stock option given to someone else that entitles that person to purchase stock in your company.

Warranties: These are items concerning your company that you have told the venture capitalist or investors are true.

ACTUAL DOCUMENTS

WHAT DO ACTUAL COMMITMENT LETTERS AND LEGAL DOCUMENTS LOOK LIKE? HERE THEY ARE.

The following documents are some of the basic documents used in a financing, except that they have been broadened in concept to include many of the standard "boiler plate" items used by most venture capitalists. After reading these documents, you will be well prepared for the ones you receive from the venture capitalist. All documents are for fictitious companies and people. The following documents are covered in this appendix:

1. Commitment letter for a loan with options for stock on Ace Electromagnetic, Inc.
2. Legal Document 1: Loan Agreement on Ace Electromagnetic, Inc.
3. Legal Document 2: Promissory Note on Ace Electromagnetic, Inc.

4. Legal Document 3: Stock Purchase Warrants on Ace Electromagnetic, Inc.
5. Legal Document 4: Stock Purchase on Ajax Computer Genetics Corp.
6. Legal Document 5: Exhibits to Stock Purchase on Ajax Computer Genetics Corp.

COMMITMENT LETTER

Venture Capital Fund
1 Green Street, Suite 600
Tyson's Corner, VA 22102

Mr. Joseph Entrepreneur, President
Ace Electromagnetic Incorporated
1234 Main Street
McLean, Virginia 2102

Dear Mr. Entrepreneur:

The Management of Venture Capital Fund (Venture) has approved a loan to your company (the Company) in the amount of $3,000,000. The approval was based on the following representations made by you:

1.01 The Company is a corporation in good standing in Virginia. You will provide Venture with a Certificate of Good Standing and a copy of the Charter and Bylaws and minutes of the organization of the Company.

1.02 The Company is primarily engaged in the business of manufacturing electromagnetic equipment.

1.03 There are no lawsuits against the Company, its directors, or its officers, personally, nor any you know of that may be contemplated. If there are any suits outstanding or contemplated, your attorney will provide Venture with a letter stating the nature of such suits and a copy of the suits. You will provide us with a copy of all lawsuits you have filed against others.

1.04 The Company is current on all taxes owed and, in this regard, you will provide Venture with a copy of the last three years' tax returns for the Company.

1.05 You have presented financial information showing that the Company, for the 12 month period just ending had sales of $1,850,000 and pretax loss of $25,000, assets of $6,000,000, liabilities of $3,000,000, and a net worth of $3,000,000.

1.06 The money borrowed will be used as follows: A. $1,000,000 to pay First National Bank, B. $1,000,000 to pay accounts payable, C. $1,000,000 to pay fees from this financing and working capital.

1.07 Upon completion of Venture's loan, you will have approximately the following assets:

1. Cash, $1,000,000.
2. Accounts receivable, $1,000,000.
3. Machinery and equipment, $1,000,000.
4. Land and building, $1,000,000.
5. Other assets, $3,000,000.

1.08 With regard to leases, you will provide Venture with a copy of every major executed lease.

1.09 The information presented to Venture is correct and you believe the projections presented to Venture are reasonable.

1.10 You will pay no brokerage fees, legal fees, or other fees on this loan without Venture's written approval, and you will indemnify Venture against all such fees.

1.11 During the past ten years none of the directors has been arrested or convicted of a material crime.

2. The terms and conditions of the loan shall be:

2.01 A loan of $3,000,000 for six years at 15 percent per annum, paid monthly on the first of each month.

2.02 The loan shall be interest only for the first 36 months and, beginning with the 37th month, you will pay principal and interest sufficient to amortize the loan over the remaining 36 months. All principal and interest outstanding at the end of six years shall be due and payable in full as a balloon payment.

2.03 The loan may be prepaid at any time in whole or part.

2.04 Takedown of the loan shall be $3,000,000 at closing.

2.05 Other terms standard for such loans.

2.06 In connection with this financing, Venture shall receive at closing separate options to purchase stock in the Company. Cost of the options to Venture will be $100. These options, when exercised by Venture and the other investment company, will provide stock ownership in the company of 35 percent at the time of exercise. The exercise price will be $100. The options will expire ten years from closing. Venture will share pro rata in any redemption of stock by the Company.

2.07 There shall be an "unlocking" provision whereby if there is a bona fide offer to purchase the Company and Venture wishes to accept the offer and you do not, then you shall acquire Venture's interest on the same terms or sell the Company.

2.08 There shall be a "put" provision whereby any time after five years from closing Venture may require the Company to purchase its options or the resulting stock at the higher of the following:

A. Ten percent of sales for the year just ended times a price–earnings ratio of eight less Venture's debt times 35 percent.

B. Ten times cash flow for the year just ended less Venture's debt times 35 percent.

2.09 Venture shall have full "piggyback" rights to register its shares any time the Company (or its management) is registering shares for sale and such registration of Venture's shares shall be paid for by the Company.

3. Collateral for the loan shall be:

3.01 A second deed of trust on the land and building of the business, subordinated as to collateral to a mortgage of approximately $1,000,000, on terms acceptable to Venture.

3.02 A second secured interest in all of the tangible and intangible assets of the Company including, but not limited to, inventory, machinery, equipment, furniture, fixtures, and accounts receivable subordinated to a revolving line of credit in the amount of $1,000,000.

3.03 Pledge and assignment of all the stock of the Company and assignment of leases listed above.

3.04 Personal signatures and guarantees of you and your spouse.

3.05 Obtaining a life insurance policy on your life for $3,000,000 with the policy assigned to Venture and with Venture as the loss payee to the extent of its loan.

3.06 Adequate hazard and business insurance, which shall include federal flood insurance if your business is located in a designated federal flood area. All such insurance shall be assigned to Venture, and Venture shall be listed as the loss payee to the extent of its interest. In this regard, you will supply Venture with a list of all business insurance, and such insurance and coverage shall be acceptable to Venture.

4. Conditions of the loan are:

4.01 Provide Venture with monthly year-to-date financial statements in accordance with generally accepted accounting standards (including profit and loss and balance sheet) within 45 days of the end of the month.

4.02 The president of the Company will provide Venture with a certificate each quarter stating that no default has occurred in the Loan Agreement.

4.03 If requested in writing, provide Venture with an annual certified audit within 90 days after the year's end from an accounting firm acceptable to Venture.

4.04 Before each year-end, provide Venture with projections of the next year in the same format as the financial statements.

4.05 Within 30 days after they are filed, provide Venture with a copy of all documents filed with government agencies such as the Internal Revenue Service, Federal Trade Commission, and Securities and Exchange Commission.

4.06 There will be no change in control of the Company, nor will there be a change of ownership without Venture's written approval.

4.07 Management will not sell, assign, or transfer any shares it owns in the Company without the written approval of Venture.

4.08 The Company will maintain in accordance with generally accepted accounting principles:

1. A current ratio of one to one.
2. Sales of $5,000,000 per year.
3. Sales of $300,000 per month.
4. Net worth of $500,000 or more.

4.09 The Company will have board meetings at least once each quarter at the Company's business offices. While a Venture representative will not serve on the board, a Venture representative will have the right to attend each meeting at the Company's expense, and Venture shall be notified of each meeting at least two weeks before it is to occur.

4.10 The Company will pay no cash dividends, and the Company will not sell any assets of the business that are not part of the regular course of business without Venture's approval.

4.11 The Company will not expend funds in excess of $100,000 per year for capital improvements, and the like.

4.12 You will live in the general Washington, D.C., metropolitan area.

4.13 The Company will not pay, nor loan, nor advance to any employee money which, in total, is in excess of $25,000 per year, without the written approval of Venture. If (1) the Company is in default for nonpayment to Venture or any senior lien, or (2) the Company is not profitable for any quarter, then the Company will not pay, nor loan, nor advance to any employee money which, in total, is in excess of $200,000 per year, without written permission of Venture.

4.14 The Company will not pay any brokerage fees, legal fees, or consulting fees in excess of $50,000 per year without the written permission of Venture.

4.15 Other conditions standard for such loans.

4.16 You will pay all closing costs and recording fees, which include all attorney's fees. You may use any attorney to draw the legal documents; however, they must be reviewed and approved by Venture's counsel. A simple review by Venture's counsel will not incur a fee; however, if the work done by Venture's counsel is beyond a simple review, a fee will be charged, and the fee will be paid by you.

4.17 In connection with this financing, Venture will receive a percent ($60,000) fee. Upon acceptance of this commitment letter, you will pay Venture $10,000 of this fee and the remainder at closing. Should closing not take place owing to the fault of Venture, then the fee will be returned less out-of-pocket expenses; otherwise, it is forfeited.

5. This commitment is conditioned upon the following, which, if not attained, will make Venture's commitment void:

5.01 Acceptance by you of this letter and the return of one copy to Venture fully executed by you, with the fee set out in 4.17, within 15 days.

5.02 Closing on the loan before year-end.

5.03 All legal documents being acceptable to Venture.

5.04 A favorable credit check of you and your business and no material adverse occurrences before closing.

5.05 A favorable visit by Venture to your business.

Sincerely,

A. V. Capitalist

President

VENTURE CAPITAL FUND

AGREED: ACE ELECTROMAGNETIC, INCORPORATED

By: _____ DATE: _____

Joseph Entrepreneur, President

_____ DATE: _____

Personally: Joseph Entrepreneur

LEGAL DOCUMENT 1

Ace Electromagnetic, Incorporated
McLean, Virginia

LOAN AGREEMENT

WHEREAS, Venture Capital Fund, a District of Columbia corporation (hereinafter "Venture") has committed under terms of a letter of _____(date) to lend to Ace Electromagnetic, Incorporated, a Virginia corporation (hereinafter "Company") the sum of Three Million Dollars ($3,000,000);

WHEREAS, the Company will issue VENTURE Stock Purchase Warrants (hereinafter "Warrants") for a total of 35 percent of the common stock of the Company.

NOW, THEREFORE, the Company and Venture agree as follows:

I. PARTIES

This Agreement shall bind and accrue to the benefit of the Company and its successors, the undersigned shareholders of the Company, Venture, and any subsequent holders of the Note, Warrants, or the stock issued there under (who are collectively referred to herein as "Holders"). The Note issued hereunder may be held by different persons, as may the Warrants. The terms of this Agreement as of the day the Company receives notice that a new party is holder of a Note or Warrant shall be binding between the Company and such new party, regardless of modifications that may subsequently be made between the Company and another holder.

II. LOAN

The Company will borrow and Venture will lend the sum of Three Million Dollars ($3,000,000) to be repaid according to the terms of the Promissory Note of even date herewith (hereinafter "Note").

III. Use of Proceeds

The Company will use the proceeds of the loan only to fund commercial electromagnetic operations with approximately $100,000 to repay a line of credit at the First National Bank, $100,000 to pay accounts payable, and $100,000 for fees and working capital.

IV. Collateral

The Note and the Holders' rights herein shall be secured pari passu against the collateral below, provided that future advances in addition to the original $3,000,000 advanced to the Company shall not be considered in determining the secured parties' shares from sale of collateral. In regard to the items in subparagraph, the Company grants Holders a security interest to attach when the Company has signed this instrument and acquired rights in the property, and when Venture has made whole or partial disbursement of loan funds to the Company, the Company's designated payee, or an escrow agent. Although other parties may become holders of the instruments secured hereby, all security interests of record will remain in the name of Venture Capital Fund, which will hold such interests in trust for the benefit of all Holders. The collateral shall be as follows:

1. A second mortgage on the Company's real estate in the Commonwealth of Virginia subject to a first mortgage to a financial institution according to terms of a separate instrument;

2. A second security interest in the furniture, fixtures, machinery, equipment, inventory, contract rights, licenses, and all tangible and intangible personal property of the Company subject to credit lines from financial institutions;

3. Assignment of accounts receivable, pledge of all the outstanding stock of the Company subject to bank lines of credit according to the terms of separate Agreements therefore;

4. Collateral assignment of the policy number 1234567 issued by ABC Life Insurance Company insuring the life of Joseph Entrepreneur in the amount of $3,000,000.00;

5. Personal guarantees of Mr. and Mrs. Joseph Entrepreneur according to the terms of a separate instrument.

V. Representations and Warranties

To induce Venture to enter this transaction the Company represents and warrants that

A. It is duly incorporated, validly existing, and in good standing under the laws of Virginia, having Articles of Incorporation and Bylaws (all of the terms of which are in full force and effect) as previously furnished to Venture; it is not and does not intend to become an investment company or passive investment vehicle;

B. It is duly qualified to conduct business as proposed by it and is in good standing as a foreign corporation in all states in which the nature of its business or location of its properties requires such qualification;

C. It has full power and authority to enter into this Agreement, to borrow money as contemplated hereby, to issue the Warrants and upon exercise thereof to issue the stock pursuant thereto, and to carry out the provisions hereof; and it has taken all corporate action necessary for the execution and performance of each of the above (including the issuance and sale of the Warrants, the reservation of shares of stock, and the issuance thereof upon the exercise of the Warrants); and each document above named will constitute a valid and binding obligation of the Company enforceable in accordance with its respective terms when executed and delivered;

D. The authorized capital stock of the Company is as set forth below, and all such stock has been duly issued in accordance with applicable laws, including federal and state securities laws:

E. The list of officers and directors of the Company previously submitted is complete and accurate. All representations made by the Company, its officers, directors, shareholders, or guarantors in any instrument described in this Agreement or previously supplied to Venture in regard to this financing are true and correct as of this date, and all projections provided are reasonable;

F. The Company has no debts, liabilities, or obligations of any nature whether accrued, absolute, contingent, or otherwise arising out of any transaction entered into or any state of facts existing prior hereto, including without limitation liabilities or obligations on account of taxes or government charges, penalties, interest, or fines thereon or in respect thereof except the debts to be paid off by the use of proceeds of this loan, and debts on open account; the accounts payable and the debts to be paid herewith have not changed materially since the date of the June financial statement previously submitted; the Company does not know and has no reasonable grounds to know of any basis for any claim against it as of the date of this Agreement or of any debt, liability, or obligation other than those mentioned herein;

G. The Company has not been made a party to or threatened by any suits, actions, claims, investigations by governmental bodies, or legal, administrative, or arbitrational proceedings except as set out in the Company counsel's letter (hereinafter "litigation letter"); neither the Company nor its officers nor directors know of any basis or grounds for any such suit or proceeding; there are no outstanding orders, judgments, writs, injunctions, or decrees or any court, government agency, or arbitrational tribune against or affecting it or its properties, assets, or business;

H. Since the date of the Venture commitment letter the Company has not suffered any material adverse change in its condition (financial or otherwise) or its overall business prospects, nor entered into any material transactions or incurred any debt, obligation, or liability, absolute or contingent, nor sustained any material loss or damage to its property, whether or not insured, nor suffered any material interference with its business or operations, present or proposed; and there has been no sale, lease, abandonment, or other disposition by the Company of any of its property, real or personal, or any interest therein or relating thereto, that is material to the financial position of the Company;

I. The Company has duly filed all tax returns, federal, state, and local, which are required to be filed and has duly paid or fully reserved for all taxes or installments thereof as and when due which have or may become due pursuant to said returns or pursuant to any assessment received by the Company;

J. The Company is not bound by or party to any contract or instrument or subject to any charter or other legal restriction materially and adversely affecting its business, property, assets, operations, or condition, financial or otherwise;

K. Except for matters set out in the litigation letter, the Company is not in breach of, default under, or in violation of any applicable law, decree, order, rule, or regulation which may materially and adversely affect it or any indenture, contract, Agreement, deed, lease, loan Agreement, commitment, bond, note, deed of trust, restrictive covenant, license, or other instrument or obligation to which it is a party or by which it is bound or to which any of its assets are subject; the execution, delivery, and performance of this Agreement and the issuance, sale, and delivery of the Warrant and other documents will not constitute any such breach, default, or violation or require consent or approval of any court, governmental agency, or body except as contemplated herein;

M. Neither the Company nor any of its officers, directors, partners, or controlling persons is an "Associate" of Venture as such terms are defined in section 107.3 of the Regulations as amended promulgated under the Act, nor an "Affiliated person" of Venture, as such term is defined in Section (a)(3) of the Investment Company Act of 1940 as amended;

N. To the best of the Company's knowledge, it has complied in all material respects with all laws, ordinances, and regulations applicable to it and to its business, including without limitation federal and state securities laws, zoning laws and ordinances, federal labor laws and regulations and the Federal Occupational Safety and Health Act and regulations thereunder, the Federal Employees Retirement Income Security Act, and federal, state, and local environmental protection laws and regulations;

O. There are no material facts relating to the Company not fully disclosed to Venture; no representation, covenant or warranty made by the Company herein or in any statement, certificate, or other instrument furnished to Venture pursuant hereto or in connection with the transaction contemplated hereby contains or will contain any untrue statement of or omits to state a material facts necessary to make the statement are misleading;

P. The Company is primarily engaged in the business of commercial electromagnetic manufacturing and is not a franchise;

Q. The Company for the 12-month period ending January 31, 1983, had sales of $850,000, pretax loss of $25,000, assets of $600,000, liabilities of $300,000, and net worth of $300,000;

R. After disbursement of the subject loan the Company will have approximately the following assets: accounts receivable $100,000, machinery and equipment $100,000, land and building $100,000, other assets $300,000;

S. Copies of leases provided are true and correct;

T. During the past ten (10) years no officer or director of the Company has been arrested or convicted of any criminal offense.

VI. AFFIRMATIVE COVENANTS

Until the Warrants are exercised and the Note repaid in full, the Company will:

A. Promptly make all payments of principal and interest as due under the Note and furnish from time to time to each Holder all information it may reasonably request to enable it to prepare and file any form required to be filed by Holder with the SBA, Securities and Exchange Commission, or any other regulatory authority;

B. Forward, or cause to be forwarded to Holders, its monthly accounting balance sheet and profit-and-loss statement within forty-five (45) days from the end of each month;

C. Forward, or cause to be forwarded to Holders, its final year-end accounting balance sheet and profit-and-loss statement within sixty (60) days of such accounting year end, which if demanded by a Holder in writing shall be prepared at the Company's expense by an independent outside accounting firm acceptable to a Holder, according to generally accepted accounting principles uniformly applied;

D. Maintain a net worth of $50,000 or more and a level of current assets (which shall be reflected in its books in accordance with generally accepted accounting principles) such that the amount of such current assets shall equal or exceed the amount of current liabilities; maintain sales of at least $500,000 per annum, $105,000 per quarter, and $30,000 per month as reflected on its books in accordance with generally accepted accounting principles uniformly applied;

E. Provide to Holders in writing each quarter the certification of the President of the Company that a default has occurred under the Warrants, Note, or this Agreement, or any debt or obligation senior to the debt of the Holders hereunder; or if any such default exists, provide Holders with a statement by the President of the Company as to the nature of such default;

F. Maintain such shares of its common stock authorized but unissued as may be necessary to satisfy the rights of the Holders of the Warrants;

G. Perform all acts as required under the Warrants including without limitation, the re-issue of replacement Warrants to a Holder upon loss or destruction;

H. Permit any authorized representative of any Holder and its attorneys and accountants to inspect, examine, and make copies and abstracts of the books of account and records of the Company at reasonable times during normal business hours;

I. Notify Holders of any litigation to which the Company is a party by mailing to Holders, by registered mail, within five (5) days of receipt thereof, a copy of the Complaint, Motion for Judgment, or other such pleadings served on or by the Company; and any litigation to which the Company is not a party but which could substantially affect operation of the Company's business or the collateral pledged for this loan, including collateral securing any guarantees, by mailing to

Holders, by registered mail, a copy of all pleadings obtained by the Company in regard to such litigation, or if no pleadings are obtained, a letter setting out the facts known about the litigation within five (5) days of receipt thereof; provided that the Company shall not be obliged by this paragraph to give notice of suits where it is a creditor seeking collection of account debts;

J. Prior to each accounting year-end, provide Holders with projected financial statements for the coming year, in the same format as used for item C;

K. Hold a meeting of the Board of Directors of the Company at least once each quarter; give Holders at least two weeks prior notice of such meeting; allow one representative designated by each Holder to attend such meeting at Company's expense;

L. Maintain all-risk hazard insurance on its assets, with mortgagee clause in favor of Holders, in such reasonable amounts and forms as required by Holders; this shall include federal flood insurance if any assets be in a designated flood plain; and supply Holders with a list of existing coverage prior to closing;

M. Give Holders notice of any judgment entered against the Company by mailing a copy to Holders within five (5) days of entry thereof;

N. Take all necessary steps to administer, supervise, preserve, and protect the collateral herein; regardless of any action taken by Holders, there shall be no duty upon Holders in this respect.

O. Within thirty (30) days of filing provide Holders with copies of all returns and documents filed with federal, state, or local government agencies including without limitation the Internal Revenue Service, Federal Trade Commission, and Securities and Exchange Commission.

P. Maintain an original or a true copy of this Agreement and any modifications hereof, which shall be available for inspection under subparagraph H.

VII. NEGATIVE COVENANTS

Until the Notes are repaid and the Warrants exercised, the Company will not without the prior written consent of all the Holders:

A. Declare or pay any cash dividend of any kind on any class of stock; make any material change in its ownership, organization, or management or the manner in which its business is conducted; authorize, issue, or reclassify any shares of capital stock except as required under the Warrants;

B. Become a party to any merger or consolidation with any other corporation, company, or entity;

C. Make expenditures for capital improvements or acquisitions in any fiscal year in excess of $10,000;

D. Make loans, advances, wage payments including salaries, withdrawals, fees, bonuses, commissions direct or indirect in money or otherwise, to any officer, director, shareholder, partner, or employee in excess of $50,000 per year, or $30,000 per year if there is a default under this Agreement;

E. Transfer, sell, lease, or in any other manner convey any equitable, beneficial, or legal interest in any of the assets of the Company except inventory sold in the normal course of business, or allow to exist on its assets any mortgage interest, pledge, security interest, title retention device, or other encumbrance junior or senior to Holders' liens except for liens of taxes and assessments not delinquent or contested in good faith;

F. Permit any judgment obtained against the Company to remain unpaid for over twenty (20) days without obtaining a stay of execution or bond;

G. Incur any declared default under any loan Agreement pertaining to another debt of the Company;

H. Pay or incur any brokerage, legal, consulting, or similar fee in excess of $5,000 per year;

I. Create or incur any debt other than that incurred hereunder, trade debt or short-term working capital debt normally incurred in the ordinary course of business;

J. Incur any lease liability or purchase any additional life insurance from business income or assets;

K. Become a guarantor, or otherwise liable on any notes or obligations of any other person, firm, corporation, or entity, except in connection with depositing checks and other instruments for the payment of money acquired in the normal course of its business.

VIII. INVESTMENT COVENANT

By accepting a Warrant, the Holder thereof represents, warrants, and covenants that it is an "accredited investor" within the meaning of Section 4(6) of the Securities Act or an "accredited person" within the meaning of Rule 42 of the Securities Act, or acquiring the Warrant and any stock issued thereunder for its own account for investment and not with the view to resale or distribution thereof except in accordance with applicable federal and state securities laws. Upon exercise of any conversion rights under the Warrant, this representation, warranty, and covenant shall be deemed to have been given with respect to the stock received.

IX. FEES, EXPENSES, AND INDEMNIFICATION

The Company shall reimburse Holders for reasonable expenses according to the terms of the commitment letter. The Company shall pay, indemnify, and hold any holders of the Warrants and Note harmless from and against any and all liability and loss with respect to or resulting from any and all claims for or on account of any brokers and from finder's fees or commissions with respect to this transaction as may have been created by the Company or its officers, partners, employees, or agents; and from any stamp or excise taxes which may become payable by virtue of this transaction or the issuance of any stock or modification hereunder. Venture warrants it has not contracted to pay any such fees.

X. UNLOCKING

If at any time after five (5) years from the date of this Agreement the Company or its shareholders receive a bona fide offer to purchase the assets of the Company or an equity interest in the Company, then the party receiving such offer (hereinafter offeree) will submit a copy of the offer and such information pertinent thereto as it may have to the Holders of the Warrants or the shares issued thereunder within three (3) days of receipt of said offer. Within ten (10) days of receipt of said copy each Warrant Holder will indicate in writing to the offeree its approval or disapproval of the offer. If a Holder approves the offer, then the offeree shall, within twenty (20) days thereafter or such shorter time if provided in the offer, accept or reject the offer. If the offeree rejects the offer then simultaneously with such rejection it shall be bound to purchase the approving Holder's Warrants or resulting stock in the Company under the same terms and conditions that such Holder would have received under the offer. If a Warrant Holder fails to communicate timely approval or disapproval, the Company may construe such failure to indicate disapproval.

XI. "PUT" RIGHTS

Beginning five (5) years from the date of this Agreement ending ten (10) years from the date of this Agreement, Warrant Holders may by written demand require the Company to purchase its Warrant or the shares of stock issued hereunder at a price of 35 percent of the higher of the following sums:

(a) Ten Percent (10%) of the Company's sales for the fiscal year immediately preceding the year of the demand times a price–earnings ratio of twelve (12), less the aggregate principal balance of the Note on the day of demand; or

(b) Ten times the Company's cash flow for the fiscal year immediately preceding the year of the demand, less the aggregate principal balance of the Note on the day of demand.

XII. DEFAULT

A. If any of the below-listed events occurs prior to maturity of the Notes, then a default may be declared at the option of any Holder without presentment, demand, protest, or further notice of any kind, all of which are hereby expressly waived. In such event the Note Holder shall be entitled to be paid in full the balance of any unpaid principal of its Note plus accrued interest and any costs thereof, including reasonable attorneys' fees, and to any other remedies which may be available under this Agreement, the Warrant, the Note, or any applicable law:

1. Occurrence of any default provision as set out in the Warrants or Note;

2. Any material representation made by the Company in writing herein or in connection herewith shall be untrue and shall remain so for thirty (30) days after written notice to the Company thereof;

3. The Company shall fail to comply with the covenants in this Agreement and such failure shall continue for a period of ten (10) days after receipt of notice thereof from any Holder of the Note;

4. The Company shall make an assignment for the benefit of creditors, or shall admit in writing its inability to pay its debts as they become due, or shall file a voluntary petition in bankruptcy, or shall be adjudicated as bankrupt or insolvent, or shall file any petition or answer seeking for itself any reorganization, arrangement, composition, readjustment, liquidation, dissolution, or similar relief under any present or future statute, law, or regulation pertinent to such circumstances, or shall file any answer admitting or not contesting the material allegations of a petition filed against the Company in any such proceedings, or shall seek or consent to or acquiesce in the appointment of any trustee, receiver, or liquidator of the Company or of all or any substantial part of the properties of the Company; or the Company or its directors or majority shareholders shall take any action initiating the dissolution or liquidation of the Company;

5. Sixty (60) days shall have expired after the commencement of an action against the Company seeking reorganization, arrangement, composition, readjustment, liquidation, dissolution or similar relief under any present or future statute, law, or regulation without such action being dismissed or all orders or proceedings thereunder affecting the operations

or the business of the Company being stayed; or a stay of any such order or proceedings shall thereafter be set aside and the action setting it aside shall not be timely appealed;

6. Sixty (60) days shall have expired after the appointment, without the consent or acquiescence of the Company, of any Trustee, receiver, or liquidator of the Company, or of all or any substantial part of the properties of the Company without such appointment being vacated;

7. The Company shall be declared in default under an Agreement in regard to the debts described in paragraph VI. E.;

8. Any guarantor or undersigned shareholder of the Company shall fail to comply with the terms of his or her undertakings to Holders;

A. No course of dealing between a Holder and any other party hereto or any failure or delay on the part of the Holder in exercising any rights or remedies hereunder shall operate as a waiver of any rights or remedies of any Holder under this or any other applicable instrument. No single or partial exercise of any rights or remedies hereunder shall operate as a waiver or preclude the exercise of any other rights or remedies hereunder;

B. Upon the nonpayment of the indebtedness under the Note or any part thereof when due, whether by acceleration or otherwise, a Note Holder is empowered to sell, assign, and deliver the whole or any part of the collateral for the Note at public or private sale, without demand, advertisement, or notice of the time or place of sale or of any adjournment thereof, which are hereby expressly waived. After deducting all expenses incidental to or arising from such sale or sales, Holder may apply the residue of the proceeds thereof to the payment of the indebtednesses, under the Notes, subject to the terms of paragraph XIII, returning the excess, if any, to the Company. The Company hereby waives all right of appraisement, whether before or after the sale, and any right of redemption after the sale. The Company shall have the right to redeem any collateral up to the time of a foreclosure sale by paying the aggregate indebtedness under the Notes;

C. Holders are further empowered to collect or cause to be collected or otherwise to be converted into money all or any part of the collateral, by suit or otherwise, and to surrender, compromise, release, renew, extend, exchange, or substitute any item of the collateral in transactions with the Company or any third party, irrespective of any assignment thereof by the Company, and without prior notice to or consent of the Company or any assignee. Whenever any item of the collateral shall not be paid when due, or any part thereof has become due, Holders shall have the same rights and powers with respect to such items of the collateral as are granted in respect thereof in this paragraph in case of nonpayment of the indebtedness, or any part thereof, when due. None of the rights, remedies, privileges, or powers of the Holders expressly provided for herein shall be exclusive, but each of them shall be cumulative with and in addition to every other right, remedy, privilege, and power now or hereafter existing in favor of the Holders, whether at law or in equity, by statute or otherwise;

D. The Company shall pay all expenses of any nature, whether incurred in or out of court, and whether incurred before or after the Notes shall become due at their maturity date or otherwise (including but not limited to reasonable attorney fees and costs) which Holders may deem necessary or proper in connection with the satisfaction of the indebtedness under the Notes or the administration, supervision, preservation, protection of (including, but not limited to, the maintenance of adequate insurance), or the realization upon the collateral. Holders are authorized to pay at any time and from time to time any or all of such expenses, add the amount of such payment to the amount of principal outstanding, and charge interest thereon at the rate specified in the Notes;

E. The security interest of the Holders and their assigns shall not be impaired by a Holder's sale, hypothecation, or rehypothecation of a Warrant or Note or any item of the collateral, or by any indulgence, including, but not limited to:

1. Any renewal, extension, or modification which a Holder may grant with respect to the indebtedness of any part thereof, or,

2. Any surrender, compromise, release, renewal, extension, exchange, or substitution which a Holder may grant in respect of the collateral, or,

3. Any indulgence granted in respect of any endorser, guarantor, or surety. The purchaser, assignee, transferee, or pledgee of the Warrants, Notes, collateral, any guaranty, or any other document (or any of them), sold, assigned, transferred, pledged, or repledged, shall forthwith become vested with and entitled to exercise all powers and rights given by this Agreement to Holders, as if said purchaser, assignee, transferee, or pledgee were originally named in this Agreement in place of the Holders.

XIII. NOTICE

All notices or communications under this Agreement of the Warrants or Notes shall be mailed, postage prepaid, or delivered as follows:

To Venture: 1666 Tyson Blvd Suite 600

 McLean, VA 22102

To Company: Ace Electromagnetic, Incorporated

1234 Main Street McLean, Virginia 22102

or, to such other address as shall at any time be designated by any party in writing to the other parties.

XIV. ENTIRE AGREEMENT

The Warrants, the Note, and this Agreement and the documents mentioned herein set forth the entire Agreements and understandings of the parties hereto in respect of this transaction. Any prior Agreements are hereby terminated. The terms herein may not be changed verbally but only by an instrument in writing signed by the party against which enforcement of the change is sought.

XV. CONTROLLING LAW

This Agreement shall be construed in accordance with and governed by the laws of the District of Columbia.

XVI. HEADINGS

The headings of the paragraphs and subparagraphs of this Agreement and the Warrants and Note are inserted for convenience only and shall not be deemed to constitute a part of this Agreement or the Warrants and Note.

IN WITNESS WHEREOF, the undersigned hereby affix their hands and seals on the year and day first above written.

ACE ELECTROMAGNETIC, INC.
VENTURE CAPITAL FUND

By:
Joseph Entrepreneur

President
A. Venture Capitalist President

Attest
John Smith, Secretary

Attest
Brenda Smith
Assistant Secretary

Agreed:
Mr. Joseph Entrepreneur
Mrs. Joseph Entrepreneur

Legal Document
Ace Electromagnetic, Incorporated
McLean, Virginia

LEGAL DOCUMENT 2

PROMISSORY NOTE

$3,000,000 Washington, D.C.

FOR VALUE RECEIVED the undersigned Ace Electromagnetic, Incorporated, a Virginia corporation (hereinafter "Company") promises to pay to the order of Venture Capital Fund, a District of Columbia corporation (hereinafter "Holder") the principal sum of Three Million Dollars ($3,000,000) together with interest as set out herein at its offices in the District of Columbia or such other place as Holder may designate in writing.

Interest from date of advance and thereafter until repayment, interest shall accrue hereunder at the rate of fifteen percent (15%) per annum.

Payments: Payments shall be due on the first day of each month after the day of this Note. Through the first thirty-six (36) full calendar months after the date hereof, payments shall be for interest only (amount). Thereafter until maturity payments shall be (amount).

Maturity: The entire indebtedness hereunder shall become due and payable in full six (6) years after the date the first payment is due.

Prepayment: Payment of any installment of principal or interest may be made prior to the maturity date thereof without penalty. Such prepayments shall be applied against the outstanding principal in inverse order of maturity.

DEFAULT AND ACCELERATION:

A. If any of the below-listed events occur prior to maturity hereof, then a default may be declared at the option of the holder without presentment, demand, protest, or further notice of any kind (all of which are hereby expressly waived). In such event the holder shall be entitled to be paid in full the balance of any unpaid principal amount plus accrued interest and any costs including reasonable attorney fees, and to any other remedies, which may be available herein in the Loan Agreement or under any applicable law:

1. Failure to pay any part of the indebtedness hereof when due;

2. Occurrence of any default as provided under the Loan Agreement pertaining hereto.

B. No course of dealing between the Holder and any other party hereto or any failure or delay on the part of the Payee in exercising any rights or remedies hereunder shall operate as a waiver of any rights or remedies of the Holder under this or any other applicable instrument. No single or partial exercise of any rights or remedies hereunder shall operate as a waiver or preclude the exercise of any other rights or remedies hereunder.

C. Upon the nonpayment of the indebtedness, or any part thereof, when due, whether by acceleration or otherwise, Payee is empowered to sell, assign, and deliver the whole or any part of the collateral at public or private sale, without demand, advertisement, or notice of the time or place of sale or of any adjournment thereof, which are hereby expressly waived. After deducting all expenses incidental to or arising from such sale or sales, Holder shall apply the residue of the proceeds thereof to the payment of the indebtedness, as it shall deem proper, returning the excess, if any, to the Company. The Company hereby waives all right of appraisement, whether before or after sale, and any right of redemption after sale. The Company shall have the right to redeem any collateral up to the time of a foreclosure sale by paying the aggregate indebtedness.

D. Holder is further empowered to collect or cause to be collected or otherwise be converted into money all or any part of the collateral, by suit or otherwise, and to surrender, compromise, release, renew, extend, exchange, or substitute any item of the collateral in transactions with the Company or any third party, irrespective of any assignment thereof by the Company, and without prior notice to or any consent of the Company or any assignee. Whenever any item of the collateral shall not be paid when due, or otherwise shall be in default, whether or not the indebtedness, or any part thereof, has become due,

Holder shall have the same rights and powers with respect to such item of the collateral as are granted in respect thereof in this paragraph in case of nonpayment of the indebtedness, or any part thereof, when due. None of the rights, remedies, privileges, or powers of the Company expressly provided for herein shall be exclusive, but each of them shall be cumulative with and in addition to every other right, remedy, privilege, and power now or hereafter existing in favor of Holder, whether at law or in equity, by statute or otherwise.

E. The Company will take all necessary steps to administer, supervise, preserve, and protect the collateral; and regardless of any action taken by Holder, there shall be no duty upon Holder in this respect. The Company shall pay all expenses of any nature, whether incurred in or out of court, and whether incurred before or after this Note shall become due at its maturity date or otherwise (including but not limited to reasonable attorneys' fees and costs) which Holder may deem necessary or proper in connection with the satisfaction of the indebtedness or the administration, supervision, preservation, protection of (including, but not limited to, the maintenance of adequate insurance), or the realization upon the collateral. Holder is authorized to pay at any time and from time to time any or all of such expenses, add the amount of such payment to the amount of principal outstanding and charge interest thereon at the rate specified herein.

F. The security rights of Holder and its assigns shall not be impaired by Holder's sale, hypothecation, or rehypothecation of this Note or any item of the collateral, or by any indulgence, including, but not limited to:

1. Any renewal, extension, or modification which Holder may grant with respect to the indebtedness of any part thereof, or

2. Any surrender, compromise, release, renewal, extension, exchange, or substitution which Holder may grant in respect of the collateral, or

3. Any indulgence granted in respect to any endorser, guarantor, or surety. The purchaser, assignee, transferee, or pledgee of this Note, the collateral, any guaranty, and any

other document (or any of them), sold, assigned, transferred, pledged, or repledged, shall forthwith become vested with and entitled to exercise all the powers and rights given by this Note as if said purchaser, assignee, transferee, or pledgee were originally named as Holder in this Note.

Definitions: The term indebtedness as used herein shall mean the indebtedness evidenced by this Note, including principal, interest, and expenses whether contingent, now due or hereafter to become due, and whether heretofore or contemporaneously herewith or hereafter contracted. The term collateral as used in this Note shall mean any funds, guarantees, or other property rights therein of any nature whatsoever of the proceeds thereof which may have been, are or hereafter may be hypothecated directly or indirectly by the undersigned or others in connection with, or as security for the indebtedness or any part thereof. The collateral and each part thereof shall secure the indebtedness and each part thereof.

IN WITNESS WHEREOF, the undersigned has caused this Note to be executed and its seal affixed on the day and year first written above.

Seal: ACE ELECTROMAGNETIC, INCORPORATED

Attest
John Smith
Secretary

BY:
Joseph Entrepreneur
President

THE SECURITIES REPRESENTED HEREBY HAVE BEEN ACQUIRED IN A TRANSACTION NOT INVOLVING ANY PUBLIC OFFERING AND HAVE NOT BEEN REGISTERED UNDER THE SECURITIES ACT OF 1933. SUCH SECURITIES MAY NOT BE SOLD OR TRANSFERRED IN THE ABSENCE OF SUCH REGISTRATION OR AN EXEMPTION THEREFROM UNDER SAID ACT.

Legal Document 3

Ace Electromagnetic, Incorporated
McLean, Virginia

Stock Purchase Warrants

I. Grant

Ace Electromagnetic, Incorporated, a Virginia corporation (hereinafter "Company") for value received hereby grants to Venture Capital Fund, a District of Columbia corporation, or its registered assigns (hereinafter "Holder") under the terms herein the right to purchase that umber of the fully paid and no assessable shares of the Company's common stock such that upon exercise and issuance of stock hereunder the Holder will hold thirty-five percent (35%) of the outstanding common stock of the Company. On the present date such number is 1,724 shares.

II. Expiration

The right to exercise this Warrant shall expire ten (10) years from the date hereof.

III. Exercise Price

The exercise price of this Warrant shall be one hundred dollars ($100.00).

IV. Effect of Redemption

Regardless of the above provision, if the Company shall redeem or otherwise purchase for value any of its shares of common stock prior to issuance of shares under this Warrant, the Holder shall be entitled to receive hereunder the same number of shares it could have received had the redemptions or purchases for value not occurred.

V. Exercise Procedure

This Warrant may be exercised by presenting it and tendering the purchase price in tender or by bank cashier's or certified check at the principal office of the Company along with written subscription substantially in the form of Exhibit I hereof;

The date on which this Warrant is thus surrendered, accompanied by tender or payment as hereinbefore or hereinafter provided, is referred to herein as the Exercise Date. The Company shall forthwith at its expense (including the payment of issue taxes) issue and deliver the proper number of shares, and such shares shall be deemed issued for all purposes as of the opening of business on the Exercise Date notwithstanding any delay in the actual issuance.

VI. Sale or Exchange of Company or Assets

If prior to issuance of stock under this Warrant the Company sells or exchanges all or substantially all of its assets, or the shares of common stock of the Company are sold or exchanged to any party other than the Holder, then the Holder at its option may receive, in lieu of the stock otherwise issuable hereunder, such money or property it would have been entitled to receive if this Warrant had been exercised prior to such sale or exchange.

VII. Sale of Warrant or Shares

Neither this Warrant or other shares of common stock issuable upon exercise of the conversion rights herein, have been registered under the Securities Act of 1933 as amended, or under the securities laws of any state. Neither this Warrant or any shares when issued may be sold, transferred, pledged, or hypothecated in the absence of (i) an effective registration statement for this Warrant or the shares, as the case may be, under the Securities Act of 1933 as amended and such registration or qualification as may be necessary under the securities laws of any state, or (ii) an opinion of counsel reasonably satisfactory to the Company that such registration or qualification is not required. The Company shall cause a certificate or certificates evidencing all or any of the shares issued upon exercise of the conversion rights herein prior to said registration and qualification of such shares to bear the following legend: "The shares evidenced by this certificate have not been registered under the Securities Act of 1933 as amended, or under the securities laws of any state. The shares may not be sold, transferred, pledged, or hypothecated in the absence of an effective registration statement under the Securities Act of 1933, as amended, and such registration or qualification as may be necessary under the securities laws of any state, or an opinion of counsel satisfactory to the Company that such registration or qualification is not required."

VIII. TRANSFER

This Warrant shall be registered on the books of the Company which shall be kept at its principal office for that purpose, and shall be transferable only on such books by the Holder in person or by duly authorized attorney with written notice substantially in the form of Exhibit 11 hereof, and only in compliance with the preceding paragraph. The Company may issue appropriate stop orders to its transfer agent to prevent a transfer in violation of the preceding paragraph.

IX. REPLACEMENT OF WARRANT

At the request of the Holder and on production of evidence reasonably satisfactory to the Company of the loss, theft, destruction, or mutilation of this Warrant and (in the case of loss, theft, or destruction) if required by the Company, upon delivery of an indemnity Agreement with surety in such reasonable amount as the Company may determine thereof, the Company at its expense will issue in lieu thereof a new Warrant of like tenor.

X. LOAN AGREEMENT

This Warrant is subject to the terms of a Loan Agreement dated today between the Company and the Holder, a copy of which is on file and may be examined at the principal office of the Company in McLean, Virginia, during regular business hours.

XI. Unlocking

The Holder or its registered assigns shall have certain unlocking rights as set out in the Loan Agreement above-mentioned.

XII. "Put" Rights

Beginning five (5) years from today and ending ten (10) years from today, the Holder may by written demand require the company to purchase this Warrant or the shares of stock issued hereunder at a price of thirty-five percent (35%) of the higher of the following prices:

1. Ten percent (10%) of the Company's sales for the fiscal year immediately preceding the year of the demand times a price earnings of eight, less the aggregate principal balance of the Note on the day of demand; or
2. Ten times the Company's cash flow for the fiscal year immediately preceding the year of the demand, less the aggregate principal balance of Note on the day of demand.

XIII. Registration

If the Company shall at any time prepare and file a registration statement under the Securities Act of 1933 with respect to the public offering of any class of equity or debt security of the Company, the Company shall give thirty (30) days prior written notice thereof to Holder, and shall, upon the written request of Holder include in the registration statement or related notification such number of Holder's shares as Holder may request to be sold on a one-time basis; the Company will keep such notification or registration statement and prospectus effective and current under the Act permitting the sale of Holder's shares covered thereby to be sold on a time-to-time basis or otherwise; such inclusion, in any event, shall be at no cost to Holder and shall be at the sole cost and expense of the Company; in the event the Company fails to receive a written request from Holder within thirty (30) days after the mailing of its written notice, then the Company shall treat such failure with the same force and effect as if Holder's failure to respond constituted notice to the Company that Holder does not intend to include its shares in such registration statement or notification; the foregoing shall not apply to a registration relating to securities of the Company covered by an employee, stock option, or other benefit plan; in connection with any notification or registration statement or subsequent amendment to any such notification or registration statement or similar document filed pursuant hereto, the Company shall take any reasonable steps to make the securities covered thereby eligible for public offering and sale by the effective date of such notification or registration statement or any amendment to any of the foregoing under the securities or blue sky laws of Virginia and the District of Columbia; provided that in no event shall the Company be obligated to qualify to do business in any state where it is not so qualified at the time of filing such documents or to take any action which would subject it to unlimited service of process in any state where it is not so subject at such time; the Company shall keep such filing current for the length of time it must keep any notification, registration statement, post-effective amendment, prospectus, or offering circular and any amendment to any of the foregoing effective pursuant hereto; in connection with any filing hereunder the Company shall bear all the expenses and professional fees which arise in connection with such filings and all expenses incurred in making such filings, and keeping them effective and correct as provided hereunder and shall also provide Holder with a reasonable number of printed copies of the prospectus, offering circulars, and/or supplemental prospectuses or amended prospectuses in final and preliminary form; the Company consents to the use of such prospectus or offering circular in connection with the sale of Holder's shares; in the event of the filing of any registration statement or notification pursuant to this Agreement or document referred to herein which includes Holder's shares, Holder shall indemnify the Company and each of its officers and directors who has signed said registration statement, each person, if any, who controls the Company with the meaning of the

Securities Act, each underwriter for the Company and each person, if any, who controls such underwriter within the meaning of the Securities Act, from any loss, claim, damage, liability, or action arising out of or based upon any untrue statement or any omission to state therein a material fact required to be stated therein or necessary to make the statements therein not misleading, furnished in writing by Holder expressly for use in such registration statement or required to be furnished by Holder.

XIV. COVENANTS OF THE COMPANY

The Company covenants that until this Warrant is exercised or expires, it will:

(a) Reserve authorized but unissued 1,724 shares of its common stock or such additional number of such shares as necessary to satisfy the rights of the Holder;

(b) Not pay any dividends in cash or in kind unless written authorization is received in writing from the Holder;

(c) Furnish the Holder consolidated financial statements of the Company, which statements shall include and be rendered as follows:

(1) Monthly year-to-date financial statements within forty-five (45) days after the close of the last previous month which statements shall include a balance sheet and a statement of profit and loss for the period in question, and

(2) If requested in writing by Holder, within sixty (60) days after the close of each fiscal year a balance sheet and a profit-and-loss statement of the Company relating to such year, certified by a firm of independent public accountants of recognized standing in McLean, Virginia, and approved by the Holder, accompanied by any report or comment of said accountant made in connection with such financial statements, and with a copy of all other financial statements prepared for or furnished to the Company.

(d) The President of the Company shall certify on each statement furnished to the Holder that the default exists hereunder, or, in the event a default does exist, the President shall submit his or her statement of such default;

(e) Maintain an office in the McLean, Virginia, area, at which its books and records will be kept and notices, presentations, demands, and payments relating to this Warrant, the Note, and the Loan Agreement may be given or made;

(f) Maintain books of account in accordance with generally accepted accounting principles;

(g) Permit the Holder through its designated representative to visit and inspect any of the properties of the Company, to examine its books and records, and to discuss its affairs, finances, and accounts with and be advised as to the same by the Officers of the Company at such reasonable times and intervals.

XV. Investment Covenant

The Holder by its acceptance hereby covenants that this Warrant is, and the stock to be acquired upon the exercise of this Warrant will be, acquired for investment purposes, and that the Holder will not distribute the same in violation of any state or federal law or regulation.

XVI. Laws Governing

This Warrant shall be construed according to the laws of the District of Columbia.

IN WITNESS WHEREOF, Ace Electromagnetic, Incorporated, has caused this Warrant to be signed on its behalf, in its corporate name, by its President, and its corporate seal to be hereunto affixed and the said seal to be attested by its Secretary, as of this 31st day of January, 2001.

Seal: ACE ELECTROMAGNETIC, INCORPORATED
By:
Joseph Entrepreneur, President

Attest
John Smith, Secretary

LEGAL DOCUMENT 4

Ajax Computer Genetics Corp.
123 Main Street
McLean, Virginia 22102

Venture Capital Corp.
125 Main Street
Washington, D.C. 20006

Stock Purchase Agreement

Dear Sirs:

You have informed us that, subject to certain conditions, you are prepared to subscribe for and purchase, at a price of Ten Dollars ($10.00) per share, two hundred fifty thousand (250,000) shares (the "Shares") of our authorized but unissued Common Stock, One Dollar ($1.00) par value (the "Stock"). In this connection, we hereby confirm our Agreement with you as follows:

1. Representations and Warranties. ("Ajax" or "we") is a corporation duly organized and validly existing in good standing under the laws of the District of Columbia and is duly qualified to transact business as a foreign corporation under the laws of Florida and California, the only jurisdictions in which the nature of the business currently transacted by us requires such qualification.

1.1 The authorized capital stock of Ajax consists of 1,000,000 shares of the Stock, all of one class, of which there are outstanding on the date hereof 972,515 shares and 7,800 shares are reserved for issuance pursuant to options held by key employees of Ajax and subsidiaries. Other than the shares (1) so reserved for stock options, and (2) the shares being purchased by you, there are no other shares outstanding.

1.2 Ajax has no subsidiaries, nor does it intend to establish any subsidiaries.

1.3 There have been furnished to you the consolidated financial statements of Ajax as of and for the years just ending. These financial statements are complete and correct and present fairly the consolidated financial condition of Ajax and the consolidated results of their operations as of the dates thereof and for the period covered thereby. Such financial statements have been prepared in accordance with generally accepted accounting principles applied on a consistent basis throughout the periods involved, subject to any comments and notes therein. Since the year end there has not occurred any material adverse change in the consolidated financial position or results of operations of Ajax, nor any change not in the ordinary course of business.

1.4 There are no actions, suits, or proceedings pending nor, to Ajax's knowledge, threatened, before any court, agency, or other body which involves Ajax, wherein Ajax is a defendant.

1.5 This Agreement and the issuance and sale of the Shares pursuant hereto have been duly authorized by appropriate and all required corporate action; such issuance and sale and Ajax's compliance with the terms hereof will not violate Ajax's articles of incorporation, bylaws, any indenture or contract to which Ajax is a party or by which it is bound, or any statute, rule, regulation, or order of any court or agency applicable to Ajax; and the Shares when issued and sold as provided herein will have been duly and validly authorized and issued, fully paid, and nonassessable.

2. Covenants. We covenant and agree with you that

2.1 Prior to your purchase of the Shares, we shall provide to you, your agents, and attorney access to the same kind of information as is specified in Schedule A of the Securities Act of 1933 (the "1933 Act"), and shall make available to you during the course of this transaction the opportunity to ask questions of, and receive answers from, ourselves and our officers necessary to your satisfaction to verify the accuracy of such information.

2.2 For a period of at least two years following the Closing Date, we will not apply more than twenty percent (20%) of the proceeds from the sale of the Shares to the business of any new products without the concurrence of all members of our Board of Directors who have been nominated by you pursuant to Section 2.3 or elected thereto pursuant to Section 5.4.

2.3 As long as you and your affiliates own combined a total of at least ten percent (10%) of the outstanding voting securities of Ajax, you and your affiliates together shall be entitled to nominate a total of two (2) persons for election as members of our Board of Directors and, if they are so nominated and legally qualify to serve in that capacity, our Board of Directors will support their election.

2.4 (a) If, at any time while you or your affiliates (collectively "you") hold any of the Shares, we shall decide to register with the SEC any issue of Stock (other than a registration of shares solely for the purpose of any plan for the acquisition thereof by our employees or for the purpose of a merger or acquisition), we will give you written notice of such decision at least twenty (20) days prior to the filing of a registration statement and will afford you upon your request the opportunity of having any Shares then held by you included in the registration if the request is made within ten (10) days after receiving such notice, to the extent and under the conditions upon which such registration is permissible under the 1933 Act and the Rules and Regulations of the Securities and Exchange Commission; provided, however, that we may exclude such Shares from a registration statement filed by us to the extent that, in the opinion of the managing underwriter of the issue being registered, the inclusion of such of the Shares or of more than a designated portion thereof would be detrimental to the public offering pursuant to such registration, and to the further extent that such exclusion is made applicable to sales by all holders of outstanding Stock, pro rata in proportion to their holdings. In the event in any registration we offer you the opportunity to sell such of the Shares which you propose to register to underwriters on a "firm commitment" basis (as opposed to a "best efforts" basis), you shall, as a condition of your participation in the registration, accept an offer to sell such of the Shares to the underwriters if the managing underwriter so requires or, in the alternative, agree not to sell such of the Shares pursuant to such registration within such reasonable period (not exceeding 120 days) as may be specified by the managing underwriter to enable those underwriters to complete their distributions; and in any event, shall enter into an Agreement with us and such underwriter containing conventional representations, warranties, and indemnity provisions. You will comply with such other reasonable requirements as may be imposed by the managing underwriter to effect the offering and an orderly distribution of the shares, including your acceptance of the same offering price as shall be accepted by us for the Stock being sold by us pursuant to such registration statement. All expenses of such registration applicable to Shares offered by you shall be payable by us, to the extent permitted by Securities and Exchange Commission Rules or policy, except for your pro rata share of the underwriters' discounts and commissions.

(b) Our obligation to accord you the right to register Shares pursuant to paragraph (a) shall apply to each and every registration which may be effected by us following your purchase of the Shares, except if at the time you shall otherwise be, both as to time and amount, free to sell all the Shares held by you. Without limitation, for the purpose of this paragraph (b), you shall be considered to be free, both as to time and amount, to sell all the Shares held by you if all such Shares may be sold within a period of ninety (90) days pursuant to Rule 144 promulgated under the 1933 Act.

(c) In the event that any registration statement relating to any Shares shall be filed and become effective pursuant to any of the foregoing provisions of this Section 2.4, then at any time while a prospectus relating to such of the Shares is required to be delivered under the 1933 act, but later than nine (9) months after the effective date of such registration statement, we will, at your request, prepare and furnish to you a reasonable number of copies of such prospectus and of such registration statements as may be necessary so that, as thereafter delivered to purchasers of any of the Shares, such prospectus shall comply with Section 10 of the 1933 Act.

(d) In the event that any registration statement relating to any Shares shall be filed pursuant to this Section 2.4, we will use our best efforts to qualify such of the Shares for sale under the laws of such jurisdiction within the continental United States as you may reasonably request and will comply to the best of our ability with such laws so as to permit the continuance of sales of dealings in such of the Shares thereunder. The filing fees with respect to such jurisdictions requested by you shall be payable to you. We shall not, however, be obligated to qualify as a foreign corporation or file any general consent to service or process under the laws of any such jurisdiction or subject ourselves to taxation as doing business in any such jurisdiction or qualify under the securities laws of any jurisdictions which we reasonably deem unduly burdensome.

2.5 If the sale and purchase of the Shares shall be consummated, we will pay the reasonable fees and disbursements of your special counsel in connection with this Agreement and the transaction contemplated herein and, in addition, will pay to you, a fee of Twenty Thousand Dollars ($20,000.00) for services in connection herewith.

2.6 We shall indemnify you and any of your affiliates against any claim for any fees or commissions by any broker, finder, or other person for services or alleged services in connection herewith or the transaction contemplated hereby.

3. Representations and Agreements of Investors. By accepting this Agreement you confirm to us that:

3.1 You and your officers have such knowledge and experience in financial and business matters that you and they are capable of evaluating the merits and risks of your investment in the Shares.

3.2 You represent that you will acquire the Shares for investment and without any present intention of distributing or otherwise reselling any of them.

3.3 You understand that the Shares will be "restricted securities" as that term is defined in the Rules and Regulations of the SEC under the 1933 Act and accordingly may not be reoffered or resold by you unless they are registered under the Act or unless an exemption from such registration is available, and you consent that any certificates for the Shares may be legended accordingly.

3.4 You represent that you have no knowledge of any fees or commissions due in this transaction, except those fees set forth in subparagraph 2.5 and any fee that may be due and payable to John Brown Brokers.

4. Closing. Subject to the terms and conditions hereof, the purchase and sale of the Shares shall take place at our office in Washington, D.C. the last day of this month, at 11:00 A.M. (the "Closing Date") by our delivery to you of a certificate or certificates for the Shares, registered in your name, and your payment to use of the purchase price therefore by wire transfer to our account with The First National Bank.

5. Conditions. Your obligation to take up and pay for the Shares on the Closing Date shall be subject to the following conditions:

5.1 Our representations and warrantees herein shall be true on and as of the Closing Date as though made on such date; we shall have performed all of our covenants and Agreements herein required to be performed on or before the Closing Date; and we shall have delivered to you a certificate to such effects, dated the Closing Date and executed by our President or Executive Vice President.

5.2 There shall have been delivered to you a letter dated the Closing Date, from our accountants to the effect that (i) nothing has come to their attention which would require them to withdraw or modify their annual report, on your consolidated financial statements as of and for the two years just ending; and (ii) they have performed a review of the interim consolidated financial statement of Ajax as of and for the three months since the audit, in accordance with the standards established by the American Institute of Certified Public Accountants. Such a review of the interim financial statements consists principally of obtaining an understanding of the system for the preparation of interim financial statements, applying analytical review procedures to financial data, and making inquiries of persons responsible for financial and accounting matters. It is substantially less in scope than an examination in accordance with generally accepted auditing standards, the objective of which is the expression of an opinion regarding the financial statements taken as a whole. Accordingly, no such opinion is expressed.

5.3 There shall have been delivered to you a favorable opinion, dated the Closing Date, of our general counsel, John Paul, Esquire, as to the questions of law involved in Sections 1.1 through 1.4 and 1.5 and covering such other questions of law as you or your special counsel may reasonably request.

5.4 There shall have been elected as a member of our Board of Directors, subject to the purchase and sale of the Shares, your President, Mr. A.V. Capitalist.

5.5 The certificates, accountants' letter, and legal opinion delivered on the Closing Date shall be deemed to fulfill the conditions hereof only if they are to your reasonable satisfaction and to that of Mr. M.S. Smith, your special counsel for the purpose of this transaction.

6. Miscellaneous.

6.1 All notices required or permitted by this Agreement shall be in writing addressed, if to us, at our address appearing at the head of this letter and, if to you, as this letter is addressed. Either party may, however, request communications or copies thereof to be sent to a different address and you may direct us to pay any dividends on the Shares to a bank in the United States for your account.

6.2 All representations, warranties, and covenants made by all the parties herein shall survive the delivery of and the payment for the Shares.

6.3 This Agreement shall be binding upon and inure to the benefit of the parties hereto and their respective successors and assigns.

6.4 This Agreement shall be construed in accordance with, and the rights and obligations of the parties hereto shall be governed by, the laws of the District of Columbia, U.S.A.

6.5 This Agreement supersedes any prior Agreement, written or oral, between the parties hereto or their affiliates regarding the subject matter hereof.

6.6 In the event the closing described in Section 4 hereof has not taken place by midyear, this Agreement shall terminate unless the parties agree in writing to further extend the same. In the event of termination, all rights, duties, and obligations of each of the parties shall cease and terminate, and this Agreement shall be considered canceled and of no effect or validity thereafter.

If the foregoing accords with your understanding of our Agreement, please sign and return to us the enclosed copy of this letter.

AJAX COMPUTER GENETICS CORPORATION

By

Joseph Entrepreneur, President

ACCEPTED: VENTURE CAPITAL FUND

By

A.V. Capitalist, President

Legal Document 5

Schedule A: Exhibits To Stock Purchase Agreement

1. Ajax (the "Company") is a Virginia corporation with its principal office at 123 Main Street, McLean, Virginia, 22102.

2. A. Exhibit 1A enclosed herewith is a copy of the Annual Report of Ajax for the fiscal year just ending, and included in said report under the same date is a copy of the Certified Audit of the Company made by its current accounting firm for the above fiscal year. Also, Exhibit 1B enclosed herewith is a copy of the preliminary unaudited Financial Statements of Ajax of the one month just ended.

B. A list of Officers and Directors of the Company and their addresses is enclosed as Exhibit hereof.

3. Joseph Entrepreneur, the President of the Company, is the sole owner owning 10 percent or more of record and beneficially of stock of the Company.

4. As of this date, Mr. Entrepreneur owns of record and beneficially 200,000 shares of stock of the Company.

5. The Company is not a holding Company and has no subsidiary corporations.

6. Ajax has 2,000,000 authorized shares of stock, all common, with a par value of $1.00 per share, and presently issued and outstanding there are 300,000 shares of stock. In addition thereto, there are options to purchase 100,000 shares of stock issued to and held by existing employees. The company has a stock option plan with 100,000 remaining unissued shares.

7. See Exhibit 3 pertaining to a list of Stock Options outstanding that have been granted to employees of the Company.

8. The Company intends to sell not less than 50,000 shares of stock in this private placement at an offering price of $10.00

per share. The Company may sell additional shares of stock to a secured venture capital firm at a price of not less than $10.00 per share, which transaction would take place in the near future if consummated.

9. Proceeds of the private placement will be used as follows; $1,000,000 in research and development, $1,000,000 in plant expansion, and $500,000 in salaries and working capital.

10. For the year-end period just ending, the Company paid salaries, bonuses, and director's fees to Joseph Entrepreneur in the amount of $51,000.00. For the current fiscal year Mr. Entrepreneur is being paid a base salary of $50,000.00.

11. The net book value per share of Ajax is $5.00 as of the year just ended. The Company anticipates receiving the entire net proceeds, with the exception of commissions and legal expenses that might be incurred under 12 below, derived from the sale of the securities being offered at $10.00 per share.

12. Commissions being paid for services rendered in the sale will be $20,000.00 to the Venture Capital Fund.

13. The Company has:

A. Employment Contract with Joseph Entrepreneur entered for a period of five years providing for annual compensation of not less than $50,000.00.

B. The other basic contracts that the Company has are for leases for office space where it maintains its offices in McLean, Virginia.

14. Enclosed herewith is Exhibit 4, a copy of the Articles of Incorporation together with all Amendments thereto of Ajax, and Exhibit 5, a copy of the existing Bylaws of the Company.

Index

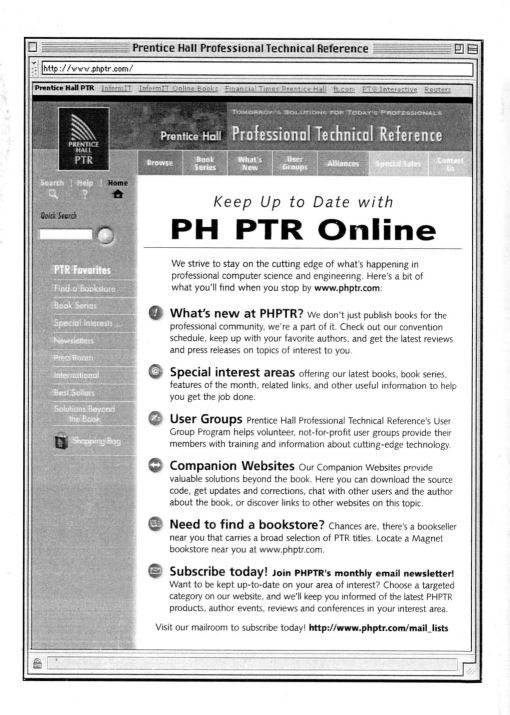

Prentice Hall Professional Technical Reference

http://www.phptr.com/

Prentice Hall PTR | InformIT | InformIT Online Books | Financial Times Prentice Hall | ft.com | PTG Interactive | Reuters

TOMORROW'S SOLUTIONS FOR TODAY'S PROFESSIONALS

Prentice Hall **Professional Technical Reference**

| Browse | Book Series | What's New | User Groups | Alliances | Special Sales | Contact Us |

Search | Help | **Home**

Quick Search

PTR Favorites

Find a Bookstore
Book Series
Special Interests
Newsletters
Press Room
International
Best Sellers
Solutions Beyond the Book

Shopping Bag

Keep Up to Date with
PH PTR Online

We strive to stay on the cutting edge of what's happening in professional computer science and engineering. Here's a bit of what you'll find when you stop by **www.phptr.com**:

What's new at PHPTR? We don't just publish books for the professional community, we're a part of it. Check out our convention schedule, keep up with your favorite authors, and get the latest reviews and press releases on topics of interest to you.

Special interest areas offering our latest books, book series, features of the month, related links, and other useful information to help you get the job done.

User Groups Prentice Hall Professional Technical Reference's User Group Program helps volunteer, not-for-profit user groups provide their members with training and information about cutting-edge technology.

Companion Websites Our Companion Websites provide valuable solutions beyond the book. Here you can download the source code, get updates and corrections, chat with other users and the author about the book, or discover links to other websites on this topic.

Need to find a bookstore? Chances are, there's a bookseller near you that carries a broad selection of PTR titles. Locate a Magnet bookstore near you at www.phptr.com.

Subscribe today! Join PHPTR's monthly email newsletter! Want to be kept up-to-date on your area of interest? Choose a targeted category on our website, and we'll keep you informed of the latest PHPTR products, author events, reviews and conferences in your interest area.

Visit our mailroom to subscribe today! **http://www.phptr.com/mail_lists**